The Fragile Thread

The Fragile Thread

THE MEANING OF FORM IN FAULKNER'S NOVELS

DONALD M. KARTIGANER

The University of Massachusetts Press   Amherst, 1979

clpw

Copyright © 1979 by
The University of Massachusetts Press
All rights reserved
Library of Congress Catalog Card Number 78–19693
ISBN 0–87023–268–1
Printed in the United States of America
Designed by Mary Mendell
Library of Congress Cataloging in Publication Data
Kartiganer, Donald M., 1937–
The fragile thread.
Includes index.
1.   Faulkner, William, 1897–1962—Criticism and
interpretation. I. Title.
PS3511.A86Z85895   813' .5'2   78–19693
ISBN 0–87023–268–1

Grateful acknowledgment is made to the following for permission to reprint copyrighted material:

Random House, Inc. and Alfred A. Knopf, Inc. for permission to qoute from the copyrighted works of William Faulkner: *The Sound and the Fury, As I Lay Dying, Light in August, Absalom, Absalom!, The Hamlet, Go Down, Moses, Intruder in the Dust, A Fable, and Requiem for a Nun;* Thomas Mann: *Essays,* and *Joseph and His Brothers;* and Wallace Stevens: "Notes Toward a Supreme Fiction," "Chocorua To Its Neighbor," "Domination of Black," "Esthetique du Mal," "The Poems of Our Climate," and "The Motive for Metaphor," all from *The Collected Poems of Wallace Stevens.*

Doubleday & Company, Inc., for material from *The Birth of Tragedy and the Genealogy of Morals* by Friedrich Nietzche. Copyright © 1956 by Doubleday & Company, Inc. Used by permission of the publisher.

Johns Hopkins University Press for material from Donald Kartiganer, *"The Sound and the Fury* and Faulkner's Quest for Form," *ELH* 37 (1970): 613–39.

The Massachuetts Review, for material from Donald Kartiganer, "Process and Product: A Study of Modern Literary Form," *The Massachusetts Review* 12 (1971): 297–328, 789–816.

Acknowledgments

I am indebted to Hyatt H. Waggoner, of Brown University, who taught me, above all else, that literature matters, that it has something important to tell us; and that if criticism is to be more than mere exercise or display, it must discuss literature seriously and with commitment. I wish to thank Martha Banta, Elizabeth Dipple, Donna Gerstenberger, Gerald Graff, and Malcolm Griffith, who read all or part of the manuscript and were generous with suggestions and encouragement. I also wish to thank Betty Feetham, Sherry Laing, Anne White, and Shirley Hanson who typed the manuscript (more than once). The Graduate School of the University of Washington provided a summer grant that allowed me to begin work on the project and an additional grant to pay for the typing. Finally I am indebted to my wife Lyn, who listened to and discussed with me most of the ideas in this book, and to my daughters Lisa, Mia, and Elizabeth—for waiting patiently (still) for me to write something they can read.

Contents

For my mother and father

—language . . . that meager and fragile thread . . . by which the little surface corners and edges of men's secret and solitary lives may be joined for an instant now and then before sinking back into the darkness where the spirit cried for the first time and was not heard and will cry for the last time and will not be heard then either

WILLIAM FAULKNER

It can never be satisfied, the mind, never.

WALLACE STEVENS

Preface

My purpose in this book is to explore the meaning of form in William Faulkner's major novels. By "form" I do not mean such technical matters as imagery, symbolism, narrative point of view, or specific devices such as stream-of-consciousness.[1] I refer rather to the significant structure of a literary work, the way in which the different units relate to each other, the way in which they become part—or fail to—of a coherent whole. Structure is the strategy of these relations, and in Faulkner, whose novels are so highly fragmented, the establishment of relations becomes a crucial issue.

The fragmentariness of Faulkner's novels is perhaps the most obvious thing about them. From the beginning of his career to the end, Faulkner arranged his novels as collections of blocks of material whose relevance to each other is, to say the least, not always clear. Sometimes there is a sequence of voices, each one the source of a unique language and perspective, as in *The Sound and the Fury, As I Lay Dying,* and *Absalom, Absalom!* Sometimes there is a juxtaposition of apparently independent stories, such as the separate lives of Lena Grove and Joe Christmas—who never meet—in *Light in August.* And once, in *The Wild Palms,* there are actually two novels set down side by side as alternating chapters, unrelated but for the fact that Wilbourne and the tall convict inhabit the same prison. This fragmentary structure is the core of Faulkner's novelistic vision, describing a world of broken orders, a world in which the meetings of men and words need to be imagined again.

The general critical response to this fragmentation has been to see it as a flaw, and either to dismiss the work accordingly or to discover in it some principle of unity. The assumption has been that if Faulkner is to have major status, his structural idiosyncrasies must be clarified: that is to say, drained of their power and made consistent with conventional notions of literary order.

Malcolm Cowley addressed the problem in his introduction to *The Portable Faulkner*, which helped reverse the critical indifference to Faulkner that had settled in during the 1940s.

> He is not primarily a novelist: that is, his stories do not occur to him in book-length units of 70,000 to 150,000 words. Almost all his novels have some weakness in structure. Some of them combine two or more themes having little relation to each other, like *Light in August*, while others, like *The Hamlet*, tend to resolve themselves into a series of episodes resembling beads on a string. In *The Sound and the Fury*, which is superb as a whole, we can't be sure that the four sections of the novel are presented in the most effective order; at any rate, we can't fully understand and perhaps can't even read the first section until we have read the other three.[2]

For Cowley, Faulkner is best as a teller of long stories, such as "The Bear" or "Spotted Horses," and his "real achievement" is the "Yoknapatawpha saga as a whole," the legend of the South that, whatever the imperfect structure of individual novels, becomes the unification and the triumph of Faulkner's fiction: "the total situation that is always present in his mind as a pattern of the South."

Cowley's approach—so appealing to Faulkner himself—is the source of a body of criticism that interprets all the books as one book, the whole corpus as a single Balzacian *Comedie*. The "weakness in structure" of individual works, the amazing variety of voice, character, and tone, the narrative innovation in virtually every novel, meld into a total fictional vision, a history, with beginning, middle, and end, of the mythical kingdom of Yoknapatawpha County. A corollary of this reading has been the discovery of a unified, consistent moral stance, more or less "traditional," more or less in keeping with the sentiments of Faulkner's Nobel Prize speech of 1950. Even as Faulkner's wayward form has been harnessed into a coherent order, so too have his thoroughly anarchic moral situations and attitudes been misread into some version of conventional moral judgment. The chief source of these distortions has been George Marion O'Donnell's attempt to dispel the charge of moral anarchy by erecting a scheme of Snopes *vs.* Sartoris, modern depravity *vs.* traditional values.[3] From the attempts to articulate a grand design in Faulkner have emerged the systems of real and imagined Southern history and the concepts of traditional community and morality that have been used to interpret the fiction.

A second approach to Faulkner, dominated by New Criticism, rejects the necessity of synthesizing the canon and instead tries to bind up the wounds of fragmentation from within the individual novels. The theoretical assumption here is that aesthetic unity is basic to successful literature, and that the superior work will always yield its sometimes submerged patterns to intelligent interpretation. Illusions of flux and paradox may abound but pattern abides in image echoes, in repeated symbols, in gradually surfacing themes, and especially in archetypal parallels that borrow the narrative coherence of a previous text.

My argument in this book is that both approaches, despite the obviously valuable results they have produced, effectively defuse the power and originality of Faulkner's work. Each of his major novels is a wrenching free from the available possibilities of literary form and a deliberate summons to the reader to attend to that fact. The novel splinters a commonly, conventionally known world into the vital reality of its separate pieces, and then makes its own recovery, its struggle for a comprehensible design, the central drama. Such a design, however, when a novel can move to it, can only be the precarious form that discloses the fact of its impending dissolution.

The critical reading of Faulkner has been the reading generally of literary modernism. Attacking this overvaluation of system, this need to rescue modernism from the disruption it continually courts, Frank Kermode has said of Yeats: "He made no order, but showed that our real lives begin when we have been shown that order ends: it is for the dreams, the intuitions of irregularity and chaos, of the tragic rag-and-bone shop, that we value him, and not for his 'system' or his 'thought.'"[4]

Richard Poirier extends this attack.

> Eliot and Joyce have been made assertive where they are vague, orderly where they have chosen to remain fragmentary, solemn where they are comic, philosophically structured where they are demonstrating their disillusionment with philosophical as much as with literary structures. The literary organizations they adumbrate only to mimic, the schematizations they propose only to show the irrelevance of them to actualities of experience—these have been extracted by commentators from the contexts that erode them and have been imposed back on the material in the form of designs or meanings.[5]

One of the blind spots of New Criticism has been its failure to take account of the process quality of much of the most important modernist writing: the quality of an emerging form, of fragments in the act of trying to generate an intelligible order. In novels like *The Sound and the Fury, Light in August,* and *Absalom, Absalom!* the traditional sense of product, of the work as completed artifact—its history whole, its directions coherent, its missteps confined to worksheets—is replaced by a sense of the novel as still going on, its author still fumbling through the fragments of character and event.

Confronted with such works, we must move from the expectation of control, the assurance that resolution is imminent, to a sense of openness. A new query of "whether" is added to the how and why we normally ask of literary closure. "We not only read the [process] book," Northrop Frye has written, "but watch the author at work writing it . . . we are not being led into a story, but into the process of writing a story: we wonder, not what is coming next, but what the author will think of next."[6] The process work is the work-in-progress: the quest, in *Song of Myself*, for a reader; in *Paterson*, for a "language"; in *Tristram Shandy*, for the articulation of a life the living of which is always at least ten steps, or ten years, ahead of the writing.[7]

In the face of such a literature, however, criticism has tended to remain product oriented, to substitute for a willful and sometimes comic chaos a coherence that is not so much the given of a work but its desire, and one it only half-wishes to fulfill. The reasons behind this critical emphasis are of some interest. To begin with, the writers themselves, in their extraliterary writing, frequently stress the existence of patterns in their poems and novels that few early readers and reviewers suspected. There is a family resemblance among such appendices and handbooks as "Notes to 'The Waste Land,' " *A Vision*, "Compson: 1699–1945," and even *James Joyce's Ulysses*, the original edition of which, its author tells us, "contains nothing . . . to which [Joyce] did not give his full approbation." In each case, somewhat after or peripheral to the literary fact, the writer has tried to construct a system for a work or body of works seemingly in shambles or, at the least, a work that looks like anything but the bearer of a coherent structure.

Of broader significance than these authorial suggestions has been the tendency of New Criticism, as Paul de Man has argued, to stress the unity of aesthetic forms as part of the Coleridgean analogy between the literary object and organic life.[8] This emphasis on unity is a commitment to what Ihab Hassan has called "the tyranny of wholes,"[9] and while it has led to an exemplary sensitivity to the most minute literary details, it always insists on subordinating these details to a totality that supposedly saves them from a "meaningless" isolation. Eliot himself, whose poem "The Waste Land" has been the frequent victim of critical

Procrusteanism, performed one of the earliest of such critical
acts when, reviewing *Ulysses* in 1923, he proposed the "mythical
method" as the possible savior of literature from "futility and anarchy."[10]

Among more recent critics there has been an attempt to assert again
the formal disruption of a literature once known for little else. Critics
like de Man, Hassan, J. Hillis Miller, Jacques Derrida, Edward Said, and
Joseph Riddell have brought to literary study a necessary sense of the
fragility of form, the problematics of all utterance, and the consequent
recognition that the achievement of modern literature begins, as Wallace
Stevens put it, in "flawed words and stubborn sounds," in that "imperfect" richer in possiblity than the totalities it dreams of.

While it is clear now that Faulkner is a novelist, a writer of "book-
length units," it is also necessary to stress that he is a modern novelist,
who must begin by dislocating the possibilities of form. My intention is
not to deconstruct the novels—they perform this act admirably themselves—but to attend to their fragments, to describe their distinct voices:
the literal voice of Benjy Compson, Darl Bundren, or Rosa Coldfield;
the voice in the story of Lena Grove or Mink Snopes. Each fragment is
a consciousness, a peculiar eloquence, a way of seeing and saying, and
each novel is the sum of these voices trying to articulate the temporary
magic of design. How Benjy Compson organizes his time-freed history,
how Jason orders his own time-ridden one, and why both versions can
signify "nothing"; how Darl Bundren's miraculous perception depends
on his distance from real things—a horse, a coffin, a fish in the dirt—
and why this vision, the deepest and most penetrating in the novel, is
one that neither family nor society can afford; or how and why
Rosa Coldfield must account for the catastrophe of the Civil War by
seeing Thomas Sutpen as a creature from hell, and how and why
Quentin Compson and Shreve McCannon must account for murder in
1865 by transforming Charles Bon into Henry Sutpen's black brother:
these are the kinds of questions I want to raise. In doing so I believe
that I can explore the larger questions of what a Faulkner novel is and
what its structure implies about consciousness, reality, and moral value.

The order achieved, when it is achieved, is not a substitution of
system for chaos, a mythic method providing the right blocks to spell
God, but the design that never denies its dubious status, its origins in
contingency.

Faulkner's concern with questions of form is in no sense a sterile
aestheticism. For Faulkner the imagination of form is a moral act, an
exploration of the possibilities and the value of human conduct. Mean-

ing and value reside in composition: the way one sees, the artfulness one devises, the love and courage one dares in order to wake the real into form. The Faulkner I try to present in this book is a Faulkner bent on describing, in the words of Roland Barthes, "how meaning is possible, at what cost and by what means. . . . not man endowed with meanings, but man fabricating meanings."[11]

In Part One: The Dislocation of Form, I discuss two novels, *The Sound and the Fury* and *As I Lay Dying*, which in very different ways lead us to a sense of the impossibility of a comprehensive form. One novel accomplishes this by refusing to allow its four distinct voices to build into a coherent narrative. The other repeats it by composing a narrative (the journey to Jefferson Addie Bundren demands) that intrudes on consciousness, that is not so much the culmination as the absurd, perhaps snickering, master of consciousness.

In Part Two: Toward a Supreme Fiction, I examine at some length *Light in August* and *Absalom, Absalom!*, the novels I consider Faulkner's best, as examples of achieved design. This design, however—always on the verge of collapse—remains linked to the disorder Faulkner insists on in the earlier novels, becoming a structure of changes: the visible crown of a constant becoming.

In Part Three: Mythos, I take up Faulkner's use of what Eliot called the mythic method, the use of a predetermined order as a means of narrative unity. In Faulkner's later novels, from *The Hamlet* to *The Reivers*, we find the sense of system that many critics have tried to see (incorrectly, I believe) in earlier novels as well: a mythos bringing all the pieces together, making the individual fragments subservient to the whole. It is this use of a mythic mode, I will argue, that leads to the serious falling off in quality of Faulkner's last novels.

In Part Four: Faulkner and Modernism, I sketch an implicit aesthetics to the novels that links them to their proper context: the high modernist mode that dominates the first third of the century. It is an account not so much of Faulkner's conscious theories of what fiction must be as of the background of my own thinking, of the assumptions about modern literature that have both influenced, and been influenced by, my reading of Faulkner.

One | *The Dislocation of Form*

1 | *The Sound and the Fury*

I

When Random House decided in 1946 to combine *The Sound and the Fury* and *As I Lay Dying* in a single Modern Library volume, the motive presumably had little to do with any formal or thematic relationship between the two novels. Faulkner did not care for the idea: "'I had never thought of TSAF and AS I LAY DYING in the same breath.'" He preferred that *The Sound and the Fury* be paired with "Wild Palms," the story from the novel by that title; "'the part of it about the doctor who performed the abortion on his own sweetheart.'"[1]

And yet the joining of Faulkner's first major novels was perfectly appropriate, and not only because, as he once said, "both of them happened to have a sister in a roaring gang of menfolks."[2] Each novel revolves around a single, sorely tried family. *The Sound and the Fury* portrays family tribulation as a decline from greatness: idiocy, madness, alcoholism, promiscuity, and theft as symptoms of a tragic Fall of Southern Princes. The Bundrens, however, with their own representatives of mental disorder, illicit sex, and double-dealing, have nowhere to go but up. Instead of family decay, *As I Lay Dying* tells a comic tale of perseverance at a price. Unburdened with governors and generals (a sure sign of degeneracy, says Jason Compson), the Bundrens need only haul Addie's moldering body to Jefferson and put her third son, Darl, on a train to Jackson in order to persuade us that they will survive. Their only war is the Great War, and rather than bullet holes in the dining-room table their souvenir is a French spyglass with "a woman and a pig with two backs and no face."

Most of the major characters of *The Sound and the Fury* are reborn in *As I Lay Dying,* in guises suited to their new social status. The tragic Caddy, whose pregnancy drives her father further into dipsomania, one brother to suicide and another to thievery, becomes the naive though equally fertile Dewey Dell. Quentin, the sensitive artist figure transforming his sister's sex life into a Byronic tale of mortal sin, becomes the articulate and impotent visionary Darl. Jason's pretense to efficiency reappears in the more attractive Cash, himself coolly competent, although as helpless as Jason in the face of extremity. And finally Benjy, childlike at thirty-three, becomes the real child Vardaman. By no means an idiot, Vardaman yet owns a child's perception that enables him to identify his dead mother and a fish—as remarkable in its own way as Benjy's ability to smell his grandmother's death or the feeling of guilt in his sister. The Compson's black servants, of course, are missing in *As I Lay Dying.* There is no Dilsey to cook, raise the children, nurse the sick, or "endure"; for these things the Bundrens need no one but themselves.

The telling of these two novels also suggests a repetition with variation. Both *The Sound and the Fury* and *As I Lay Dying* come to us as a succession of stream-of-consciousness monologues, each novel a version of Faulkner's usual reversed picaresque structure: not a sequence of bizarre incidents happening to a single hero, but a sequence of bizarre heroes happening to a single incident. But here as well the two novels diverge, becoming parodies of each other. In *The Sound and the Fury* individual consciousness assumes an extreme freedom, nearly unbounded by the pressure of plot. The Easter weekend which is the novel's present, whether from the point of view of its Christian implications or its secular events such as Benjy's birthday or Jason's habitual chasing of his niece, scarcely amounts to a controlling structure. The tale each of the four narrators is trying to tell, the history and meaning of four children growing up in the South in the first quarter of this century, is the tale that fails to come clear. This is the point Faulkner made in his account of the writing of the novel.

And that's how that book grew. That is, I wrote that same story four times. None of them were right, but I had anguished so much that I could not throw any of it away and start over, so I printed it in the four sections. That was not a deliberate *tour de force* at all, the book just grew that way. That I was still trying to tell one story which moved me very much and each time I failed, but I had put so much anguish into it that I couldn't throw it away, like the mother that had four bad children, that she would have been better

off if they all had been eliminated, but she couldn't relinquish any
of them. And that's the reason I have the most tenderness for that
book, because it failed four times.[3]

In *As I Lay Dying* the rambling interior monologues become short
staccato bursts, as if consciousness, faced with the obstacles of fire
and flood, can spare only moments for sensibility. Moreover, a complete *action* takes place, and with a clarity rather startling for a
Faulkner novel: a death and a movement from one place to another,
curbing the isolated minds and motives into a service of that action.
There is nothing in *The Sound and the Fury* like the journey to Jefferson, an easily paraphrased plot that begins with Addie Bundren's
request to be buried with her people and concludes with a fitting tran-
quillity of bananas, graphophones, and the appearance of an odd little
woman introduced as Mrs. Bundren. Action, in other words, becomes
a form of control, urging the Bundrens—as voices and as actors—
toward the completion of a tale and a quest. This external pressure on
consciousness is also the source of the novel's absurd comedy.

Faulkner's comments on the writing of *As I Lay Dying* are as instructive as those on *The Sound and the Fury*. The two novels eventually came to represent for him two kinds of writing, one in which a
book "grows," as if possessing a life of its own, another in which a book
is more deliberately composed, everything in it predetermined. He
called *As I Lay Dying* tour de force, which he insisted the earlier novel
was not. "Sometimes," Faulkner said, "technique charges in and takes
command of the dream before the writer himself can get his hands on
it. That is *tour de force* and the finished work is simply a matter of
fitting bricks neatly together, since the writer knows probably every
single word right to the end before he puts the first one down. This
happened with *As I Lay Dying*."[4] *A Fable*, a much bigger and more
ambitious book, was also tour de force because "I knew exactly what I
wanted to do, but it took me nine years to find how to do it. But I
knew what I wanted to do." "I simply used a formula," he said, "a
proven formula in our western culture to tell something which I
wanted to tell."[5]

The formula that assisted the writing of *As I Lay Dying* and *A
Fable* is comparable to, if not identical with, the pressure of plot that
organizes these novels, whether in the form of the journey or the life
and death of Christ. *The Sound and the Fury*, for the most part, is
without such pressure; it is the book that struggles, with all the signs
of its struggles showing, toward wholeness.

5

Yet both novels, despite the differences, are about failures of telling, about what Michael Millgate calls "the problem of the elusiveness of truth."[6] They are like tragic and comic masks of a single meditation on the mysteries of absence: the departed sister, the dead mother, both of whom bring to life the imaginations of bereft families. It is as if the vacant space in which Caddy or Addie once stood is now the dark silence of significant speech, an absence waiting to be filled with meaning.

The Sound and the Fury is more obviously this kind of novel, for its sorrow is rooted in the failure of each of its four voices to summon up, singly or collectively, a persuasive account of what it is that has happened to the Compsons. "When I began it," Faulkner wrote, "I had no plan at all. I wasn't even writing a book";[7] and the novel suggests nothing so much as its own effort to discover the plan implicit to itself, the book it might become were language eloquent enough, were the telling of stories free enough of bias and imposition, were the human mind capable of imagining the truth.

As I Lay Dying keeps its secret better hidden. After all, the journey is completed, the body has been placed in the ground where it belongs; a story has been enacted and told. But the story and the journey may comprise an empty form, for the motives of each of the Bundrens (with the exception of Jewel) vary so greatly from the alleged motives of that journey that the design is at least partially detached from the consciousnesses that give it life, from the people who implement it through their actions. More important, the most incisive vision in the novel—that of Darl—has nothing whatever to do with the controlling action. The clear-cut structure of *As I Lay Dying*, in other words, becomes a symbol of rigidity, of the imagination imprisoned in an action remote from its own deepest motives. The quest has been carried out, but what has been won?

In the two novels we find a radical questioning both of the possibilities of effective human effort and the possibilities of fiction: whether the novel of consciousness, of process, can complete itself in some kind of coherent whole, or whether the novel of action, of product, can be the culmination rather than the violation of consciousness.

II

The Sound and the Fury is the four-times-told tale that opens with a date and the disorder of an idiot's mind and concludes with "post and tree, window and doorway, and signboard, each in its ordered place." But this final order is one that has meaning only for the idiot: a sequence of objects that, when viewed from one perspective rather than another, can calm Benjy into a serene silence. The reader remains in a welter of contradictory visions.

None of the four tales speaks to another, each imagined order cancels out the one that precedes it. Truth is the meaningless sum of four items that seem to have no business being added: Benjy plus Quentin plus Jason plus the "narrator." "'You bring them together,'" as Faulkner wrote in *Absalom, Absalom!,* "'. . . and . . . nothing happens.'" This atomized Southern family, caught in the conflicts of ancient honor, modern commercialism, self-pity, cynicism, diseased love, becomes Faulkner's impassioned metaphor for the modern crisis of meaning. And *The Sound and the Fury* becomes, paradoxically, a vital expression of the failure of imagination, an approximation of what, for Frank Kermode, is no novel at all: "a discontinuous unorganized middle" that lacks the beginning and end of novel-time.[8]

Neither in the figure of Caddy, for some an organizing center of the novel, nor in the well-wrought fourth narrative do we find an adequate basis of unity in the work. The former possibility has been encouraged in several places by Faulkner himself, who claimed that the story began with the image of Caddy in the tree, and that she is its center, "what I wrote the book about."[9] But rather than a means of binding the fragments together, the image is itself complicated by the fragmentation. It moves into that isolation within the memory, eternal and not quite relevant, that all the major images of the novel possess. Millgate reveals a common uneasiness about this problem: "The novel revolves upon Caddy, but Caddy herself escapes satisfactory definition."[10] The accumulation of monologues results in neither a unity of vision nor a unity of envisioners.

The Benjy section represents extreme objectivity, a condition impossible to the ordinary mind and far in excess of even the most naturalistic fiction. In their sections Quentin and Jason are extremely subjective, each imposing a distorted view on experience, in exact contrast to Benjy, who can abstract no order at all. The fourth section is the voice of the traditional novelist, combining in moderation the qualities of the first three sections: objective in that it seems to tell us faithfully and credibly what happens (our faith in Quentin and Jason is, of course, minimal), and at the same time interpretive but without obvious distortion. Following upon the total immersion in experience or self of the three brothers, the last section is told entirely from without, and establishes the kind of comprehensive but still fixed clarity we expect to find in fiction. And yet for those very qualities, which for many are its strengths, it does not—even as the others do not—tell us what we most need to know.[11]

The Benjy section comes first in the novel for the simple reason that Benjy, of all the narrators, cannot lie, which is to say he cannot create. Being an idiot, Benjy is perception prior to consciousness, prior to the human need to abstract from events an intelligible order. His monologue is a series of frozen pictures, offered without bias: "Through the fence, between the curling flower spaces, I could see them hitting"; " 'What do you want' Jason said. He had his hands in his pockets and a pencil behind his ear"; "[Father] drank and set the glass down and went and put his hand on Mother's shoulder." His metaphors have the status of fact: "Caddy smelled like trees."[12]

The quality of Benjy's memory is the chief indicator of his non-human perception, for he does not recollect the past: he relives it.

> "Wait a minute." Luster said. "You snagged on that nail again. Cant you never crawl through here without snagging on that nail."
> *Caddy uncaught me and we crawled through. Uncle Maury said to not let anybody see us, so we better stoop over, Caddy said. Stoop over, Benjy. Like this, see. We stooped over and crossed the garden, where the flowers rasped and rattled against us. The ground was hard. We climbed the fence, where the pigs were grunting and snuffing. I expect they're sorry because one of them got killed today, Caddy said. The ground was hard, churned and knotted.*
> *Keep your hands in your pockets, Caddy said. Or they'll get froze. You don't want your hands froze on Christmas, do you.*
> "It's too cold out there." Versh said. "You dont want to go out doors." (P. 3)

The sequence begins in the present, April 7, 1928, with Benjy and Luster crawling through a fence to get to the branch, where Luster hopes to find a golf ball. It shifts to a winter day of Benjy's childhood, when he and Caddy are also crawling through a fence on their way to deliver a note from Uncle Maury to Mrs. Patterson. The scene shifts again to earlier the same day, before Caddy has come home from school.

These shifts are triggered by a nail, a fence, the coldness—some object or quality that abruptly springs Benjy into a different time zone, each one of which is as alive and real for Benjy as the present. Strictly speaking he "remembers" nothing. As Faulkner said of Benjy in 1955, "To that idiot, time was not a continuation, it was an instant, there was no yesterday and no tomorrow, it all is this moment, it all is [now] to him. He cannot distinguish between what was last year and what will be tomorrow, he doesn't know whether he dreamed it, or saw it."[13]

Time as duration—Bergsonian time—is what Faulkner is alluding to here; and it is this sense of time that Benjy, by virtue of his idiocy, has abandoned. Memory does not serve him as it serves the normal mind, becoming part of the mind and integral to the stream of constantly created perception that makes it up: the past which, as Bergson put it, "gnaws into the future and which swells as it advances."[14] Benjy does not recall, and therefore cannot interpret, the past from the perspective of the present; nor does the past help to determine that perspective. Instead of past and present being a continuum, each influencing the meaning of the other, they have no temporal dimension at all. They are isolated, autonomous moments that do not come "before" or "after."

This freedom from time makes Benjy a unique narrator indeed. He does not perceive reality but is at one with it; he does not need to create his life but rather possesses it with a striking immediacy. There is a timelessness in the scenes Benjy relives, but it is not the timelessness of art, abstracting time into meaning. It is the absence of the need for art.

Benjy's monologue, then, does not constitute an interpretation at all; what he tells us is life, not text. Emerging as if from the vantage point of eternal stasis, where each moment lived (whether for the first or fiftieth time) is the original moment and the only moment, unaffected by any of the others, this telling is an affront to the existence of narration or of novels. As Bleikasten says, it "is the very negation of narrative."[15] This is one of the reasons why the Benjy section has such a hold on us, why we attribute to it an authority we never think of granting the others, especially the narratives of his two brothers. Spoken with the awareness that time is always present, and thus missing that sense of consecutiveness necessary to our quick understanding, Benjy's monologue is difficult; yet the cause of that difficulty persuades us that this is truth, not art.

The irony, however, and the reason why the novel does not simply end with this section, is that while Benjy is not himself formulating an interpretation, his succession of lived images passes over into *our* interpretation, becomes a temporal fiction of Compson history that is so clear it is unbelievable. Benjy's scenes, despite fractured chronology and abrupt transitions, meld into a set of clear and consistent character portraits—two-dimensional figures with the sharpness of allegorical signposts that elicit from us simplistic evaluations empty of deep moral insight. "But for the very reason of their simplicity," one critic has written, "Benjy's responses function as a quick moral index to events."[16] This is indeed the effect of Benjy's monologue and its danger.

The following passage, taken from the end of Benjy's monologue, is typical. This is the night of Damuddy's death, when Quentin, Caddy, Jason, and Benjy (between the ages of three and eight) are being put to bed:

> There were two beds. Quentin got in the other one. He turned his face to the wall. Dilsey put Jason in with him. Caddy took her dress off.
> "Just look at your drawers." Dilsey said. "You better be glad your ma aint seen you."
> "I already told on her." Jason said.
> "I bound you would." Dilsey said.
> "And see what you got by it." Caddy said. "Tattletale."
> "What did I get by it." Jason said.
> "Whyn't you get your nightie on." Dilsey said. She went and helped Caddy take off her bodice and drawers. "Just look at you." Dilsey said. She wadded the drawers and scrubbed Caddy behind with them. "It done soaked clean through onto you." she said. "But you wont get no bath this night. Here." She put Caddy's nightie on her and Caddy climbed into the bed and Dilsey went to the door and stood with her hand on the light. "You all be quiet now, you hear." she said.
> "All right." Caddy said. "Mother's not coming in tonight." she said. "So we still have to mind me."
> "Yes." Dilsey said. "Go to sleep now."
> "Mother's sick." Caddy said. "She and Damuddy are both sick."
> "Hush." Dilsey said. "You go to sleep."
> The room went black, except the door. Then the door went black. Caddy said, "Hush, Maury," putting her hand on me. So I stayed hushed. We could hear us. We could hear the dark.
> It went away, and Father looked at us. He looked at Quentin and Jason, then he came and kissed Caddy and put his hand on my head.
> "Is Mother very sick." Caddy said.

"No." Father said. "Are you going to take good care of Maury."
"Yes." Caddy said. (Pp. 91–92)

Within the space of a single, short scene, each member of the Compson household is definitively characterized. Quentin is the figure of
impotence, the one who turns his face to the wall, expressing his futile
outrage at all that has gone on that day. Jason, meanness personified,
has already told on Caddy—without particular benefit, although he
does not realize this. Dilsey is the loyal retainer, the embodiment of
responsible affection, who undresses and cleans up Caddy, and sees to it
that all the children are in bed. Mother's lack of responsibility is defined
by her absence: she is "sick." Father makes his appearance, to look at
Jason and Quentin, and to kiss Caddy and touch Benjy (still named
Maury): *almost* the responsible parent but playing his favorites and, in
his last words, delegating responsibility for Benjy to Caddy. Caddy
herself is love, the one who can quiet Benjy down with the touch of
her hand. She is also the boldness of youth as both her dirty underwear
and confident assumption of the mother's role indicate.

What is so striking about this scene is not only that the meaning of
each character can be summarized in an abstract word or two, but that,
although the scene comes at the end of Benjy's monologue, the characters are the same as they were in the beginning. They exhibit little
change or development; nor can Benjy develop significantly his understanding of them. Each character must be himself over and over again,
bearing, like a gift of birth, his inescapable moral worth.

Life—for the scenes Benjy witnesses are at one level the most authentic in the novel—retains the power of its rawness, its freedom from
structure; yet simultaneously it passes into the order of our interpretation: a coherent fiction implying all-too-clear moral attitudes. And the
demands of our own reader's role are such that it is impossible for us
to reverse the process, to return this charged but implausible text to its
state of pure presence in the mind of the nonnarrator where it originates.

The most difficult task in reading *The Sound and the Fury* is to get
beyond this opening section, for finally Benjy is demonstrating the
poverty of the pure witness of what is unquestionably there. Benjy's
monologue is never less, or more, than truth. We must pass on to the
next three sections in which this truth confronts deliberate distortion:
vested interests organizing, plotting—consciously or unconsciously,
violently or subtly. And with these distortions the cautionary fable we
have gleaned from Benjy's images collapses into new complexities:
Caddy's promises succumb to need, Jason's ruthlessness turns over into

psychotic paranoia, Quentin's futility rages in dreams of murder and incest.

Yet the collapse is not total, as much of the criticism of the novel attests. Not the least irony of *The Sound and the Fury* is that we are tempted most by an absolutism that the whole structure of the novel teaches us to dismiss: not because it is not true but because it is not the truth of what it means to be human in that world which, so this novel asserts, is the one that exists.

III

Following Benjy's freedom from time and interpretation comes the time-possessed Quentin, who wants nothing more than to *replace* life with interpretation. Reality for Quentin is primarily change—in particular the change implicit to the sexual identity of his sister Caddy—and interpretation, metaphor, is the created ground of permanence in which change is eliminated. Caddy's development from child to adolescent and her subsequent loss of virginity epitomizes that change which, in Quentin's mind, is the essence of confusion.

> until after the honeysuckle got all mixed up in it the whole thing came to symbolise night and unrest I seemed to be lying neither asleep nor awake looking down a long corridor of grey halflight where all stable things had become shadowy paradoxical all I had done shadows all I had felt suffered taking visible form antic and perverse mocking without relevance inherent themselves with the denial of the significance they should have affirmed thinking I was I was not who was not was not who. (P. 211)

Against this vision of formlessness Quentin props a Byronic fable of incest between himself and Caddy, thus gilding what Father calls her "natural human folly" (p. 220) into a horrific one. Through metaphor he informs his confusion with the clarity of hell: *"the pointing and the horror walled by the clean flame"* (p. 144). But what is most important is that this hell, and the incest that enables Quentin and Caddy to deserve it, is purely imaginary. In the crucial interview that brings Quentin's monologue to a close, Father asks him: "did you try to make her do it and i i was afraid to i was afraid she might and then it wouldnt have done any good but if i could tell you we did it would have been so and then the others wouldnt be so and then the world would roar away" (p. 220).

"if i could tell you we did it would have been so. . . ." It is not an actual hell reserved for actual sinners that Quentin wants, but his invented one whose unreality frees it from a confusing and disappointing world. Purity for Quentin lies in a fiction, *known* as a fiction and priding itself on its indifference to reality. He is trying to transform life from within its midst, to convert dull promiscuity to sin, his dreary frustrations into a hell of rich and well-defined despair. It is a hell necessarily unreal: actual incest with Caddy "wouldnt have done any good."

Confronted everywhere with his impotence, Quentin is desperate to believe in the power of words alone: to substitute for what-is the names of what-is-not. He wants to convince Caddy of the reality of his fantasy, not that they have literally made love but that words have a substance more real than bodies.

> *I'll tell you how it was it was a crime we did a terrible crime it cannot be hid you think it can but wait   Poor Quentin youve never done that have you   and I'll tell you how it was I'll tell Father then itll have to be because you love Father then we'll have to go away amid the pointing and the horror the clean flame I'll make you say we did I'm stronger than you I'll make you know we did you thought it was them but it was me listen I fooled you all the time it was me* (P. 185)

Quentin tries to get Caddy to accede to this fantasy, to see words as the originator rather than the imitator of deeds. This is Quentin's willful decadence, a version of his subsequent suicide in that it puts the world away, using metaphor as a wedge between language and life. As Mr. Compson says, Quentin is trying to make "a temporary state of mind . . . symmetrical above the flesh" (p. 220). In this sense he is like the three young boys in Cambridge talking about what they might do with the prize money for a fish they neither have caught nor have any hope of catching: "They all talked at once, their voices insistent and contradictory and impatient, making of unreality a possibility, then a probability, then an incontrovertible fact, as people will when their desires become words" (p. 145).

Quentin's need to alter an unbearable reality through language owes much to the teachings of his father. On the first page of Quentin's monologue we read: "Because no battle is ever won he said. They are not even fought. The field only reveals to man his own folly and despair, and victory is an illusion of philosophers and fools" (p. 93). And shortly before the end: "Father was teaching us that all men are just accumulations dolls stuffed with sawdust swept up from the trash heaps where all previous dolls had been thrown away" (p. 218). Mr. Compson's theme has been the futility of human action.

Anxious to believe his father is wrong, Quentin clings to the moral codes of Southern antebellum myth: if a woman has been deflowered it can only be because "he made you do it let him he was stronger than you," and a loyal brother will avenge her: "tomorrow Ill kill him I swear I will" (p. 187). But finally this melodramatic interpretation of events will not do, and so Quentin escapes the cynicism of his father by embracing fully the idea of impotence: the pure fantasy of incest that signals the abandonment of time and his entrance into a world of words.

Quentin's behavior on June 2, 1910, parallels his quest for an irrelevant language. He moves toward a stylization of his life by separating his deeds from his purposes, the conduct of his last day from the impact of its destination. Cutting his thumb on his broken watch crystal, Quentin administers iodine in order to prevent infection; he attends to the matters of packing his belongings, writing farewell notes, stacking books, like someone going on vacation or moving to another town. At the end he carefully removes a blood stain from his vest, washes, cleans his teeth, and brushes his hat, before leaving his room to drown himself.

Both forms of metaphor, verbal and behavioral, move toward suicide. Driving words further and further from facts, style from purpose, art from meaning, Quentin is inside his death—the place without life—for much of his monologue. And yet, since the pride of his fiction-making is its admitted distance from the real, Quentin cannot help but acknowledge the agony of what is: that he has not committed incest with Caddy, that she has had several lovers, that she is pregnant with one man's child and is married to another, a "blackguard." There is in all this an affront that Quentin's artistry cannot conceal or bear. His only triumph is that he has proved his father wrong at least about one thing: "no man ever does that [commits suicide] under the first fury of despair or remorse or bereavement" (p. 221).

The deliberate flight from fact that dominates Quentin's monologue reverses the effect of Benjy's monologue that precedes it. Benjy has made us aware of the distortions of the *literal;* his language is exact, free of bias. It is truth, not metaphor. Yet this exaggerated objectivism results in the most simplistic of moral designs. Quentin, on the other hand, has plunged into metaphor; but in doing so he reduces subjectivism to an art of decadence: "symmetrical above the flesh."

IV

"The first sane Compson since before Culloden," Faulkner said of Jason in the Appendix to *The Sound and the Fury* written sixteen years after the novel. This is a view that has been adopted wholly or in part by many readers of the novel, although one wonders how anyone, especially Faulkner, could have considered Jason sane or rational.[17] Surely Jason is as removed from what we generally consider sanity as any character in *The Sound and the Fury*. He is in fact far less aware of what is actually real than his brother Quentin. Such is our quickness in the twentieth century to polarize rationality and emotion, intellectual and intuitive responses, that critical interpretation of *The Sound and the Fury* has found it easy to set Jason up as its rational villain, the opposite number of the high-minded, intuitive Sartorises and Compsons, and probably, with white-trash Snopeses and invading Yankees, the secret of the fall of man in the Faulkner world. Such a thesis is hardly adequate for the kind of complexity Faulkner offers us here and elsewhere in his fiction. Faulkner may indeed be on the side of intuition, particularly as Bergson described it, but in his best work he does not demonstrate that preference by neat categories of the kind in which Jason has been pigeon-holed.

A man who says, "I wouldn't bet on any team that fellow Ruth played on. . . . Even if I knew it was going to win" (p. 314)—to pick out only one example—is hardly the epitome of cold-hearted business-like behavior. And that he could ever have "competed with and held his own with the Snopeses" (p. 420), as Faulkner writes in the Appendix, is incredible. No man who is fooled and humiliated so many times in one day by everyone from Miss Quentin to Old Man Job, is going to be a match for Flem Snopes, whose coldly analytic inhumanity has so often been wrongly identified with Jason. The latter's insistence that he would not bet on a sure winner is not only irrational, it is even the mark of a curious idealism. It is also a significant, usually ignored, side of this pathetic man who spends his Good Friday crucifying himself on the crosses he alone provides.

A psychotic, some wit once said, is a man who honestly believes that two plus two equals five; a neurotic knows very well that two plus two equals four—but it bothers him. Let this be our hint as to the difference between Jason and Quentin, for Quentin deliberately composes an incest fable in order to deal with a reality he cannot face. That it *is* a fable is something he himself insists on. Jason, however, confuses the real and the illusory, and is quite unaware of the way he arranges his own punishment. Standing between him and reality is his need to hold on to two opposing views of himself: one is that he is completely sufficient, the other is that he is the scapegoat of the world. On one hand Jason considers himself an effective operator, family head, market speculator, brainy swindler of Caddy and her daughter, a man of keen business sense. On the other hand he nurtures the dream of his victimization, his suffering at the hands of the Compsons, the Gibsons, his boss Earl, even the telegraph company.

Jason's entire monologue wanders through a maze of contradiction that cannot be reduced to mere hypocrisy or rationalization. With $7,000 stashed away, the accumulation of fifteen years of theft, Jason thinks "money has no value; it's just the way you spend it. It dont belong to anybody, so why try to hoard it" (p. 241). Regretting that he must be a detective (p. 297), he yet makes the pursuit of his niece Quentin a major project. Insisting only that she show "discretion," fearing that someday he'll find her "under a wagon on the square" (p. 299), he nevertheless chases her far out into the country on a day when nearly everyone else is at the traveling show in town, when there is no one to see her but himself. He scoffs at Compson pride in blood (p. 286), yet later it is his and his mother's name that Quentin is making "a byword in the town" (p. 291). He firmly believes that it is Caddy who has deceived *him,* who has broken her promises to him, and that Quentin, in letting the air out of his tires, has given back far more than she has received: "I just wouldn't do you this way. I wouldn't do you this way no matter what you had done to me" (p. 303). And in the midst of all this double-dealing and plain fraud, Jason can sincerely say, "If there's one thing gets under my skin, it's a damn hypocrite" (p. 285).

Within this web of opposed purposes—is it comfort or suffering that he seeks?—Jason seems absent of any objective awareness of those realities most relevant to him. He is confusion incarnate, guilty of all he seems to hate, hating his own image in others, the least sane and the most perversely imaginative of all the Compsons. When the world threatens him with satisfaction, when his niece heeds his insistence on discretion by driving with her man friend into an abandoned country-side, Jason chases after her, contradicting his own wishes so that his pain can be adequate to his unintelligible need. Quentin creates in order to avoid suffering, Jason, to experience it.

Surely we cannot match criteria of sanity or cold logic with what goes on in Jason's mind on April 6, 1928. For Bergson, the analytic mind is capable of the "ingenious arrangement of immobilities."[18] It is the kind of perception that orders reality rather than entering into sympathetic union with it. But Jason's organization of things is so confused and contradictory that we can hardly observe in him the sense of conscious control that Bergson identifies with the analytic mind. Jason's most obvious quality, visible in all his pratfalls, is his inability to *utilize* reality, to make it integral to a specific design. To compare him with Faulkner's master of analytic reasoning, Flem Snopes, is to see how absurdly distant he is from Flem.

The meanness with which Jason confronts the world is the cover that scarcely conceals his lack of self-knowledge. His agony is real, but he cannot begin to explain its source or its meaning. The only language he can risk is the stream of impotent insult he inflicts on everything around him. The result, after the pathos of Benjy and the occasionally burdensome rhetorical self-indulgence of Quentin, is some uproarious invective: "I haven't got much pride, I can't afford it with a kitchen full of niggers to feed and robbing the state asylum of its star freshman. Blood, I says, governors and generals. It's a damn good thing we never had any kings and presidents; we'd all be down there at Jackson chasing butterflies" (p. 286). Following Benjy and Quentin, this sort of thing comes as bracing, if low, comedy. And it reminds us, even in this grim study of family distintegration, of the variety of Faulkner's voices and his daring willingness to use them.

Thus Faulkner adds still one more piece to his exploration of the possibilities of vision. Still subjective, as opposed to the more objective first and fourth sections, but substantially different from Quentin's, Jason's is the mind that seems to have dissolved the boundaries of fact and invention, not as they might be dissolved in the collaboration within a supreme fiction, but as in the furthest stages of paranoia. The great irony of the section is that Jason is the one Compson who creates the appearance of ordinary social existence: he holds a job, wears a hat, visits a whorehouse regularly, and manages to fool his mother into burning what she believes are Caddy's checks. But his existence is actually a chaos of confused motion, utter disorder within the mind. Quentin, preparing methodically for suicide, is a study in contrast.

V

With "April Eighth 1928" the novel moves outward, away from the sealed monologues of Benjy, Quentin, and Jason. The telling of the Compson history from within passes to the telling from without. It is the last possibility Faulkner must exhaust in order to make his wasteland of sensibility complete: the traditional fictional method of the removed narrator describing objectively the characters and the events and, without a sense of excessive intrusion, interpreting them for us.

For the first time in the book we get novelistic description: weather, place, persons, the appearance of things as from the eye of a detached but interested spectator: "The day dawned bleak and chill, a moving wall of grey light out of the northeast which, instead of dissolving into moisture, seemed to disintegrate into minute and venomous particles, like dust that, when Dilsey opened the door of the cabin and emerged, needled laterally into her flesh, precipitating not so much a moisture as a substance partaking of the quality of thin, not quite congealed oil" (p. 330). And with this description a new voice enters the novel: "She had been a big woman once but now her skeleton rose, draped loosely in unpadded skin that tightened again upon a paunch almost dropsical, as though muscle and tissue had been courage or fortitude which the days or the years had consumed until only the indomitable skeleton was left rising like a ruin or a landmark above the somnolent and impervious guts . . ." (p. 331). It is a rhetorical voice, set apart from the chaos and the distortion we have already seen. And from its secure perch, intimate with the events yet aloof from the pain of being a Compson, this voice seeks to tell us the meaning of what has come before.

Benjy, so brilliantly rendered in his own voice in the first section, is now described from the outside.

> Luster entered, followed by a big man who appeared to have been shaped of some substance whose particles would not or did not cohere to one another or to the frame which supported it. His skin was dead looking and hairless; dropsical too, he moved with a shambling gait like a trained bear. His hair was pale and fine. It had been brushed smoothly down upon his brow like that of children in daguerrotypes. His eyes were clear, of the pale sweet blue of corn-flowers, his thick mouth hung open, drooling a little. (P. 342)

One is almost shocked by the description—is this Benjy? Having wrestled with the processes of his mind, we find this external view like the portrait of someone else, another idiot from another novel. Not only described, he is also interpreted: "Then Ben wailed again, hopeless and prolonged. It was nothing. Just sound. It might have been all time and injustice and sorrow become vocal for an instant by a conjunction of planets" (p. 359).

Jason, once again in pursuit of Quentin, this time for the $7,000 she has taken from his room, is also described, "with close-thatched brown hair curled into two stubborn hooks, one on either side of his forehead like a bartender in caricature" (p. 348), and his meaning is wrested from the confusion of his own monologue. The narrator focuses chiefly on the bank job promised Jason years ago, which he never received because of Caddy's divorce from Herbert. It is supposedly neither Quentin nor the money that he is really chasing: "they merely symbolized the job in the bank of which he had been deprived before he ever got it" (p. 382). What has been stolen from him this time is simply "that which was to have compensated him for the lost job, which he had acquired through so much effort and risk, by the very symbol of the lost job itself" (pp. 383–84).

With both Benjy and Jason a great deal has been lost in the abstraction of meaning from movement. From the total immersion of the private monologue we move to the detached external view; from confused and confusing versions of reality we get an orderly, consistent portrait of the Compson family. And yet this clarity does not explain; these interpretations of Jason and Benjy seem pale and inadequate beside their respective monologues. Can Jason's terrible confusion, for example, really be embraced by the motive attributed to him in this section? There is a curious irrelevancy here, as if in this achieved meaning one were reading about different characters entirely. And yet in the earlier monologues we have already seen the inadequacies of personal distortion and the two-dimensional clarity of pure perception.

My point here is not simply a determined refusal to admit the comprehensiveness of what I am reading. It is rather to recognize that in this fourth attempt to tell the Compson story we are still faced with the problems of the first three, namely, a failure of the creation of a sufficient form. And this failure becomes itself the form, and therefore the meaning, of *The Sound and the Fury*. The four fragments, each a fully achieved expression of voice operating within the severest limitations, remain separate and incoherent.[19]

The fourth section is, of course, the easiest to read. It is divided into four parts: the scene in the house Easter morning, showing Dilsey at work and the discovery of the stolen money; the Easter service at church; Jason's pursuit of Quentin; and the short scene in which Luster tries to take Benjy to the graveyard through town. The polarities of Dilsey's and the Compson's existence are emphatic, especially in the juxtaposition of the Easter service, in its celebration of God's time, and Jason's mad chase, his striving in the context of human time. Dilsey, understanding the broken clock in the kitchen or the "beginning and the ending" in church, has a sure grasp of both.

Dilsey has been pointed to as the one source of value in the novel, supported by the comment in what seems to me an invariably misleading appendix, and it is clear that she embodies much that the Compsons lack, especially a sense of duty to her position as servant and her total faith in God.[20] It is also clear that her service to the family has not been enough to save it, and that even her own children disobey her often, in certain instances emulating the Compson sin of pride. Her religious faith is remote as far as the Compsons are concerned. If the Christian myth is being put forth here as a source of order in the world, it clearly has only ironic reference to them.

> "I know you blame me," Mrs. Compson said, "for letting them off to go to church today."
> "Go where?" Jason said. "Hasn't that damn show left yet?"
> (P. 348)

But Dilsey is irrelevant not only to the Compsons but to those assumptions of the nature of reality basic to the novel. Unlike the other members of the Compson household, and unlike the perspective implicit to this fragmented novel, Dilsey possesses a "mythic" view of the world, the assurance of an enduring order that presides over human existence, organizing it into an intelligible history. It is an order she has not invented but inherited, a traditional Christianity providing meaning and direction to her life. Outside the dissonance and distortion of the first three narratives, the grotesque visions we can never dismiss or corroborate, Dilsey's orthodoxy is a controlled and clear point of view—yet it is remote from that complexity of existence by which the novel lives.

Dilsey transcends chaos by her vision of Christian order.

> "I've seed de first en de last," Dilsey said. "Never you mind me."
> "First en last whut?" Frony said.
> "Never you mind," Dilsey said. "I seed de beginnin, en now I sees de endin." (P. 371)

This is what Quentin wishes he could do: see in the midst of action the direction of action, understand the living moment because it is part of a history that has already, and always, ended. Dilsey has this gift because she is a Christian. She exists not as one whose life unfolds in surprise, each moment a new and frightening Now, but as one who knows every step of the way because there is in fact only one history.

The traditional narrative form of this section of *The Sound and the Fury* rests on similar assumptions. Its externally placed perspective, its clear plotting, its coherent analysis of what the behavior of Benjy and Jason means—all of these are basic to a fiction that believes in endings and their power to press into service, and thus make intelligible, each single moment. Dilsey is the center of "April Eighth 1928" because she is the spiritual embodiment of the fictional tradition in which it is told.

Dilsey has what Frank Kermode calls a sense of an ending. For her, the deterioration of the Compsons only confirms the demise of the godless and prideful, and brings still nearer the moment toward which all history moves. Yet the whole of *The Sound and the Fury* does not subscribe to the implications of ending, in terms of either the resolution of action into meaning or the reconciliation of fragments into a controlling system. Dilsey's special understanding, as Frony's question makes clear—" 'First en last whut?' "—is unavailable to any of the major characters in the novel. Nor is it available to the reader unless he ignores three-fourths of that novel, which flatly juxtaposes the last section against the three others that are inconsistent with it, and even confronts Dilsey (and the Easter service that articulates her mode of belief) with the spectacle of Jason's frantic chase after Quentin.[21]

Challenging Dilsey's religious vision is the same sense of time in motion, of a reality intractable to any mental construct, that lays bare the distortions of Quentin and Jason and transforms Benjy's timeless perspective, free of distortion, into a frozen imitation of experience. Neither in the Dilsey section, whatever the power of her characterization or sheer attractiveness as a human being, nor anywhere else in the novel do we see demonstrated the ability of the human imagination to render persuasively the order of things. Instead there is the sense of motion without meaning, of voices in separate rooms talking to no one: the sound and fury that fails to signify.

The Sound and the Fury reads like an anthology of fictional forms, each one of which Faulkner tests and finds wanting. The novel insists on the poverty of created meaning, although in doing so it possesses, like "The Waste Land," a power that for many readers the later works cannot equal. There is Benjy's unmediated vision of pure presence, that makes of art a kind of impertinence. There are the grotesque orderings of Quentin and Jason—one an effete escapism that seeks a reality dictated by the word, the other subjectivism crippled by paranoia. Both are parodies of the possibility that art might illuminate, not merely distort, the real. And there is the conventional nineteenth-century fiction: the orderly telling of a tale that retreats from all those suspicions of language, concept, external point of view, imposed order, that made the modern possible and necessary.

The achievement of the novel is the honesty of its experiment; we take its "failure" seriously because the attempt seems so genuine and desperate. The basic structure of a compilation of voices or discrete stories is one Faulkner returned to again and again, but never with such a candid admission of the limitations of art. Behind the novel is some as yet vague conception of what literature in the twentieth-century might be. Acknowledging, insisting on decreation, making real the time prior to prearrangement, *The Sound and the Fury* yet strives for whole-ness, an articulation of design: the form not imposed like a myth from the past, but the form that is the consequence of contingent being.

Nearly two decades later, Wallace Stevens expressed the hope of an age.

> To discover an order as of
> A season, to discover summer and know it,
>
> To discover winter and know it well, to find,
> Not to impose, not to have reasoned at all,
> Out of nothing to have come on major weather,
>
> It is possible, possible, possible. It must
> Be possible. It must be that in time
> The real will from its crude compoundings come[22]

The impressiveness of *The Sound and the Fury* is that it accepts nothing it cannot earn. It will have only "major weather." And so the novel sits like a stillborn colossus, always on the verge of beginning.

2 | *As I Lay Dying*

I

The comedy of *As I Lay Dying* grows out of the collision between an outrageous plot and the improbable group of actors selected to carry it out. A plot means action—its most common form is the journey—while for the most part the Bundrens would prefer to stay put. But his wife's wish forces Anse, his four sons (one turns out to be the preacher Whitfield's), and one daughter on to the road to Jefferson where, nine days after Addie Bundren has expired, they succeed in getting her rotting corpse into the ground.

But the Bundrens as helpless agents in a plot they never made is only part of the joke. Compounding it is the fact that, under the guise of a fidelity so unwavering it often seems brainless, most of the Bundrens have purposes of their own for the journey: Anse covets a new set of teeth, Dewey Dell, a pill to bring on a miscarriage; Vardaman longs for a toy train, and Cash, a "talking machine." The comedy turns to their advantage as they transform this long funeral procession into a journey of self-serving aims. Addie Bundren becomes both prime-mover and a convenient excuse; and the remaining Bundrens are pathetic vassals, serving the dead at the expense of the living, as well as a group of resourceful deceivers, who force the journey-plot to satisfy intentions that have nothing to do with the burial of Addie.

Unlike *The Sound and the Fury*, in which the stream of consciousness technique impedes development of a clear narrative line, *As I Lay Dying* builds the clearest, most coherent plot in all of Faulkner's writing.[1] Despite the fact that the entire novel is told in fifty-nine monologues, divided among fifteen speakers, the thread of the journey is always a dominant structure. It is the public cause of everything that happens in the novel. In this respect *As I Lay Dying* seems to conform to very traditional notions of fiction, in which, as Northrop Frye has said, "characters exist primarily as functions of the plot."[2] In his important essay on the plot of *Tom Jones,* R. S. Crane identifies plot as "the particular temporal synthesis" of action, character, and thought. The novel is "a dynamic whole which affects our emotions in a certain way through the functioning together of its elements in subordination to a determinate poetic form."[3]

But in *As I Lay Dying,* of course, the subordination of character to "a determinate poetic form" is only half the story. This is not because, like Tom Jones, the characters have mistaken the pattern that is governing their lives, but because they knowingly fill that pattern with purposes that have little to do with it. Consciousness completes itself in an action that does not quite fit, resulting in an absurdity that reflects on both.

Alien to all this is one of the sons, Darl Bundren. He is neither comic victim nor comic actor. He lacks both private *and* public motives, serving neither the dead nor himself. He is fundamentally different from the other members of the family because he can find no link whatever, not even a selfish one, between his vision and the long trek to Jefferson. Darl's predicament is the one stated by Addie Bundren: "I would think how words go straight up in a thin line, quick and harmless, and how terribly doing goes along the earth, clinging to it, so that after a while the two lines are too far apart for the same person to straddle from one to the other."[4] This division between words and deeds is the division between consciousness and narrative that underlies the whole novel, achieving its most extreme expression in the condition of Darl. It is his presence that shifts the novel from the comic play between motives and plot, neither of which does mortal damage to the other, to the potential tragedy of forces deadlocked in opposition. Beneath the journey and all its purposes opens a threat of madness and annihilation. The novel moves closer to *The Sound and the Fury,* to that quality of a fiction coming apart in the spaces between well-made lines. Again, despite the vast differences of these two works in tone, action, and setting, we see exemplified the limitations of mind in the effort to know itself in an appropriate and fitting form.

II

Darl's expansive vision, transcending the limits of space and time, is the difference between himself and the others. He describes in detail scenes he does not even see. He is our reliable witness at crucial events whether he is present, as he is in the crossing of the river, or absent, as he is at the death of Addie. Yet he has no substantial sense of himself: "And before you are emptied for sleep, what are you. And when you are emptied for sleep, you are not. And when you are filled with sleep, you never were. I dont know what I am. I dont know if I am or not. Jewel knows he is, because he does not know that he does not know whether he is or not" (p. 76). The wagon loaded with wood standing in the rain slips from his grasp: "Beyond the unlamped wall I can hear the rain shaping the wagon that is ours, the load that is no longer theirs that felled and sawed it nor yet theirs that bought it and which is not ours either, lie on our wagon though it does, since only the wind and the rain shape it only to Jewel and me, that are not asleep. And since sleep is is-not and rain and wind are *was,* it is not." Darl has to "prove" through cause-effect logic the reality of what is irrevocably *there,* including his own being: "Yet the wagon *is,* because when the wagon is *was,* Addie Bundren will not be. And Jewel *is,* so Addie Bundren must be. And then I must be, or I could not empty myself for sleep in a strange room. And so if I am not emptied yet, I am *is.*"

The rest of the Bundrens, untroubled with ontology, confine their awareness to the plainly real, either to those objects that attract them to Jefferson or, in the cases of Jewel and Cash, to the horse and coffin that become essential parts of the trip. In these objects they discover themselves as well as a focus for whatever grief the death of Addie Bundren invokes, and thus reduce that grief to the human dimensions that make it tolerable. Jewell and the horse he has bought by working both day and night for five months, Cash and the coffin he builds for Addie with such painstaking care, Vardaman and the fish he substitutes for the body of Addie and later the toy train that waits in Jefferson, Dewey Dell and the abortion she fumblingly seeks, Anse and his long-desired teeth—these are the channels of grief and the hard foundations of new purpose. It is easy enough to mock the poverty of such images as vessels of consciousness, but these are the things that save by becoming the crude limit to the nothingness of death. Most important, they are the images that enlist the Bundrens in the journey to Jefferson; for this is the narrative that preserves the family unit, fulfills (almost incidentally) the promise to Addie, and brings *As I Lay Dying* to a coherent end—however circuitous the trip.

Outside the body of these images, like a Nietzschean Dionysos, beckons the madness of a vision that rejects image, that cannot (or refuses to) convert feeling into object, motive into action. Darl's remoteness from things is his remoteness from the journey, from the family, and from that half of *As I Lay Dying* which is its narrative line. What appears at times to be the only rational voice among the Bundrens— " 'She wants Him to hide her away from the sight of man' " (p. 204)— is also the voice of insanity, rejecting the forms that sanity requires.

Of all the Bundrens, Vardaman is the one whose transformation of death is the purest. The shortest monologue in the novel is this: "My mother is a fish" (p. 79). Vardaman lacks the cunning of Anse and the doggedness of Cash, which enable them to replace the shock of death with what they well know is self-interest or the mind-consuming practice of craft. In his innocence Vardaman resorts to a basic primitivism: my mother is dead but she lives still, as the body of a fish. This identification of Addie and the fish is the act of a mind prior to metaphor, prior to the need to imagine rather than simply to receive an immediate substitution of body for absence. Addie must be somewhere, in some sensual form. There can be no idea of Addie that does not take the shape of something in Vardaman's world. The huge fish he has caught that morning, chopped up with his axe, and subsequently eaten, becomes the reality beside which death cannot stand.

Vardaman exemplifies the kind of primitive mind Ernst Cassirer discusses in several works: the mind that, not yet educated to the ways of scientific thought, sees life "as an unbroken continuous whole," and can move without self-deception from the mother to the fish.

> The limits between the different spheres are not insurmountable barriers; they are fluent and fluctuating. There is no specific difference between the various realms of life. Nothing has a definite, invariable, static shape. By a sudden metamorphosis everything may be turned into everything. If there is any characteristic and outstanding feature of the mythical world, any law by which it is governed—it is this law of metamorphosis.

Even Vardaman's hostile response to Peabody is part of the primitive mentality.

> The feeling of the indestructible unity of life is so strong and unshakable as to deny and to defy the fact of death. In primitive

thought death is never regarded as a natural phenomenon that obeys general laws. Its occurrence is not necessary but accidental. It always depends upon individual and fortuitous causes. It is the work of witchcraft or magic or some other personal inimical influence. . . . A man who dies has of necessity been killed by some other man or perhaps even by a woman.[5]

Addie must be *someone's* victim, and Peabody, as the last one outside the family to see her, must be the evil force.[6]

From the purity of this kind of metamorphic vision Vardaman moves to the indirections of metaphor and displacement. From his conviction that Addie is not in the coffin—*"My mother does not smell like that. My mother is a fish"* (p. 187)—he eventually resigns himself to the fact that she is: " 'I can smell her,' I say. 'Can you smell her, too?' " (p. 206). Displacing his obsession with the fish is the toy train that he hopes is waiting in Jefferson: "It goes round and round on the shining track. Then the track goes shining round and round" (p. 206). The difference between Vardaman's understanding of the fish and his understanding of the train is the difference between a primitive sense of the unity among things and the civilized sense of discontinuity: the recognition that unities are not given but must be established through metaphor. The train is no more miraculous a conception than Cash's coffin or Jewel's horse. Like those images, however, it is Vardaman's physical prop in the confusion of Addie's death. His progress toward the train, and Jefferson, becomes the same narrative line that binds him to the rest of the family and to the plot his mother has imposed. That finally the train is *not* in the window where he expected it to be is of no more importance than the fact that Dewey Dell fails in her quest for an effective drug. They are in Jefferson and through these images, they have survived. As Vardaman says of Darl: *"He went crazy and went to Jackson both. Lots of people didn't go crazy. Pa and Cash and Jewel and Dewey Dell and me didn't go crazy. We never did go crazy"* (p. 241).

By understanding the primitive tradition behind Vardaman's initial reaction to Addie's death, we can understand the background of what it is the other Bundrens are doing. Faced with the problem of death, the Bundrens instinctively resort to images and gestures only once removed from Vardaman's awareness of a world of magic. Jewel's horse is, like the fish, a totem figure. And although he knows the difference between his mother and the animal, Jewel has been able to transfer to the horse, and thereby to some extent control, his jealousy and rage regarding Addie. This transference is clearly the vehicle of his sanity. When Addie dies, the horse remains as Jewel's point of control; it becomes the agent of his involvement in the journey, the possession he, though grudgingly, contributes as part of a trade with Snopes for a team of mules. The slow, ill-managed journey violates Jewel's need for decisive action, yet it is still the plot that holds the family together, and the necessary ritual that answers his potential madness with therapeutic form.

With increasing distance from the mother, the obsessive images of Dewey Dell and Anse still function similarly to those of Vardaman, Jewel, and Cash. The fetus that troubles Dewey Dell, the teeth that will enable Anse to eat "God's appointed food' " (p. 182)—these are still the physical things that occupy mind, images that more than words become the shapes of identity.

The coffin Cash makes so lovingly for Addie may not be as familiar a totem figure as the fish and horse, but it is an image equally effective in enabling Cash to form the limits of his grief. In his role as carpenter, Cash converts that grief into what is for him the far more comprehensible dimensions of a box. Cash has been pointed to by more than one critic as the figure who goes the furthest in this book in bringing together its disparate motifs: "Cash [is] the one character in the novel who achieves his full humanity in which reason and intuition, words and action merge into a single though complex response."[7] It is Cash who, in his devotion to the well-made thing, "is man defining himself, declaring his human dignity through the perfection of his work."[8]

Though Cash is certainly more compassionate than all the other Bundrens, I think such claims for him are too extreme. André Bleikasten writes in his excellent study of the novel, "Seeing Cash so thoroughly engrossed in the making and transportation of the coffin, one wonders if he has not forgotten what it contains. Unless the coffin is for him what the horse is for Jewel and the fish for Vardaman: the object of a transference."[9] Cash's obsession with the coffin shows a concern more with the specific totem than with Addie. The thirteen reasons for beveling— "1. There is more surface for the nails to grip. 2. There is twice the gripping-surface to each seam," including such items as "6. Except" and culminating with "13. It makes a neater job" (pp. 77-78) —indicate not only care but narrowness of mind, an involvement in craftsmanship so deep as to ignore or trivialize the questions of love and grief. Cash's box holds Addie all right, but *backwards*—the body reversed to make room for her flare-bottomed dress (p. 82).

There is much truth in Cash's conviction that "there just ain't nothing justifies the deliberate destruction of what a man has built with his own sweat" (p. 228). But the emphasis here is the single-minded devotion to what a man has *built,* the well-wrought image more basic to sanity than the spirit one sweats into it, because it erects arbitrary walls for one's identity. What Cash has done, as all the Bundrens do but Darl, is praise the image beyond the human life it is built to sustain. The price of a barn is the life of Darl Bundren, who can identify himself at last only by his confinement behind the walls of Jackson.

While one may be sympathetic to various forms of artfulness—particularly, as in Cash's case, when it involves such large sacrifice—I think we must examine more critically the character of this "human dignity" which Cash declares "through the perfection of his work," as well as the character of the work itself. "Against such dematerialization of the human," Bedient writes, "the construction of the coffin, which looks so merely mechanical, is actually a passionate protest, a fierce assertion of human value."[10] And yet we must ask, what kind of human value? and what kind of construction?

Faulkner made clear on numerous occasions outside his fiction (and, less explicitly, on numerous occasions within it) his reservations about well-made things. One example of these reservations I quoted in the previous chapter—the comments on tour-de-force fiction. Another is his well-known tendency to rank authors and books in terms of their failure rather than their success. This was the reason Hemingway was second to Wolfe, *Huckleberry Finn* to *Moby-Dick:* "*Huckleberry Finn* is a complete controlled effort and *Moby-Dick* was still an attempt that didn't quite come off, it was bigger than one human being could do."[11] It was also the reason Faulkner came to prefer *The Sound and the Fury* to all his other novels.

While these reservations cannot be offered as evidence of Faulkner's attitude toward Cash, perhaps they point to things in this novel that can be—the basic differences between Darl and Cash. Darl is the man who rejects the physical, rejects form, pursues a self already committed to absence. Cash is the most artful of all those Bundrens who, knowing little else, know themselves in the impoverished images they have created. Yet we can scarcely ignore the fact that achieved form for Cash is only a coffin for love, a skillfully made box for a rapidly decaying body, and disturbingly close to what Addie Bundren means by "a significant shape, profoundly without life like an empty door frame" (p. 165).

This is the central irony of *As I Lay Dying,* the gaping distance between vision without form and form without vision, or, as Bleikasten puts it, between "[c]onsciousness without identity or identity without consciousness."[12] It is an irony that I think must prevent us from suggesting either Darl or Cash as the bearer of a "full humanity" or a full awareness. Between them lies the novel's weight and the anguish issuing from the fact that neither can propose a way of seeing or a way of acting that approaches the richest possibilities of order, or what I believe Faulkner hoped were those possibilities.

So it is not a full humanity Cash achieves. Confronted at last with the laughter of his brother's full insanity, he can only say, "It was bad. It was bad so. I be durn if I could see anything to laugh at" (p. 228). Yet much of the vitality and resilience that is part of the meaning of *As I Lay Dying* is vested in the figure of Cash, Faulkner's first and only artist to be convinced that "it's better to build a tight chicken coop than a shoddy courthouse" (p. 224).[13]

III

Darl's alienation from the other members of the family is the price of his remarkable vision. For all the clarity of what Darl sees, the uncanny reports of events he cannot witness, he reveals also a total lack of involvement with those events.

> "You, Cash," she shouts, her voice harsh, strong, and unimpaired. "You, Cash!"
>
> He looks up at the gaunt face framed by the window in the twilight. It is a composite picture of all time since he was a child. He drops the saw and lifts the board for her to see, watching the window in which the face has not moved. He drags a second plank into position and slants the two of them into their final juxtaposition, gesturing toward the ones yet on the ground, shaping with his empty hand in pantomime the finished box. For a while still she looks down at him from the composite picture, neither with censure nor approbation. Then the face disappears.
>
> She lies back and turns her head without so much as glancing at pa. She looks at Vardaman; her eyes, the life in them, rushing suddenly upon them; the two flames glare up for a steady instant. Then they go out as though someone had leaned down and blown upon them. (P. 47)

The vision is sharp, but with the clarity of the disengaged; one would scarcely guess that the speaker is talking about the death of his mother.

Darl's descriptions of the Bundrens are full of metaphor, but his real search is for a meaning divided from image, identity free of the body that confines. He desires a oneness with the mother beyond what he sees as the insane structure of the journey she herself has chosen.

Darl's quest, the opposite of Vardaman's, is to attain what Cassirer describes as a religious consciousness, epitomized in the Old Testament prophets, which chooses to liberate itself from things, to move "from the sphere of material existence to the true religious sphere of meaning, from the image to the imageless." Like Quentin in *The Sound and the Fury,* Darl is pressing toward the supremacy of words, toward a realm of language "beyond all intuition of the given, the merely existent."[14] This "merely existent" is the world of the Bundrens, the world of the journey, the body of narrative. The journey is both a linear form and a social action designed to make death tolerable. It builds a ceremony in the presence of nothingness. This journey, in all its implications, is closed to Darl. It is closed to him because he has no concrete sense of self that can become the bridge for his participation in it, no vein of self-interest for which he can find the appropriate physical formula. Darl is of little help in making the coffin, placing it in the wagon bed, or getting it across the river. Nor does he contribute anything of his own, no horse, no tools, no shattered leg, no money patiently saved away for a new set of teeth, a graphophone, or an abortion. His act of arson is his single attempt to convert his unimaged consciousness into deed, and of course it must be a negative deed: he cannot build, but only burns down. His dream here is not the fulfilled image but the annihilation of image, the coffin and body cremated and the narrative of the long interment stopped.

Darl's description of the barn fire and Jewel's rescue of the animals and the coffin is striking because of his remoteness from the event. He presents the fire as a piece of art, a kind of stage play at which he is only a spectator. He erects a series of frames in which characters act, or out of which they leap: Jewel "springs out like a flat figure cut [c]leanly from tin against an abrupt and soundless explosion"; "The front, the conical façade with the square orifice of doorway broken only by the square squat shape of the coffin on the sawhorses like a cubistic bug, comes into relief"; "They are like two figures in a Greek frieze, isolated out of all reality by the red glare"; "We watch through the dissolving proscenium of the doorway"; "For an instant he looks up and out at us through the rain of burning hay like a portiere of flaming beads"; "he appears to be enclosed in a thin nimbus of fire. Without stopping it overends and rears again, pauses, then crashes slowly forward and through the curtain. This time Jewel is riding upon it, cling-ing to it"; "the widening crimson-edged holes that bloom like flowers in his undershirt" (pp. 208–12).

Jewel's mother and horse are now identical, as the coffin "rears" and Jewel "is riding upon it," while Darl remains the artist who has ar-ranged it—having literally started the fire and now describing it in metaphor. But in the telling of the event he excludes himself from it. The irony is that Jewel's success in resolving his own division between mother and horse is here only a metaphoric one, the invention of his insane brother who can work out no comparable resolutions for himself.

Society may occasionally mock the Bundrens in their journey, but Darl, who tries to stop it, is its real enemy, the stranger to image and the subverter of structure. Family and society combine at the end of the novel to send Darl to the asylum because, as Cash says, "This world is not his world; this life his life" (p. 250).[15]

Such are the complexities of this the most ambiguous, even as it is the least difficult, of all Faulkner's major novels. The ambiguity cannot be resolved but only recognized. As I Lay Dying, from the point of view of its narrative, is, like Cash's coffin, well-made and tight. But, also like the coffin, it holds the body backward. The price of its completion is the eviction of the most profound vision in the novel.

We never forget the grotesqueness of the journey: "folks couldn't stand it. It had been dead eight days, Albert said. They came from some place out in Yoknapatawpha County, trying to get to Jefferson with it. It must have been like a piece of rotten cheese coming into an ant-hill" (p. 193). And while the novel may affirm an awesome courage and en-durance, it also confirms the poverty of human creation. In this respect, as in others, it echoes *The Sound and the Fury*.

Of the achievement of *As I Lay Dying* there can be no question. The novel has, as Bedient has said, an "opacity," a mysterious and terrible "immediacy" that casts a shadow.[16] But the meaning of its form, of its internal relations, suggests, like *The Sound and the Fury*, the failure of coherence: the discovery that Addie Bundren makes "that words are no good; that words dont ever fit even what they are trying to say at" (p. 163). Vision tears itself loose of the earth, free at last in the country of the mad; while action, prisoned to a corpse, preserves the sanity of the mundane.

As I Lay Dying and *The Sound and the Fury* span between them what, to Faulkner in 1928–1929, seemed to be the possibilities of fiction:

the strong controlling plot, somehow irrelevant to consciousness, and plot vanished, leaving consciousness without an action in which to know itself. A book of words and a book of deeds; a book of air, whose words outrun events, "making of unreality a possibility," and a book of earth, in which words and the central guardian of words are overrun by an implacable motion. In *The Sound and the Fury* event is made dim by the explaining word, is lost in the voices of unrestrained monologue. In *As I Lay Dying* event checks voice; the short, staccato utterances comically punctuate the steady movement toward Jefferson. Both novels are about a break in expression, some failure of the imagination to reconcile form and vision, to create a shape that is not a stasis, change that is not chaos.

But what would it look like—a fiction in which order is the edge of consciousness, where an imagined reality exists and redeems, yet revolves endlessly?

Two | Toward a Supreme
Fiction

3 | *Light in August*

I

Light in August is the strangest, the most difficult of Faulkner's novels, a succession of isolated, brilliantly etched characters and scenes that revolve around, finally blur into, an impenetrable center—the character Christmas. As remote from us and his author as he is from the society around him, Christmas withholds some ultimate knowledge of himself, some glimpse into the recesses of being which we feel necessary to understanding. Yet just as obvious as his distance is the fact that he epitomizes every character and movement in the book. Whatever is in *Light in August* is here archetypally in this figure whose very name begins his mystery: Joe Christmas. He is, as Alfred Kazin has observed, "compelling rather than believable," a character who "remains as he is born, an abstraction."[1] Like an art image that has never had the privilege of being human, he is never to be merely "believed"; yet at the last he is to "rise soaring into their memories forever and ever. They are not to lose it. . . ."

The mystery of Christmas, which doubtless for Faulkner begins, prior to the novel's turning it to account, with the opacity of the mulatto and an uneasiness concerning miscegenation, would appear at first to be the weakness of the novel. Yet this mystery is the meaning of *Light in August,* for the impenetrability of Christmas becomes the only way Faulkner can articulate a truly inhuman, or larger-than-human, wholeness of being of which the others—Lena, Hightower, Byron, Joanna, Hines, Grimm—are the human shadows. For us, they are the recognizable figures for which we read novels; they explain Christmas in their freedom from his special agony of seeming not quite born. In reality it is he who explains them, these "characters" who solidify into crisp, static shapes only because they are less than he. Dimly aware of the pursuit of self that ensures Christmas's isolation, they assume the roles that guarantee their place at least on the edge of society, and to those roles, as well, of the comprehensible figures of fiction. They are not only the visible, partial reflections of the wholeness which is Christmas's suffering, but what Faulkner himself returns to at last: the people he must portray as the bright fragments of the mystery in his book that is necessarily beyond him.

Although *Light in August* is not told as a series of voices, its structure retains the fragmentariness of Faulkner's earlier novels. Through a narrative that juxtaposes blocks of seemingly unrelated material, *Light in August* creates a quality of incoherent mosaic. Despite the fragmentation, however, *Light in August* moves toward a resolution of the problems of *The Sound and the Fury* and *As I Lay Dying*: the broken form, the incompatibility of twin commitments to flux and design, process and product. *Light in August* is dominated by the imagery of dualism: whiteness and blackness; hardness and softness; the "cold hard air of white people" and "the fecundmellow voices of negro women"; "the far bright rampart of the town" and "the black pit . . . the original quarry, abyss itself": all the patterns in which people confine their lives and the violence that threatens and finally breaks loose.[2] This dualism, however, transforms itself into a dynamic in the figure of Joe Christmas.

At the center of *Light in August* is the mulatto—more important, the *imagined* mulatto. This is the role that Christmas, never being sure of what his origins are, has chosen. Able to "pass," to choose a single identity, Christmas chooses instead his doubleness. The only identity that will satisfy him is the one which, in Faulkner's South, is no identity at all, but rather an image of disorder. As a black worker at the orphanage to which Christmas is sent as a child says to him: " 'You dont know what you are. And more than that, you wont never know. You'll live and you'll die and you wont never know' "(p. 363).[3]

Missing from Christmas is the kind of stable and consistent meaning that fictional characterization and the context of the novel insist on: a stability based, as we shall see, on repression and commitment to a fixed pattern. Being neither black nor white, Christmas is doomed to indefiniteness. And yet he is more than a blankness. On the one hand he *is* a life, a structure, a single character—difficult yet visible, lacking the clarity of Hightower and Lena and Joanna, yet capable of being summoned up in our minds by the words "Joe Christmas." On the other hand, he is the disorder that lives always at or near the surface of *Light in August,* the chaos of mixed bloods that brings forth from the life of Jefferson an inevitable violence. The mulatto is the Faulknerian symbol of what is beyond comprehension or art; Joe Christmas is the expansion of that symbol into a precarious yet memorable design that both confronts, and is made of, its own disorder.

In other words, Faulkner begins to move toward a more complex idea of fictional meaning, of a way in which a human life and a fictional creation can unveil a vacancy that yet projects a signifying form, a form that is more than a vacancy. The fragmentariness of *The Sound and the Fury* is echoed in the uneven development of *Light in August*— the juxtaposed but incongruous incidents, the major characters (Lena and Joe) who never meet—but these fragments now begin to cohere in a tragic dialogue, a modern form in which design emerges as the voice of a chaos that is signified by and subverts that design.

This modern form is epitomized for us in the figure of Christmas, in the process of his fictional existence. His possible black-white division suggests a reality of perpetual making: a reality of forces whose individual identity is problematic and whose projected meeting is an outrage. The stable dialectic of the rest of the novel encounters in Christmas a dynamic that it finds intolerable. The society of Jefferson and the novel *Light in August* are equally threatened by the meaning of Christmas, for the mode of his being and his characterization are equally destructive to society and to fiction. This opposition of town and text to their own center is an irony underlying the whole novel, for Christmas as a character is as inaccessible to the community of Jefferson as he is to *Light in August,* even as he generates the most profound meanings of both. "This face alone," Hightower thinks, "is not clear" (p. 465). He represents an interaction of forces that the novel and Jefferson can only compartmentalize. Black and white, and all they imply, are distinct sectors, carved in stone, except in the example of Christmas.

The book is about this difference between itself and Christmas, its failure to be equal to his story, to live its life in the same struggle between oppositions as he lives his. Failing to portray Christmas according to traditional criteria of characterization, Faulkner yet suggests to us the struggle of which Christmas is made, and thus makes clear the inadequacy of the portrayal. We are given the general shape of Christmas's contradictory actions, but we are never provided full insight into his inner drama.

Faulkner compels his novel to revolve around a shadowy figure, in whom a strange union of forces represents the impossibility of his existence in verbal form. Yet the *fact* of that impossibility is alive in the novel as a palpable guilt: the awareness of a failure to grasp no more surely than society the truth of the man who becomes its victim; the failure to recognize who Joe Christmas really is.

This may sound more complex than it is, for in certain ways we are on familiar modern ground: the articulation in language of the difficulties of language, in this case the creation of a fictional being, the failure of whose portrayal is something like a strategy. The novelist implies the further range of meaning that both undermines the creation yet compounds the significance.

F. R. Leavis, dealing with Conrad's *Heart of Darkness* (an author and work similar to the Faulkner I am trying to describe) and its attempt to suggest levels of horror beyond articulation, makes what is still a forceful argument against this sort of thing: "He is intent on making a virtue out of not knowing what he means. The vague and unrealizable, he asserts with a strained impressiveness, is the profoundly and tremendously significant."[4] The answer to such an argument can only be that an art form (the opposite of incoherence) can describe the struggle toward, and even the qualified failure of, art forms. In *Light in August* the failure of the writer to give his central figure a complete fictional life is mirrored by a situation in which society fails to include this figure in its own structure, yet is deeply marked by his life and death. The man who can have no part in the community, who is in fact cast out of it, finally has a most important part. So too, the figure who is never "realized" in the novel comes to dominate it, casting over its strikingly peopled surface an unearthly light that alters everything.

II

Christmas then is clearly the key: in one sense insufficiently developed as a character, he supplies the rest of the novel with significance. For most readers he is a victim who never frees himself from the circle of his crossed blood (real or imagined), and who is killed by a society enraged at his flaunting of the mixture. But Christmas is more than this, more than his victimization. The conflict driving him toward a violent death is also the conflict he in part creates. This death and the form it takes are what he chooses: his own version of "It is finished."

Readers have always been aware of the parallels between Christmas and Christ, yet have rarely known what to do with them. The tendency among Faulkner's best critics has been to avoid clear-cut identification between the two; there seems little enough in common between the personality of the Christ of the Gospels and the central figure in *Light in August*. Yet it appears to me that the daring of Faulkner's creation here is that Christmas *is* a Christ in the novel, a figure whose form—the antithesis in which his personality is rooted, the struggle for a whole-ness of identity unknown to human beings—repeats the structure of the life of Christ.

Joe believes that he may be part black, part white. Blackness is for him what it is for the South in which he lives: an unpredictability, an abyss where life is perpetual flow; passive, yet faintly hostile, and never quite understood. Whiteness is the essence of design: cold, hard, man-like, as predictable as behavior in the context of Simon McEachern's iron laws of good and evil, or the cool and lonely street that stretches before Christmas.

Light in August is permeated with the idea of division, but Christmas is unique among the characters in that he is the only one who insists on unifying the forces rather than accepting, indeed depending upon, their separation. Not, as in Lena's case, by having sufficient faith to do away with the duality or, as in Joanna's, by living that duality one ele-ment at a time. Rather he searches for a wholeness that serves alike the dual sides of himself.

This quest for wholeness is to some extent a *given* one for Joe: as he is the model of the division known to all, he is also the most extreme example of the novel's pervading fatalism. Of all the characters his life seems the most arbitrarily determined, as if he were invented by minds prior to the maturity of his own. Referring to the circumstances sur-rounding Joe's birth—Milly's affair with a man possibly part Negro, Hines's assumption of the role of witness to God's inevitable ven-geance—Olga Vickery writes that "Joe is born into a myth created for him by others."[5]

This myth that precedes Joe into existence involves more than the mad assumptions of Hines that he is part Negro, the anti-Christ, the incarnation of sin and corruption. It is also formed by the dietician and McEachern. From the dietician Joe learns a relationship blending women, sex, unpredictability, and secrecy; for the five-year-old boy she is an image of disorder, completely unfathomable behavior that explains itself only by shouting " 'You nigger bastard!' " (p. 117). From Mc-Eachern, however, he learns the example of rigid definition, the oppo-site of what he has learned from the dietician. Joe's foster father provides him with a powerful image of predictability, rooted in the belief in a design fashioned by God of the destined elect and the destined damned. This Calvinistic sense of a preordained order results in an absolutist belief that there are distinct roles prepared for each man and in an insistence, as if a duty to the God who has created those roles, to fulfill them.

To the black-white division, created by Hines and complicated by the dietician, McEachern's Calvinism adds a commitment to self-knowledge and self-fulfillment. This evolves into the need for Joe to complete his given identity, whatever its nature.

It is in the combination of these influences on Joe's development that we can begin to see the strange dilemma that has been prepared for him. On the one hand he has been informed that his nature is divided between what he will eventually realize are the opposite poles of existence: the black and the white, the fearfully free and the coldly, permanently ordered. On the other hand he has learned a commitment to being what he is, and a hatred of that hypocrisy and cant that would allow him the peace of accepting less. Christmas is committed, then, to a design rooted in contradiction, a narrative whose completion is impossible according to the terms of the world into which he has been born. His quest for order is fatally bound to an endless process, the hopeless reconciliation of black and white.

In one sense he is the inheritor of an externally conceived plot, yet we must note the difference between the situation here and that of *As I Lay Dying*. Addie Bundren's imposed funeral journey, despite the Bundrens' private motives, has much more of the structural priority common to narrative than does the identity Christmas receives from his various inventors. It is not Hines or the dietician but Joe himself who supplies weight to that possible identity, giving it most of whatever strength it comes to possess. The "given" of Joe's blackness, unlike Addie's journey, does not function as an arbitrary pattern to limit consciousness; and the behavior of Christmas is different from the Bundrens' willingness to honor publicly and dismiss privately the given plot. Joe transforms this pattern into something larger than its origins. He at once obeys and enlarges its outlines, making it responsive to his own emerging identity, completing the narrative of the anti-Christ even as he lifts it to its sublime opposite. Plot in this novel is not the "determinate poetic form" controlling character energy but the unfounded fable that Christmas reinvents and transforms through a continuing act of consciousness.

Christmas is comprised of what Nietzsche called the Dionysian and the Apollonian, the will to destruction and the will to order. Nietzsche's understanding of those concepts and his insistence on the dynamic relationship between them captures the dynamic of Christmas's character and the tragic conflict he epitomizes. Christmas is both the Dionysian force and its verbalization by an Apollonian force, that difficult fusion that Nietzsche said was the focus of every Greek tragedy: "the one true Dionysos appears in a multiplicity of characters, in the mask of warrior hero, and enmeshed in the web of individual will. The god ascends the stage in the likeness of a striving and suffering individual. That he can *appear* at all with this clarity and precision is due to . . . Apollo."[6]

In Faulkner's terms, this hero is the black man in the appearance of a white, the god in the guise of a human being. He is the meeting ground of the elements that form him: a commitment to a stable design that the chaos of content is forced to deny. Joe Christmas well knows, as does Faulkner, that there is no language, no action, no available myth or version of reality, that will allow him to live the entirety of his contradictory being. His life is spent in the quest for such a possibility, but not in the north or south of his universe does there exist a name for his wholeness. If there is a wholeness available to him at all, it can lie only in the process of his life, a life gathering itself from the polarities of white and black, design and motion: visible, if still beyond discourse or reason, only as the crossed sticks of his conflict and crucifixion.

Yet he drives incessantly toward identity, fiercely defying all attempts to define him by reduction to less than his awareness of himself. To say "toward identity," however, is to suggest possibility of a kind that doesn't really exist in the novel. By the time Joe has arrived in Jefferson, he knows there can be no conclusion to his particular quest; for it is not a quest to achieve, to win, to bring back, but a quest simply to *be*. Design as an unchanging order that seals its identity forever, like Hightower's adolescent memory of daring boys in wartime he can review again and again, always the flames of burning stores in Jefferson, always the same sound of the shotgun concluding a romantic tale— there can be no such design for Christmas because he can never accept the conclusion of a tale. The whole meaning of his life is that it has no such conclusion. Christmas must create his black-whiteness in every action, destroying each action in the next, the white of the black man's prison, the black of the white man's desire. He can conclude nowhere, for the wholeness he embodies is superior to language, conception, society, art, to all the articulations of action; he can only be the perpetual process of himself. Each motion is no more than a momentary definition, a fragment, a lie, but each joins the *succession* of motions that is the identity of Christmas. His life is always living, never has it *been lived;* he exists in persistent change, and pattern is nowhere but in the act of his becoming.

If there is ever a time when Christmas believes that the unity he desires is something he can know within the contexts society and people provide, it is during his relationship with the waitress-prostitute Bobbie Allen. Prior to that relationship Joe is convinced not only that black and white are separate, for there is no question yet of reconciliation, but that he can prevent the invasion of certain forms of that blackness into his own life (despite the fact that he is aware of his own possible blood division). Blackness in this case is the menstruation of women which Joe, influenced by the dietician, easily connects with unpredictability and chaos: the "periodical filth" that fatally mars "the smooth and superior shape" (p. 173) of women. Despite what is told him of menstruation, Joe is still adolescent enough to be able to think, *"All right. It is so, then. But not to me. Not in my life and my love"* (p. 174)

But on the first of his evening meetings with Bobbie, Joe discovers she is having her period and he responds by striking Bobbie and fleeing to the woods, there to find the trees, "hard trunks . . . hardfeeling, hardsmelling" (p. 177), like the hardness of McEachern's ruthless design but now imperfect. The trees are like "suavely shaped urns in moonlight. . . . And not one was perfect. Each one was cracked and from each crack there issued something liquid, deathcolored, and foul" (pp. 177–78). But unlike Hightower, who also worships the possibility of a pure life, "complete and inviolable, like a classic and serene vase" (p. 453), Christmas gives up this particular version of what order and design mean. He becomes involved with Bobbie despite his initial disgust; more than that he reveals his suspicions about his black blood, not as a weapon as in subsequent encounters, but simply as a part of his identity: the blackness he discloses to her even as he has received and accepted hers.

He even dares to accept favors from Bobbie (or what he assumes to be such), the "mercy," associated with the dietician, which he has come to associate with all women as a part of chaos. Since mercy is a redemption from design, a reprieve from that order of things every fact points toward, Christmas sees it as the enemy of order, creating dependencies difficult to honor because one's expected role has been changed. The meaning of mercy to Christmas corresponds to the meaning of his own blackness; faced with an undeserved favor, Christmas usually resists as doggedly as if he were contesting the triumph of the blackness within himself. In part this is because he associates the *need* for mercy with

44

the degraded condition of the Negro; the food Joanna Burden prepares for him is *"Set out for the nigger. For the nigger"* (p. 224). To accept such mercy becomes then a retreat from his insistence on living the whole of his identity, the whiteness as well as the blackness of his being. It is therefore remarkable that he *is* prepared to accept favors from Bobbie Allen, even as he is prepared to accept the menstruation symbolizing her female imperfection, or to share with her the suspected truth of his blood division. And so when Joe begins to visit Bobbie in her room, "he did not know at first that anyone else had ever done that. Perhaps he believed that some peculiar dispensation had been made in his favor, for his sake" (p. 185).

Joe discovers that Bobbie is a prostitute, but he is still prepared at the last to marry her, as if his notions of black and white could actually coexist, cancel each other out in the love of a man and a woman. It is this belief of Joe's that gives the episode with Bobbie a curiously idyllic quality, as if his commitment to identity were somehow not hopelessly complicated by his inner division, as if he could actually be, on earth, the black-white man who is loved and accepted as such, and who can find in that acceptance the necessary language with which to know and accept himself. Bobbie, however, faced with the embarrassment of McEachern's attack at the dance hall and with the deeper problem of Joe's possible murder of his foster father, must revert to the categorizations of her society: she must free herself of the relationship with Joe and return him to his unacceptable divisions: " 'Bastard! Son of a bitch! Getting me into a jam, that always treated you like you were a white man' " (p. 204).

The fifteen-year street of Joe's quest for identity begins here, an identity that depends on his refusal to accept all possible versions of it. His life—the one he insists he has chosen—becomes the series of alternating roles that seem to divide him, but that are really the difficult terms of his wholeness.

The actions of Christmas from that time on are extremely complex, never allowing the kind of simplistic definition society requires. Invariably these actions combine white and black aspects, subtly bringing together opposing characteristics that allow Joe to remain distinct from white and black, even as he includes the wills of each. This is not simply a matter of challenging whites with his blackness, blacks with his whiteness, but with his capacity, his need, for deliberate reversals, to make of contradictory actions a single seam of personality.

Upon his appearance at the sawmill in Jefferson, in the second chapter of the novel, we find him carrying his name like "an augur of what he will do," yet no one can interpret it: " 'Is he a foreigner?' 'Did you ever hear of a white man named Christmas?' . . . 'I never heard of nobody a-tall named it' " (p. 29). Apparently a white man—allowing himself to be thought that anyway—he takes a "negro's job at the mill" (p. 31) as if in subversion of that whiteness. Yet he counters the effect of a menial job with a contemptuous look that is at odds with it. And while no one understands the meaning of these reversals, everyone senses their strangeness.

The climax of his life is the murder of Joanna and his subsequent behavior as he endures his own Passion Week, his every action appearing to contradict the previous one, yet the whole a sequence of man moving in a tortured harmony. The murder is a blend of determinism and deliberateness. Completed in Joe's mind before he performs the act—"*I had to do it. She said so herself*" (p. 264)—it is still an act of self-assertion as well as self-imprisonment. As he remarks earlier, musing over the ease and security of marriage to Joanna: " 'No. If I give in now, I will deny all the thirty years that I have lived to make me what I chose to be' " (pp. 250–51).

In hiding from his pursuers, in his capture and his subsequent escape, Christmas reveals his commitment to dual forces. In choosing to stay in the area, he demonstrates, according to some, his blackness: " 'show he is a nigger, even if nothing else' " (p. 292). But though he refuses to leave the county, he has little trouble avoiding his pursuers, and so his believed ignorance becomes his arrogance, the two combining to make clear categorizations of Joe impossible. Putting on the black brogans for which he has traded his city shoes, Christmas "could see himself being hunted by white men at last into the black abyss which had been waiting, trying, for thirty years to drown him and into which now and at last he had actually entered" (p. 313). But as he senses himself moving toward that primal abyss, which is chaos to him—and toward which he has partially moved all his life—he also tries to maintain an *order,* to keep intact an "orderly parade of named and numbered days like fence pickets" (p. 314). Such, of course, is his conception of whiteness, the dry, firm design that closes off a space, marking the boundaries between the understood and the unknown. He inquires about the day of the week, and it becomes evident that in the wildness of his behavior since the murder—fleeing without really trying to escape, pausing to curse God in a Negro church—he is also carrying out the required actions of some ritual in his own mind, completing some design. This design will strike the reader as in some ways similar to the life of Christ (driving the money-changers out of the church, for instance), but its prime importance, it seems to me, is simply the fact of design itself: Christmas is trying to time his capture according to some idea in his own consciousness, according to some pattern that exists prior to the act and that must be fulfilled. Whatever the precise reason—and there is no way of telling what it is—it is important to Christmas that his arrest take place on a certain day, and he chooses the day like a man whose primary concern is not to give himself up on Friday or Wednesday because it is that day, but who is creating an illusion of life *as the fulfillment of an order.* This is a gesture entirely opposed to his sense of an enveloping blackness, the coming chaos where order is annihilated. Yet, even as he moves in the wagon toward Mottstown with his chosen pattern established, the black shoes keep their symbolic import: "the black tide creeping up his legs, moving from his feet upward as death moves" (p. 321).[7]

Joe's capture sustains the dual style which, in his last days especially, becomes so emphatic. His getting a haircut and shave prior to capture, the calm and passivity with which he accepts capture (he doesn't actually give himself up), imply the meekness of a Negro or the contemptuousness of a white man, deliberateness or indifference. The categories of human behavior accepted by the southern community are all evident in Christmas's conduct, yet in such a mixture that Christmas is behaving as neither black nor white: " 'he never acted like either a nigger or a white man. That was it. That was what made the folks so mad' " (p. 331). He is now the process of both callings, a confluence of forces that violates the foundations of community life and all the individuals in that community.

And he sustains that variation of styles right to the end. Having allowed himself to be captured, without even trying to get out of the county, he seizes the first opportunity to break away from his captors when they reach Jefferson. Supposedly having agreed to accept a life sentence, he then arranges what is likely to mean an immediate execution. Christmas is moving now in a continuous motion of conflicting orders, a motion that Gavin Stevens, commenting on Christmas's last hours, must break into blocks acceptable to the dualistic logic of the community: " 'Because the black blood drove him first to the negro cabin. And then the white blood drove him out of there, as it was the black blood which snatched up the pistol and the white blood which would not let him fire it. And it was the white blood which sent him to the minister. . . .' " Stevens's analysis of Christmas's dilemma depends on the assumption that black and white are irreconcilable: " 'his blood would not be quiet, let him save it. It would not be either one or the other and let his body save itself' " (p. 424). But the safety and peace Stevens presumes here is the peace Christmas could never accept. This is not his failure but his triumph, not weakness that deprives him of the security of structure, but an inhuman strength that is his rise to a condition above it: design and darkness at one in the supreme fiction of his life.

In the catastrophe of his murder and castration, Joe Christmas becomes the completed paradox of conception and change, the image of what he is and has been:

> soaring into their memories forever and ever. They are not to lose it, in whatever peaceful valleys, beside whatever placid and reassuring streams of old age, in the mirroring faces of whatever children they will contemplate old disasters and newer hopes. It will be there, musing, quiet, steadfast, not fading and not particularly threatful, but of itself alone serene, of itself alone triumphant. (P. 440)

Like an image of supreme art, a revolving fiction of disparate forces no longer disparate, he is now that which is beyond struggle or the endless arguments with self of which the struggle has been made, beyond dogma and dialectic, crucified into the black-white man—and therefore beyond the separation on which that poor phrase of dualism rests. He will be interpreted in the discourse of those who are in life rather than in art; Gavin Stevens's systematic version of Christmas's oppositions is the first of these interpretations. But Christmas, as he has always been, although not in a language available to him or us, simply is: "of itself alone triumphant."

Joe Christmas is a Christ figure in this novel because he grows into manhood with a conviction both of an unintelligible, unresolvable split within him and a need to live this split into definition, one that is available, as far as he can determine, nowhere on earth. He owes this conviction to the existence of a narrative created independently of him, a mythic structure, fatal, foretelling, in which he believes and on the basis of which he acts, although he is aware that this tale of his origins may be false. The biblical Christ, like Joe, is born into a narrative that precedes him. Also like Joe, his consciousness is not the plaything of a myth, but rather the source of a courage to fulfill what has been foretold, to *be* that atonement of man and God that he believes is the task of his life and death. We may see Christ as merely the completion of a structure created centuries before his existence, the victim not so much of the men who crucify him as he is of the iron narrative that requires his death in order for the world to complete its pattern. But we must see him also as the arbiter of his destiny, not only the God who becomes a man in order to endure the unwinding of a design, but as the man who becomes the God through his willingness to fulfill that design. It is as if in choosing to complete what has been foretold he invests the ancient prophecies, spoken by the lips of men, with meanings larger than they contain.

Christ berates the man who would save him from the disaster ahead: "But how then should the scriptures be fulfilled, that it must be so."[8] And yet he also prays, "My Father, if it be possible, let this cup pass from me; nevertheless, not as I will, but as thou wilt." His words from the cross, "My God, my God, why hast thou forsaken me?" are the triumphant combination of man and God, the outcry of man caught in the chaos of seeing his death without end, and the whisper of God who composes the meaning of that death by quoting a psalm centuries old, transposing chaos into a unifying design. The quotation confirms the oneness of past and present: from the cross it establishes both the validity of prophecy and the identity of the man who speaks: "Jesus was quoting," Thomas Mann has written, "and the quotation meant: 'Yes, it is I!' "[9]

Christ's identity as the man-God can be established only by his pursuing the dualism to the end: for him to be rescued from his fate by "twelve legions of angels" would establish only his divinity but not his humanity. On the cross the anguished sufferer and the God who has fulfilled the prophecies are one, suspended in space like a divine image of the experience and meaning of being human. The death confirms the unique wholeness of his life, in which the human and divine, flesh and spirit, have become the inseparable languages of each other.

The basic form of Christ and Christmas is the same; and both come to horrify those communities whose insistent divisions they have chosen to resolve. This element of outrage is, of course, more emphatic in the case of Christmas, whose agony and confusion drive him to murder, whose tale is not told by a believer, as in the Gospels, but by the writer doomed to membership in the community. The violence of introducing a new vision to a world convinced it can do without it is everywhere in the story of Christmas. Faulkner's Christmas, unlike the dull echo of Christ we find in *A Fable,* is a new and striking creation of the *act* of vision, of what it might mean to invent and live a meeting of contradictions: of man and God, of design married to the darkness that destroys and signifies.

III

To move from Christmas to the "characters" of *Light in August*
is to move to what is more properly the language of fiction and to
fuller, more conventionally realized figures. These characters depend
for their identities, in the context both of society and the novel, on the
existence of certain patterns: the illusions of order that allow them to
live their lives. Each character inherits or creates a pattern that, although
it restricts movement and choice, remains a last defense against a reality
not to be faced unarmed. These are Apollonian structures built to protect against a chaos too difficult to understand or bear, and thus the
characters come to them in gratitude and relief. In Hightower's words,
they are the "shapes and sounds with which to guard [themselves] from
truth" (p. 453).

Such a use of illusion also characterizes the Jefferson society Faulkner
sets up in the novel: a rigid system of white and black, where the
black—symbolically the unconscious, the "lightless hot wet primo-
genitive Female" (p. 107)—is calmed into impotence by being locked
within the confines of the city walls. The town has a name for its
"reality"—it is called "nigger" and lives in Freedman town—and thus
has stabilized it, believing like Hightower (and with considerably more
reason) that it has bought its immunity. The black community, in other
words, has been drawn into the white-dominated Jefferson community
and made subservient to it. If blackness is in this novel a Dionysian or
process principle, it has become clearly the servant of an Apollonian or
product order. Blackness is in Jefferson an *image* of chaos and therefore
its very opposite, a verbal and social prison for chaos.

All the characters in the novel but Christmas follow the model of
Jefferson: they commit themselves to a clear pattern, designed to resist
the complexity of actual conditions. One means of carrying out this
commitment is the strategy of objectifying an inner reality, transferring
fear or desire, a chaos scarcely to be met as one's own, to an object
outside the self. The imagination creates illusory patterns that identify
and eject those parts of the self too difficult to bear. In several instances
Christmas himself becomes the living figure of someone else's inner
reality. McEachern and Percy Grimm's identification of Joe as Satan
or black rapist is a strategy of psychic survival.

This is not to say that repression is absolute, or illusion invulnerable.
On the contrary, it is the frailty of illusion that creates the action of the
book. Chaos reveals itself often, sometimes as the temporary anger, a
holiday of vengeance, through which community releases its locked up

energy; sometimes as that glimpse of the real that even the most dream-ridden, like Hightower, occasionally require. And sometimes we see it as the mad edge of those fanatic orders created by Hines and McEachern: orders which, like all the others, are fed by the fires of chaos, so much so that any relaxation of design must be the outbreak of insanity.

These strategies of survival are the writer's strategies of characterization as well. Their inner chaos objectified, as it can never be for Christmas, McEachern and Grimm gain a certain fixity that allows us to see them. Christmas insists on a total self: he will not know himself, as the others do, in the image of that which he must eventually destroy. His remoteness from us, as opposed to the clarity of McEachern and Grimm, Hightower and Hines, is owing to his unwillingness to accept a split life. Chaos is himself, not a sacrificial object. In creating Christmas, Faulkner challenges an idea of consistency in character for the sake of an idea of change and movement. As Kazin puts it, Faulkner attempts "the tremendous feat of making us believe in a character who in many ways is not a human being at all—but struggling to become one."[10] Character as a struggle toward being becomes Faulkner's subversive act in a novel of otherwise conventional characterization, just as Christmas's insistence on oneness is his own subversive act.

The figure of Hightower is the clearest version in the novel of the human need to encounter reality through protective fantasies. As with Christmas and Joanna Burden, Hightower has inherited the particular forms his need for order will take, his childhood memories of the Civil War experiences of his grandfather and his father. Referring to the horror with which the young Hightower first notices the patch of Yankee blue on his father's black coat worn during the war, Edmond Volpe observes, "He associates his father with the real world; the story of his grandfather releases him from the terrors of reality."[11] The father's coat, with its array of patches—"Patches of leather, mansewn and crude, patches of Confederate grey weathered leafbrown now" (p. 444) and the patch of blue—is the motley costume of comedy. But the story of the grandfather's raid on Jefferson and his subsequent death in a henhouse is of the single color and clear line of an adolescent's notion of glory:

> "they were boys riding the sheer tremendous tidal wave of desperate living. Boys. Because this. This is beautiful. Listen. Try to see it.

Here is that fine shape of eternal youth and virginal desire which makes heroes. . . . It's too fine, too simple, ever to have been invented by white thinking. A negro might have invented it. And if Cinthy did, I still believe. Because even fact cannot stand with it." (P. 458)[12]

Hightower presents the story as a magnificent artifact of color and touch and sound, with the whole circumstance of the war, " ' with all that for background, backdrop: the consternation, the conflagration' " (p. 458). The death at its close, the disgrace of chicken-stealing, only enhances its beautiful unbelievability for Hightower: " 'It's fine so. Any soldier can be killed by the enemy in the heat of battle, by a weapon approved by the arbiters and rulemakers of warfare. Or by a woman in a bedroom. But not with a shotgun, a fowling piece, in a henhouse' " (p. 459).

Spurred from the beginning by a tale, Hightower at first attempts to imitate its form by going to seminary, as if in Church he can live in a context where "truth could walk naked and without shame or fear," where life could be "intact and on all sides complete and inviolable, like a classic and serene vase" (p. 453). His aim is to convert his life into the purity of the tale. But the seminary has to give way to a parish, then to the need for a wife; at last he comes to Jefferson, where, as it turns out, he has been headed all the while.

But Hightower's devotion to his bright dream is a process well-told by several of Faulkner's critics.[13] What I would like to concentrate on here is the division in Hightower between his need for design and his still existing need to live, however superficially, in a real world. " 'I am not in life anymore' " (p. 284), Hightower muses, but his peculiar pathos is that he is, that he is suspended between dream and reality, completely absorbed in neither; and unlike Christmas, he cannot perform the difficult art of bringing them together.

Hightower's sole link to a world outside himself is Byron Bunch, but through Byron he becomes gradually involved with Lena Grove, with the grandparents of Joe Christmas, and finally with Christmas. Reality, it appears, is not easily put aside, and Hightower's delivery of Lena's baby is the culmination of his grudging surrender to its temptation. It is as if he has been goaded back into life, tempted to think it can prove less violent, more manageable than before.

In his return, however, he still must heighten his real action into illusion, his engagement with the real never to be free of the imagination's embellishments: "And then he says it, thinks it. *That child that I delivered. I have no namesake. But I have known them before this to*

be named by a grateful mother for the doctor who officiated" (p. 384).
He can even think that " 'luck and life [have] returned to these barren
and ruined acres' " (p. 385), and that he, Gail Hightower, the outcast,
the scorned, has been a part of that returning.

These particular extensions of the real are more wedded to action
than Hightower's memory of his grandfather's war exploits. Yet in the
midst of this new sense of having put aside his ghosts for the flesh of
reality, his new pride in falling asleep over *Henry IV* instead of Tenny-
son, Hightower still gloats over the fact that Byron has abandoned his
courtship of Lena and left town (p. 391). In this respect Hightower is
still harboring an addiction to purity, in the wake of new life caressing
uncomplex things: " 'If you must marry, there are single women, girls,
virgins. It's not fair that you should sacrifice yourself to a woman who
has chosen once and now wishes to renege that choice. It's not right.
It's not just' " (pp. 298–99).

But the temptation of the real continues its work on Hightower, and
he makes his gesture at the end to save Christmas from Percy Grimm
by insisting that Christmas was with him the night Joanna Burden was
murdered. It is the climax of his self-abasement, for both the homo-
sexuality and the mulatto murderer must be for Jefferson the maddest
kinds of violation of its well-guarded order.

Hightower's confession, however, cannot be seen as a full meeting
of the real and the abandonment of illusion. For with this admission,
Hightower is also insuring the latest community rejection that will
drive him back to the safer confines of his dreaming. Exploiting the
image of Joe as black rapist and murderer, and adding a hint of homo-
sexuality, Hightower's confession is motivated not only by humanitarian
purposes but by hunger for the bitter privileges of his imaginary world.

So we see him at the end of the novel confronting, one by one, the
darkest realities of his lifetime, only to conclude, as always, with the
persistent dream that puts realities aside. In chapter 20 he confronts
everything: his horror at a coat, his hypocrisy at the seminary, his
service to a church that he believes is a barricade "against truth and . . .
peace" (p. 461), his misuse of his pulpit—"a charlatan preaching worse
than heresy" (p. 462), the masochistic pride in his torment at the hands
of the townspeople—"that patient and voluptuous ego of the martyr"
(p. 464). Then the most awful reality of all, that he has been the " 'instrument of [his wife's] despair and shame' . . . *I don't want to think
this. I must not think this. I dare not think this*" (p. 464).

At the conclusion of this confession of perverse desire, Hightower
has only summoned new energies to serve the illusion that is still

paramount. The ugliness of his life and the ensuing guilt support and provide the power for that enduring illusion which is "honor and pride and life" miraculously distilled from impurity: "It is as though they had merely waited until he could find something to pant with, to be reaffirmed in triumph and desire with" (p. 466). Once again the imaginary riders rush by, dividing illusion from the darkness that has strangely inspired it: "the wild bugles and the clashing sabres and the dying thunder of hooves" (p. 467).

Joanna Burden would appear to be a typical instance in the novel of the need to possess a pattern for existence, in her case the inherited conviction that the Negro is the curse of the white man. This is the pattern that envelops her, and like Hightower's it begins to operate while she is still a child. Leaving little room for consciousness, it ensures a recognition of the forces of black and white as a *duality,* and thus weakens from the beginning any power consciousness might have for breaking through to some version of interaction. This polarity is the result of her father's efforts to derive some meaning from the murder of her grandfather and brother: " 'Your grandfather and brother are lying there, murdered not by one white man but by the curse which God put on a whole race before your grandfather or your brother or me or you were even thought of. A race doomed and cursed to be forever and ever a part of the white race's doom and curse for its sins' " (p. 239).

To contain violence in a pattern that will justify violence, that will convert it from some eruption of human hate and madness into a comprehensible part of a larger scheme—this is the dominant structure not only of Joanna's life but of the novel in general. The nature of violence is altered: the Dionysian is made not only to serve the Apollonian impulse toward design, but in so doing to lose its brief identity as Dionysian.

As a result of the pattern her father describes, Joanna likewise imagines an absolute narrative: " 'But after that I seemed to see them for the first time not as people, but as a thing, a shadow in which I lived, we lived, all white people, all other people' " (p. 239). The meaning of her life becomes the effort to rise: " ' "But in order to rise, you must raise the shadow with you" ' " (p. 240).

There is an important difference, however, between Joanna and the other inheritors of pattern, and it is this difference that helps explain why Joe Christmas stays with her for three years, and why he releases himself from her only because he has decided to bring his life to its own meaning and conclusion. Upon meeting Joe, Joanna divides her life in half: a being of day and a being of night, the spinster who methodically carries out her destiny by advising and aiding Negro colleges—by helping black people "rise"—and the frustrated middle-aged woman who spends her nights in sexual orgy with a man she believes or hopes is part Negro. By day she raises the Negro of her imagination to her level and at night lowers herself to his, as if trying in fact to *become* what is for her the principal meaning of the word damned: "'Negro! Negro! Negro!'" (p. 245).

In one role she is "hard, untearful and unselfpitying and almost manlike" (p. 221), in the other, free of the manlike passion for order, an image for Christmas of a "bottomless morass" (p. 246). By day she remains true to the pattern forced on her by her father, adopts the role of a white woman hung on a cross of blackness; by night she undermines the pattern in the only way she knows how: by becoming the cross itself, with Joe as the instrument of her transformation.

Because of this division, she is the only one in the novel who can believe in and accept Joe's own suspected division. She is not indifferent to his black blood, like the white prostitute in Detroit; yet she is still able to draw Joe into the context of her own design. He contains within himself the polarity of her vision of the world, the saved and the damned, and for a time she is willing, as if in partnership with him, to taste both: salvation by day, damnation by night. Joanna's is by no means a "whole" life, since she takes her design and her chaos one at a time; but she is the closest to Joe in the novel.

Finally, however, she belongs with the believers in order; by the "third phase" of her relationship with Joe she has decided that damnation is done, and the time has come to ascend, this time for good. Having accepted him as a divided being for the purposes of her own tour of hell, Joanna must now nail Joe down as Negro, marry him and/or send him to a Negro college, force him to study with a Negro lawyer and to take over from her the task of raising the Negro: he must raise himself as if he were both Christ and cross. At the end, she wants only for him to kneel with her, to allow her to retreat back to her given role of the white savior of Negroes by letting her pray for him and his black soul. For this is the only way she can redeem her period of damnation, convert it from an indulgence in nymphomania into a necessary humiliation of the self which consumes part of the path to salvation. That she has actually enjoyed her sex with Joe she does not even hide from herself: "What was terrible was that she did not want to be saved. . . . 'Don't make me have to pray yet. Dear God, let me be damned a little longer, a little while' " (pp. 249–50). But finally she *must* pray, and must raise Joe to college graduate and respectable lawyer; must solidify him into the black role that will justify her sexual relationship with him. More important, she must secure herself in her own original role, the circle of her life she too has never been able to break out of. At the end she does not challenge this given pattern at all, but hopes to reassert it with a clarity consistent with her heritage.

She does not reckon, however, on the stubborn integrity of Joe. For if her life has been lived in the design of a white Christ redeeming the black cross to which she is nailed, then Joe's has been lived in the insistence that he has not succumbed to an imposed design of any sort: that he is black *and* white, and that he will know the full nature of this complexity in his quest for identity. Joanna tries to force Joe to that single side of him which is his blackness; his killing her is, in more ways than one, an act of self-defense.

In McEachern, Hines, and Percy Grimm we see examples of the most mindless commitments to pattern in the novel: not pattern as the heroic, adolescent poem Hightower distills from his past, or as the social commitment Joanna Burden has created out of her conviction of the Negro's God-bestowed inferiority, but pattern as an implacable machine in the shape of God, carving a complex reality into the clear names of good and evil. To be sure, Hightower's fable and Joanna's hope to raise the Negro, like all patterns, must have their victims, the instruments of a wife or a mulatto lover (not to mention the inner being) that are necessary to the service of these designs. Yet McEachern, Hines, and Grimm are possessed by their orders to an extreme not found elsewhere in the novel. In the end, however, these frozen products are invaded, if only momentarily, by the Dionysian chaos that pattern has been intended to close off. This invasion is comparable to the uncharacteristic recklessness of Hightower in moving again toward life, or in risking the lie that Christmas was with him the night of the murder, or to Joanna's three years of nighttime debauchery with Christmas. In the lives of Joe's two "fathers" and his murderer, however, it erupts with a unique savagery, for theirs have been the most regimented and locked-in lives, and the ones in which the spectre of madness has always loomed.

Grimm, we are told, "had been for a long time in a swamp, in the dark" when "his life opened definite and clear. . . . uncomplex

and inescapable as a barren corridor, completely freed now of ever
again having to think or decide" (p. 426). The National Guard becomes
his design, its order, honor, and uniform become the language, the
"austerely splendid scraps of his dream" (p. 432). Throughout the chase
after Christmas, Grimm maintains a perfect calm and composure
appropriate to his chosen vocation: "He ran swiftly, yet there was no
haste about him, no effort. There was nothing vengeful about him
either, no fury, no outrage" (p. 436). But at the close, confronting the
nigger-murderer-homosexual-seducer of white men and women, Grimm
is no longer the composed guardsman, joyful in the rigidity of duty,
but the maddened avenger whose protective shield has been dislodged
for a moment by the sight of Christmas, who is at this point not so
much his own Dionysian darkness as Percy Grimm's.

For Hines and McEachern, the last encounter with Joe Christmas is
a meeting with the Devil himself: Christmas transformed into a crude
Satanic incarnation of his creators' madness. McEachern expresses his
discovery of Joe in the last of the sins he has predicted for him—sloth,
ingratitude, irreverence, blasphemy, lying, and lechery—with only a
sigh, "a sound almost luxurious, of satisfaction and victory" (p. 154).
In fulfilling completely the terms of folly, Joe confirms McEachern's
place on the side of right, and confirms as well his foster father's polar
vision. But McEachern's calm and assurance are only a delusion of
mind when he confronts Joe at the dance hall with Bobbie: "Very
likely he *seemed to himself* to be standing just and rocklike and with
neither haste nor anger. . . . Perhaps they were not even his hands
which struck at the face of the youth" (p. 191, my emphasis). This is
McEachern at the edge of lunacy: "it was not that child's face which
he was concerned with: it was the face of Satan, which he knew as
well" (p. 191).

Hines has also tried to escape an inner violence through the mad
fable of his grandson as the Devil's child. As Volpe has pointed out,
"His daughter's sexual adventure provides a focus for his tensions, and
his violence is transformed into a blend of religious and racial fanaticism." With such a pattern in mind "the once violent Hines can now
sit quietly in the orphanage for five years to watch his grandson."[14]
Immersed in the illusion of his own godliness, Hines can wait, "watching and waiting for His own good time" (p. 120); yet at the end, when
Joe quietly allows himself to be captured in Mottstown—"the captive
was the only calm one" (p. 326)—Hines is no longer an agent of God
but madness maddened: "Impotent and raging, with that light, thin

foam about his lips. . . . 'Kill the bastard!' he cried. 'Kill him. Kill him.' " (p. 327).

The eruption of chaos into the once secure limits of order is, generally in a much less furious manner of course, a pattern repeated several times in the novel, for *Light in August* is not only about the attempts of people and societies to preserve an Apollonian-like pattern to their lives, to replace chaos with art, but about the necessary re-emergence of that chaos. This is one of the several meanings of the novel's enigmatic title; for the light of August is a "savage summer sunlight," a "shameless savageness" (p. 438). Every figure in the novel must live his moment in this August light when an inner savageness, like the fury of a god long quelled, temporarily destroys the existing orders. And the source of this eruption, *in every case,* is Joe Christmas who, like the hero of Greek tragedy, brings to everyone the knowledge that annihilation looms, that the inevitable wreckage of design must disclose the destructive self.[15]

IV

We come, and none too soon, to less strenuous matters: Lena Grove and Byron Bunch; the very names abolish rage and pain. Lena and Byron are the sources of comedy in *Light in August* and of a kind of affirmation, although perhaps this last has been too uncritically emphasized by readers. Their meeting and subsequent relationship is a triumph of human action in the novel: good, gentle people, winning for themselves a deserved happiness amidst the extremity and obsession surrounding them. And yet it is doubtful that this sense of acceptance and even delight, which opens and closes *Light in August,* relieves the novel from its grimmer sense of human fate, or redeems Jefferson, whose citizens are as happy to see the departure of Lena and Byron as they are of Lucas Burch and Christmas.

There is a kind of irrelevance in Lena. The world of *Light in August* is not her world, and her faith and the luck it brings her are as remote from this novel as Dilsey's faith is from the main thrust of *The Sound the Fury.* That these are good people and frequently even happy people—old Dilsey singing away over the breadboard, Lena in constant delight at the mere passage of miles—does not alter the fact that they are not quite central to most of what goes on in their books or to the notion of reality those books insist on.

The comedy of Lena Grove is a comedy of faith, a conviction of order
so firm that it can hardly be said to be a conscious choice. Walking
with assurance out of Doane's Mill as if signposts marked "Lucas Burch,
10 mi." will be set alongside the road; pleased with her ladylike behavior at Armstid's breakfast table; fascinated with the variety of
countryside, people, reactions to her—Lena beholds a world she cannot
imagine as hostile. The comedy of it all is simply our recognition of
that faith as being not only irrelevant to reality but superior to it. Lena's
belief that " 'a family ought to all be together when a chap comes' "
(p. 18) is the assurance that it will be. The distance between this faith
and what we know to be the truth of Lucas Burch and his ilk would
normally result in pathos. Here it is comedy because we know that
although Lena is obviously wrong about the intentions of her lover,
she is also right about her own destiny; we know that contradictions
will somehow resolve themselves in her favor, regardless of Lucas
Burch. There is a part of Lena, Byron says, that " 'knows that [Lucas]
is a scoundrel' " (p. 285); yet she is not to be bothered with rationalizing
the difference between this knowledge and her larger faith. Her attitude
is much like Byron's: " 'if the Lord don't see fit to let them two parts
meet and kind of compare, then I ain't going to do it either' " (p. 285).

In a novel primarily about the violent collisions between illusion and
reality, Faulkner dares to give importance to the woman who recognizes no disparity between them: illusion *becomes* reality in the comic
vision of Lena Grove. Her outlook, as pleasantly and resolutely unswerving as Hines's is fanatically and hatefully unswerving, is the least
imaginative creation in the novel, for it is simply a social and religious
platitude she has adopted whole. Good girls don't have bastard children—"I reckon the Lord will see to that' " (p. 18)—and it isn't going
to occur to Lena that she deserves less from God than the next good girl.

Lena's place in *Light in August* has been acutely perceived by Irving
Howe, who looks beneath the usual platitudes about Lena: "She stands
for the outrageous possibility that the assumption by Faulkner and
his cultivated readers may be false: —the assumption that suffering
finds a justification in the growth of human consciousness. For Lena is
and does 'right' with a remarkably small amount of consciousness or
suffering, neither of which she apparently needs very much; she is
Faulkner's wry tribute to his own fallibility, a tribute both persuasive
and not meant completely to persuade."[16] Insofar as consciousness is
concerned and the modernists' grasp of life as a struggle toward full
awareness, Lena Grove is the character least relevant, for she is herself
barely conscious at all.

There is another, by no means contradictory, way of looking at Lena. This is as the representative of that which makes a struggle toward consciousness quite unnecessary: namely, pure faith. In this respect she is the counterpart of Dilsey, whose faith in *The Sound and the Fury* is the source of the most effective vision in the book—not because it is true to the kinds of reality that novel presents, but because it sustains her, where all other visions are inadequate even to their owners. Like Dilsey, Lena knows within the midst of becoming the being that designs the whole. As Dilsey can say " 'I seed de beginnin, en now I sees de endin,' " so Winterbottom can say of Lena, " 'I reckon she knows where she is going. . . . She walks like it' " (p. 7). It is characters like Lena and Dilsey who, in the midst of Faulkner novels of chaos and a persistent fragmentation, live lives that are like lives remembered, lives with beginnings, middles, and ends. They move from known beginnings to known conclusions, always aware of the full scope of the history they are in the process of completing.

Opposed to the wholeness Lena represents is Christmas, whose own wholeness is not a given, like grace, but a struggle with divisions he is all too aware of. The chaos that Christmas must engage is the chaos that Lena cannot even see. She possesses by faith what Joe can have only through the Faulknerian route, that is to say, through the tragic route of defining an individual history. Joe ends whole because crucified; crucified because he has dared to create his wholeness. Lena is born into a condition that Joe has had to prove. In more ways than one she inherits her "family" at the end because he has lived and died for it.

Behind Lena, dogged, persevering, is Byron Bunch, the most flexible of men and the most resourceful in breaking out of his self-styled patterns and risking the no-man's land of possibility. At the beginning of *Light in August,* Byron has walled himself into a tight structure of weekday work and Sundays in a country church, created out of a simple acknowledgment that "a fellow is more afraid of the trouble he might have than he ever is of the trouble he's already got" (p. 69). Infatuated at his first meeting with Lena, Byron breaks a prime habit— " 'In town on Sunday night. Byron Bunch in town on Sunday' " (p. 70)—thus quietly but emphatically opening himself to a world of contingency and the need to submit all his carefully built codes to the awkward demands of loving Lena Grove.

He invents new illusions to protect himself from those demands, but he discards them when reality beckons. He pretends that the pregnant Lena is a virgin, only to accept at last, with the cry of her baby, *"that she is not a virgin. . . . It aint until now that I ever believed that he is*

Lucas Burch. That there ever was a Lucas Burch" (p. 380). Following his request to the sheriff to send Lucas Burch to see Lena, Byron leaves Jefferson, mistakenly assuming that Lena and Lucas will get married. At the sight of Lucas climbing out the back window of Lena's cabin, he dreams of bringing Lucas *back:* " 'And I may not can catch him, because he's got a start of me. And I may not can whip him if I do, because he is bigger than me. But I can try it. I can try to do it' " (p. 403). After his beating at the hands of Lucas, and after seeing Lucas ride off on a train, Byron is left with the reality that Lena is, at long last, available.

At this point his imagination comes to a halt, for he is either unable or unwilling to create a fantasy about what is to follow. He can see himself at the door of her cabin easily enough: *"Then I will stand there and I will. . . .* But he can get no further than that" (p. 418). Byron has opened himself to the unpredictabilities of reality in a manner duplicated by no one else in the novel except Christmas. Most of the other characters have never discarded their protective illusions; Lena, of course, has never had any need to. But in the name of love, Byron submits himself to the road, the road Lena travels with equanimity because her faith is greater than its surprises, but which Byron must endure as an ordinary man.

If Byron were a more impressive figure, his power at least to begin a course of action free of imaginary preconceptions (apart, of course, from the hope that he will eventually make Lena his wife) might have greater significance in the novel. As it is, Byron has merely tied himself to Lena's larger vision, whose authenticity we certainly do not question, but whose relevance to Faulkner's world continues to escape us.

And what of Jefferson, locale and backdrop for all these events? Its division of white and black is an echo of the destructive dualities of the leading characters. We shall not reach the deepest meanings of *Light in August,* however, by attacking the community. It is, for the bulk of the novel, a quiet, peaceful place, precisely because it has worked out a modus vivendi of pattern and desire that enables it to endure and to protect its members. Jefferson may be said to represent the most stable possibilities of an existence basically full of contradiction. Not that it has achieved a genuine interaction of forces by any means, but its illusions are less desperate, less fanatic than those of Hines, McEachern, Joanna, or Grimm, and less remote from reality than those of Hightower.

Significantly enough, Jefferson is able to accommodate even its out-casts—the Hightowers, the Joanna Burdens, the Hineses—allowing all of them (with the important exception of Christmas) to remain within the community, even if on the outskirts. And while some, like High-tower, are made to feel its disapproval, most are the beneficiaries of its tolerance and charity. Hines is considerately escorted home by towns-people who find his fanaticism no saner than do we. Byron Bunch, whose deliberate self-isolation renders him merely invisible for part of the novel, and whose courting of the pregnant Lena makes him into "wellnigh a public outrage and affront" (p. 398) for the rest of it, is in no danger from society. And Joanna and Hightower, whose patterns vary the most from Jefferson's codes, are, until the final days of Christ-mas, allowed the peace and occasionally even the small generosities of the community.

Most of the life of Jefferson is in fact the life of order, of people who believe that "no matter what a man had done with his Sabbath, to come quiet and clean to work on Monday morning was no more than seemly and right to do" (p. 37). And when violence is at last set loose, aroused by the image of the black murderer Christmas, the town soon reverts to the tranquility of "suppertables on that Monday night" (p. 419), the citizens of Jefferson eating and calmly talking about the strange be-havior of Christmas, following his arrest. Jefferson is what is possible and plausible in *Light in August;* its vision is not equal to Christmas, but in this respect it follows a deep precedent. In short, Cleanth Brooks is quite right when he emphasizes the condition of Jefferson as a matrix, the life of a little Southern community, one which, whatever its limitations, faults, and cruelties, is a true community."[17] Between the religious visionary, Lena, who frames the novel, and the evolving Man who lives at its center, we have nowhere to stand but in the community of men and women. As Hightower says, "all that any man can hope for is to be permitted to live quietly among his fellows" (p. 69).

This recognition, however, returns us to the tragedy of the novel, for the failure of Jefferson to comprehend Christmas is a crucifixion. And the need for clarity at the expense of truth which that crucifixion ex-emplifies is a need implicit not only to the structure of community but to the structure of art as well. The great guilt of Jefferson is that it can find no room within it, not even on its periphery, for Joe Christmas. It has no place for him for the simple reason that he is the one figure in the novel whose sense of the necessary relationship between design and energy is different from its own. But this is the guilt, one must add, of the novel *Light in August* and its author, whose failure to bring

Christmas fully into the context of the human becomes a moving admission that community's repressive division may find an echo in the nature of fictional language.

V

All of Faulkner's major novels are studies in fragmentation, experiments in the nature and cause of disorder and in the possibility of working through it to some sense of coherence. As I hope I have already established, the making of coherent form in Faulkner is of prime significance, involving the most crucial issues of consciousness and the possibilities of human community.

In *As I Lay Dying,* following the persistent refusal of *The Sound and the Fury* to accept any of its various imaginative modes, Faulkner uses the long funeral journey of the Bundrens as a means of avoiding the disintegration that befalls the Compsons. With the same structural device he also alters the shape of *As I Lay Dying* from a succession of remote, self-interested voices into a coherent action. The irony, of course, is that awareness, so much of what Addie calls "the duty to the alive, to the terrible blood," has been purged from the novel for the sake of its order, even as the rich consciousness of Darl must be purged from the family as the price of the completion of the journey.

In *Light in August,* however, Faulkner uses far subtler means of ordering disjointed materials. Unlike the "voice" novels, this narrative is told from outside, and from this external point of view Faulkner creates an intricate network of mirror images and metaphoric relationships that unify the book. Despite the novel's considerable fragmentariness, its unrelated characters, its juxtaposition of incongruous events, not to mention Faulkner's usual chronological shifting, *Light in August* achieves a high degree of coherence almost entirely through the use of metaphor: an elaborate series of echoes bringing together in the reader's mind, if not in that of the participating characters, the whole sprawling canvas of *Light in August.*

Michael Millgate has observed:

Any search for underlying patterns in *Light in August* might well begin with a consideration of the extensive series of parallels and substitutions which appear in the course of the novel and which again establish thematic and even narrative links between its different strands. An obvious example is Mrs. Hines' confused identification

63

of Lena's baby with Joe Christmas when he was a child, and her further reference to the baby as being actually Christmas's son. One thinks also of the similarities between the apparently opposed backgrounds of Hightower and Miss Burden, fanatics of the South and of the North; of the parallelism between the tragic encounter of Joe Christmas with Percy Grimm and the primarily comic encounter of Byron Bunch with Lucas Burch, which takes place at the same moment in time; of the reverberations set up in the reader's mind by the incident of Christmas breaking into a Negro church like an impersonation of the devil, recalling as it does both the mad forays into Negro churches made by his grandfather, Doc Hines, and the moment of Satanic glee caught by the camera as Hightower leaves his empty church.

Most important of all, however, is the relationship between Miss Burden and Lena Grove and Lena's replacement of Miss Burden at the plantation after the latter's death.[18]

These links are indisputable; and one can go even further in itemizing them since they exist, usually in less striking manner, all through the novel.

Lena's four-week journey from Doane's Mill to Jefferson, for example, "is a peaceful corridor paved with unflagging and tranquil faith" (p. 4); Joe Christmas's earliest memory is that of a "quiet and empty corridor" (p. 111); and the orphanage dietician who has such a profound effect on Joe's life, though she has nothing whatever to do with Lena, comes to see her life as "straight and simple as a corridor with [Hines] sitting at the end of it" (p. 118). Finally, Percy Grimm also comes to "see his life opening before him, uncomplex and inescapable as a barren corridor" (p. 426). Although the meanings are different and even contradictory in each context, the literal and metaphoric corridors become a connecting link among the four characters.

Hines and McEachern accost the dietician and Bobbie Allen with similar outbursts: "'Answer me, Jezebel!'" (p. 123) and "'Away, Jezebel!'" (p. 191); Percy Grimm's "certitude, the blind and untroubled faith in the rightness and infallibility of his actions" (p. 434) suggests nothing so much as the faith of Lena Grove; Hightower and his bride-to-be make use of "a hollow tree in which they left notes for one another" (p. 454), in innocent anticipation of Christmas and Joanna, who "insisted on a place for concealing notes, letters. It was in a hollow fence post below the rotting stable" (p. 245); and when Hightower says abjectly " 'So this is love. I see' " (p. 455), he repeats in delusion Christmas's ecstatic discovery: " 'Jesus. Jesus. So this is it' " (p. 183).

Lena and Joanna both discover their pregnancies at the same time, "Just after Christmas" (p. 251); if Joanna were in fact pregnant, she and Lena would both give birth in August. Given the confusion by Mrs. Hines and Lena herself as to who her baby really is and who is its father, it is as if Lena has borne not her own child by Lucas Burch, but Joanna's by Joe Christmas. The story of Lena's conception of her baby is also like that of Milly Hines, while Joanna's grandfather, Calvin Burden, is a more sympathetic McEachern, beating the loving God into his children. Byron's weekend treks into the country repeat those of Hightower's father, who was secretly "riding sixteen miles each Sunday to preach in a small Presbyterian chapel back in the hills" (p. 442).

Characters are constantly replacing each other, moving into squares on the board reserved for someone else, or repeating unwittingly the behavior of an unknown antecedent. Expecting to find Lucas Burch, Lena discovers Byron Bunch at the mill; when Hightower enters Lena's cabin, hopeful of receiving some reward for his services, he also comes as a poor substitute for Lucas.

This kind of substitution results at times in a bitter irony. During the initial chase after Christmas, prior to his arrest in Mottstown, the sheriff and his men are led by bloodhounds to a Negro cabin where the scent of Christmas's shoes has guided them. With pistols drawn, expecting to encounter the dangerous black murderer, the sheriff "kicked open the door and sprang, pistol first, into the cabin. It contained a negro child. The child was stark naked and it sat in the cold ashes on the hearth, eating something" (p. 311). Returning to the cotton house where Christmas apparently exchanged shoes with the child's mother, the men find "one astonished and terrified field rat" (p. 312).[19]

Through such a tissue of echoes and repetitions Faulkner draws the fragments of his novel together, yet he does so at a huge price, deliberately paid, in truth as well as power. For this kind of order is an imposed one; it does not emerge from the action of the novel, and it is seldom realized by the characters. Instead they are metaphoric orders devised by an ingenious narrator and made available only to the reader of the tale, not to the people who have lived those echoes. The order achieved here is in the realm of what Coleridge meant by fancy, not imagination: relationships are established simply as structural gestures, a poetic order imposed on unpoetic and scattered materials. No transformation through metaphor occurs; we are not led by the work into a knowledge of a new order of things previously unseen. On the contrary, our logical sense of the novel's disorder remains intact, and our poetic sense of its order points more to the cleverness of the novelist than to a new vision of reality.

The pressure of genuine metaphor welding together what is logically irrelevant, gives way here to less assertive simile, suggesting resemblance while remaining securely aware of the actual differences between things. As Murray Krieger writes, "The test of poetry is whether or not it solicits us to end in another way of apprehending, whether or not it builds intramural relations among its elements strong enough to transform its language into new meanings that create a system that can stand up on its own."[20] The aim of Faulkner's fiction is to approach such a way of apprehending, to create from chaos orders of reality that assert not only the power of the poet's consciousness but propose an entirely new truth.

But in the many figurative links of *Light in August* the novelist seems to provide nothing more than an ostentatious display of his prowess, of the skill with which he controls the fragments of his work. This is wild and disordered existence, the technique implies, saved only by the writer's manipulations creating what is obviously an illusion of order. The triumph, if triumph there be, is his; and the consolations of form appear to be not quite authentic.

Occasionally, it is true, these links are imagined not by a superior, outside intelligence, but by the characters themselves, as when Hightower links Joe and Byron by believing that both, in their "immoral" activities, are being guided by the devil (p. 291). Most of the examples in the novel of this kind of metaphoric connection, the characters' conscious creation of relationships unfounded in fact, occur toward the end of the book; and it may well be that this is calculated to express a growing power on the part of such characters to break out of the novel's heavy fatalism and create, with whatever degree of illusion, the terms of order. The relationships between Lena's baby and Christmas are of this kind: Mrs. Hines imagines that the baby is actually Joe, born again, with the stain of his past and his murder of Joanna momentarily redeemed; and Lena occasionally finds herself believing that Christmas is her baby's father. For most of the novel, however, order is an external achievement imposed with almost Joycean care on material that is itself quite mindless of the connections and relationships it is serving.

This elaborate use of metaphoric form, much more prevalent here than in any other Faulkner novel, is consistent with the heavy fatalism that dominates *Light in August*. Characters come alive only in the restricted possibilities of their pasts. Many are caught in the fixed patterns bestowed on them by ancestors; others discover quickly the need for such frozen models and fashion these for themselves, quickly transforming them into prisons as solid as if they were conceived in the blood.

"And this too is reserved for me" (p. 380), Byron Bunch thinks, pondering the fact that he must tell Lucas Burch he is now a father; and Hightower receives his new sense of vitality, of potency: "It would seem that this too was reserved for me. And this must be all' " (p. 392). It is the narrator who mutters the grim refrain: "But it is not all. There is one thing more reserved for him" (p. 392). With nearly all the characters, even Burch, who can envision the "Opponent" who moves them all like chessmen on the board (p. 414), life is little more than what is "reserved" for them. It is as if all were designed and done with before hand, the events of a life waiting patiently, like chairs in a wood, for their proper owner to happen upon them.

Both the action of *Light in August* and its method of structure through image patterns suggest, on one level, nothing so much as an enormous trap. In his role as narrator Faulkner becomes a detached sovereign, composing from a distance a network of figurative schemes that the characters unwittingly perform. The rigid patterns they *have* chosen find their fitting echo in those metaphoric links only author and reader are aware of.

The genuine fragmentariness of the fictional material—Lena and Joanna, to choose one example, have in *fact* nothing to do with each other—is altered only by the writer's superior establishment of order-making links. In the same way, the characters of the novel learn that the only protection against reality is the acceptance of solid patterns, inherited or created, with which they can shield themselves.

But this is only part of *Light in August,* for at the center of the novel, in this respect as in all others, is Christmas. In the midst of imposed orders is the figure of the man who challenges and expands the limits of his own given narrative, who both accepts and revitalizes the myth bestowed on him by his crazed grandfather, enlarges it to the structure of that self he is in the process of creating. Given the extreme dubiousness of the origins of the myth and Christmas's creative drive to expand it, we discover that we are not dealing with myth at all but with its transformation into a fiction: the authority of myth is not superior to but identical with the living structure of a creating mind.

And so it is Christmas who frees the novel from the innumerable links in which it is imprisoned. He does this, not as Lena does, by being blind to the chaos against which pattern is conceived, but by living a life whose pattern, the black and the white, he can sustain only by exploding first one part of the duality, then the other. This is pattern *in process,* the Apollonian confirmed and annihilated by the Dionysian. Through the forces of Christmas, *Light in August* drives, as no other Faulkner novel before it, toward a new fictional status: toward the idea of a supreme fiction, the form that feeds on its own dissolution.

The product quality of narrative, the pattern that precedes consciousness, is delivered over to the processes of consciousness. Narrative does not predetermine but draws forth the inventiveness that must complete the fiction. The narrative of Christmas begins with the not very-well-founded assumptions of his grandfather, but becomes a dynamic questing for identity: a fiction which is supreme because it retains a given shape even as it dissolves into expanding configurations of meaning.

Light in August comes to us then as the most enigmatic of Faulkner's novels. In its presentation of characters who require nothing so much as the security of imprisoning pattern, in its own metaphoric ordering of typically fragmentary materials, the novel presents a narrow view of the potentialities of human consciousness—and even extends that view to society in the form of Jefferson. Yet at the center of the novel, as if he were a god-figure enduring his necessary crucifixion at the hands of those who must see less for fear that they will see more than they dare to comprehend, is Christmas. The novel demonstrates that the ranges of human imagination are terribly restricted—its fairest model, the small town that has merely learned to live peacefully with its division; yet it also contains a figure who pursues the limits of consciousness. Faced with Christmas's intolerable pressures toward vision, community can only absorb him into its crude logic, call him by the name of blackness, and kill him. Yet is he not at the same time comparable to Stevens's hero, who rises "because men wanted him to be"?

. . . large in their largeness, beyond
Their form, beyond their life, yet of themselves,
Excluding by his largeness their defaults.[21]

He is the victim of their fear of vision, yet in their memories—expanding those integers of black and white they thought they had understood—he is the man who endures "forever and ever."

4 | *Absalom, Absalom!*

In *Light in August* Faulkner made the first of his most significant attempts to free himself from the idea of the necessary failure of fictions, of the unbridgeable distance between any human construct and reality. He did this not by asserting a referential relation between formulation and fact but by suggesting new ways of fictional meaning. Joe Christmas is a character in whom illusion and flux are wedded together. His enactment of the roles of black and white is a process of making into flesh the ungrounded fable of his origins. The figure of his life remains a mystery, a metaphor, for it revolves around a center—the blackness—which may be imaginary. Indeed the power of the figure resides in that very possibility, and in the fact that Joe is aware of it and does not conceal it. This possible invention of the blackness that gives Joe his special distinction and his special agony is not an evasion of complexity, as in the case of Quentin Compson's fantasy of incest, "symmetrical above the flesh." It is rather the means by which Joe confronts and illuminates that complexity, his own and his society's. Joe comes to exemplify the activity of the supreme fiction that Faulkner is trying to create: the fiction that claims both the precariousness and the relevance of forms, not as opposition but as a dynamic whose terms feed on and fuel each other.

Absalom, Absalom! is another and even more successful attempt to construct a significance of fictions without giving up the sense of a fundamental discontinuity between art and life that is basic to the modern. Faulkner's method is comparable to the design-process dynamic of *Light in August,* but now focuses on the relationship between the teller of a tale and its principal actor. *Absalom, Absalom!* is part of a major tradition in modern fiction, including such novels as *Moby-Dick, Heart of Darkness, Lord Jim, The Great Gatsby, Doctor Faustus,* and *All the King's Men,* in which the spheres of the imagined and the real are first divided, then fused. Teller and actor become mirrors of each other, both exploiting and serving their opposites; and the exploration of the relationship between imagining and acting, illusion and reality, is lifted to the dramatic surface of the text. Telling, on the one hand, is a means of exploitation as the narrator forces the actor to become the incarnation of his own fantasies and desires. At the same time the actor is the narrator's model, whose action the latter *imitates,* even as he provides that action with verbal form, establishing motive and meaning. In fact the teller must become in some way the subject of his imaginative reconstruction in order to give validity to his telling. Marlow's act of narration in *Heart of Darkness,* for example, its defiance of narrative convention, its risks of incoherence, its pressing of the facts of barbaric behavior into the forms of tragic vision and victory, is a partial repetition and justification of the acts of Kurtz: Marlow's source, his predecessor, and the beneficiary of his imaginative talents. Marlow's tale and Kurtz's life, apparently separate entities, derive their reality and validity from each other. The relationship they establish is a metaphor for the action of modern fictional meaning.

The narrator celebrates his own life by transforming his hero into a dramatic version of it. At the same time he celebrates the life of his hero by relegating his own to the repetition of what he takes to be the truth of that life. That truth, that interpretation, is both the means and the end of the repetition.

The deeds of the actor are the ground from which the narrator builds his fable; yet the act of creation, involving form and interpretation, must contain the motives of the teller as well. The result is a novel about the making of a fiction centered on an impressive actor, yet imbued with the attitudes of an equally impressive creator. The narrator invents himself indirectly, finds his identity in his own fiction, even as the actor—like a character searching for a novel—finds a home and a meaning in this created world. Fiction and fact are interdependent and indistinguishable: both are present but which is which?

At the center of *Absalom, Absalom!* there is a known fact, like a real stone enduring centuries of words: in 1865 a man named Henry Sutpen, the son of Thomas Sutpen and Ellen Coldfield, killed a man named

Charles Bon. The fact is inhuman not only because it has to do with violent death but because it is without meaning; it covers everything with chaos. This fact is what makes imagination necessary; and imagination is limitless, with the single exception that it cannot drive the fact from existence, from having occurred.

The lives of Miss Rosa Coldfield, Mr. Compson, Quentin Compson, and Shreve McCannon, retelling the story of the Sutpen family in 1909–1910, take root and grow into unique shapes through the different ways they approach this fact. Each must invent the structure that will satisfy the conditions of fact and the conditions of the self as well. The novel is one of four "educations"; the narrators must each learn the processes by which they can master imaginatively the enigma of murder in 1865.[1] The test of that mastery is the degree to which imagination and fact can coincide in a supreme fiction: it is fact metamorphosed into a figure for subjective desire, yet it is still fact. This is the climax of Nietzschean tragedy: "Dionysos speaks the language of Apollo, but Apollo, finally, the language of Dionysos."[2]

Listening to the last sentence of Miss Rosa's long and urgent recapitulation of her life, Quentin realizes that "there was . . . something which he . . . could not pass." The story he has just heard does not fully explain to him the imagined picture of Judith and Henry striking one another with their blowlike words: *"Dead? / Yes. I killed him."* Similarly, all the speakers must "pass" what appears to be some meaningless sequence of human affairs, must strive to explain the shockingly clear but still incoherent facts.

In order to achieve that explanation, each narrator must pass some enigma of the self as well. Meaning rests on what the self dares to imagine, and what it dares is crucially involved with how much knowledge of self it can risk. There is a familiar Freudian truth here that the imagination, like dreams, is always a function of our deepest personality traits; and that it rises in order to resolve symbolically tensions otherwise irreconcilable, perhaps unendurable. Familiar or not, that truth comes to vivid life in *Absalom, Absalom!* as each narrator tells the Sutpen story in accordance with his own private needs. In *The Philosophy of Literary Form,* Kenneth Burke proposes an approach to literature *"in terms of a situation and a strategy for confronting or encompassing that situation."* The language and structure of the work are the poet's means of identifying and coping with a significant personal dilemma. Form, in other words, is symbolic: "The motivation out of which [the poet] writes is synonymous with the structural way in which he puts events and values together when he writes."[4]

Burke is thinking, of course, of real poets, not imaginary ones, yet strategies of composition are what *Absalom, Absalom!* is all about; and the relevant materials are not in diaries and letters, but solely within the work. We must examine what the narrators tell us for its motivation if we are to arrive at its full meaning, for one is the symbolic language of the other. Our questions must not be merely *what* each narrator believes or *how* they have come to believe it, but *why* they find it *necessary* to believe in the way they do. The question is not how, for example, Quentin and Shreve discover that Charles Bon is Henry's half-brother, but why it is necessary for them to *make* Bon his half-brother, for that "discovery" is as much a strategy as Miss Rosa's need to see Sutpen as a demon. And strategy, as Burke tells us, always contains attitude.

Each version of the Sutpen history we receive, each interpretation of the available facts into a particular plot, equipped with motive and meaning, is an exercise in symbolic extrication from some condition of anxiety. The success of that extrication, both in terms of the relief it provides the teller and the assent it gains from the listener, depends on the degree of candor it demonstrates. Pretty tales which simply pretend that false is true satisfy neither listener nor teller. The genuine symbolic form must create the strongest opposition possible for the speaker to pass. A convincing extrication, in other words, depends on the power the poet can give those elements in his structure that are most threatening to the resolution he is trying to achieve. This, of course, is part of the strategy.

In each narration in *Absalom, Absalom!* we see the speaker's attempts to deal with the potential opposition within his tale to his own interpretation: Miss Rosa's demonic view of Sutpen must consider the possibility of his humanity; Mr. Compson's sense of human folly and meaninglessness must cope with Charles Bon's apparent altruism in dying for love and honor; Quentin and Shreve's idealistic approach to Bon must contend with his possible exploitation of Judith as a means of getting even with his "father," Sutpen. Strategy demands as much tension as the teller's own version of truth will allow.

But where does self-serving strategy end and "truth" begin? When, if ever, does art cease to temper guilt, to exonerate the poet's own life, and when does it become more? Imagination must begin in personal need, but when and how does it produce a fiction that comprises a truth for us all? At what point does fiction intersect with reality even as it preserves a discontinuity we have come to insist on?[5]

II

The heart of Miss Rosa Coldfield's narrative is her re-creation of Thomas Sutpen as a diabolical and therefore incomprehensible being, *"from abysmal and chaotic dark to eternal and abysmal dark completing his descending"* (p. 171). His motiveless behavior accounts for the decline not only of his and Miss Rosa's families but of the entire South. Miss Rosa's interpretation of Sutpen's character as demonic is perfectly consistent with her understanding of the story as a whole. Like Sutpen's refusal to allow his daughter Judith to marry Charles Bon, this story is for Miss Rosa " 'without rhyme or reason or shadow of excuse' " (p. 18). The basic irrationality of all the events is further proof of her conviction that the devil has been at work. Miss Rosa's narrative, however, like all the versions of the story we get, is rooted in her own personality, and we must read her interpretation as a text of that personality, its symbolic outline, even as it is a text grounded in certain facts about Sutpen.

Miss Rosa's is a tale of remoteness, of a gap between herself and a sensual world whose primary image is Thomas Sutpen. She divides existence in half, between class and custom, *"the devious intricate channels of decorous ordering"* and physical reality, *"the touch of flesh with flesh"* (p. 139). It is this second realm that remains closed to her. Quentin Compson says that Miss Rosa talks about Sutpen in order to let people know *"why God let us lose the War"* (p. 11). More crucial is her need to exonerate herself from the guilt of not having completed her passage into a real world. The Sutpen she invents is the cause of her aborted life; at the same time that life is a major impulse to the invention.

Sutpen's mulatto daughter, Clytie, plays a role comparable to Sutpen's in Miss Rosa's imagination. She is the blackness that corresponds to Sutpen's powerful virility, and Rosa has as much trouble literally passing Clytie as she does imaginatively and literally passing Sutpen. Following the murder of Charles Bon—whom she loved in the only way possible for her, in fantasy—Miss Rosa rides out to Sutpen's Hundred but is prevented from seeing the body of Bon. Blocking her way on the stairs is Clytie, *"something monstrous and immobile . . . that black arresting untimorous hand on my white woman's flesh"* (p. 139). Rosa knows here what she has always known: *"let flesh touch with flesh, and watch the fall of all the eggshell shibboleth of caste and color too."* But this is a meeting she cannot accept. She retreats to the conventions that protect her against Clytie and which she will eventually use to

save herself from Sutpen: *" 'Rosa?' I cried. 'To me? To my face? . . .*
Take your hand off me, nigger!' " (pp. 139–40).

Miss Rosa's basic fear of life is easily traceable; she is born into the
old age of a man widowed by her birth, a man who disapproved not
only of the war but of life: "That night he mounted to the attic with
his hammer and his handful of nails and nailed the door behind him
and threw the hammer out the window" (p. 82). The Coldfield in-
heritance is, according to Mr. Compson, a " 'cluttering of morality and
rules of right and wrong' " (p. 120), and is a major source for Rosa's
life-long inability to move from preconceived orders to an encounter
with the real.

In several ways Miss Rosa is comparable to the Quentin of *The Sound
and the Fury,* who is also terrified of blackness, sex, and the mundane
realities of men who cheat at cards and women who fornicate in the
woods. Mr. Compson, ever aware of the need to ease the truth with a
tale, comments in the earlier novel on Quentin's assertion that he and
Caddy have committed incest: "you are contemplating an apotheosis in
which a temporary state of mind will become symmetrical above the
flesh." Miss Rosa hardly needs Compson to supply such information, for
she well knows *"there is that might-have-been which is the single rock
we cling to above the maelstrom of unbearable reality"* (pp. 149–50),
even as she must always believe that the Civil War was fought—*"what
else worth dying for?"*—to preserve the meanings of *"love and faith at
least above the murdering and the folly"* (p. 150). The gap between
some "symmetrical" order and living flesh, the "might-have-been" and
an "unbearable reality," is what provokes the earlier Quentin to suicide
and, for all her attempts to engage that reality, drives Miss Rosa continually back to the "single rock" of her illusions. Despite her fear,
however, she tries again and again to "awake," to know on her pulses
those Sutpen truths that have always fascinated and frightened her. This
eagerness persists to the very end, to 1909, as once again she journeys
out to Sutpen's Hundred, this time with Quentin rather than Wash
Jones as her escort, again to confront the *"inscrutable coffee-colored
face"* (p. 138) of Clytie on the stairs, and, at the top, not the dead Bon
but the dying Henry.

The drama of Miss Rosa's life lies in these unsuccessful attempts to
escape the Coldfield heritage, that "cluttering of morality"; and the
drama of her narrative is her attempt to provide a portrait of Sutpen
that goes beyond a Gothic fable. Both of these attempts, for the success of one is clearly bound up with the success of the other, reach their
climax when, after the war, Sutpen returns home and proposes marriage

to Miss Rosa. Astonishingly enough she accepts that proposal. Her great hope is that Sutpen, for all the reek of brimstone that she herself has set round him, is indeed but a man, and she is to know at last what it means to be the wife of a man: *"There was an ogre of my childhood which before my birth removed my only sister to its grim ogre-bourne . . . and I forgave it . . . and I did more than just forgive: I slew it"* (p. 167). She decides that Sutpen may be *"villain true enough, but a mortal fallible one less to invoke fear than pity"* (p. 167). It may just be possible that he is only a man, and that he has done only what men do, if more boldly, and that it is his violent engagement with the land, his black slaves, and a community both fascinated and outraged by him, that constitutes the reality Rosa is reaching out for.

This admission that Sutpen may be only human is the "opposition" of her version of the story. It gives rise, hardly by coincidence, to the richest, most compelling part of her tale, as her fear of Sutpen's diabolism is absorbed into the strange love story of the ruthless plantation owner and the frightened sister-in-law determined to waken from sleep. But the seeds of her impending disappointment, indeed horror, are already set in the fantasy with which she cannot help but gild this marriage: *" 'O furious mad old man, I hold no substance that will fit your dream but I can give you airy space and scope for your delirium' "* (p. 168).

Sutpen shatters this fantasy with the suggestion—which Miss Rosa cannot even put into words—that he and Miss Rosa have a child, testing for gender, before considering marriage: *"as if he were consulting with Jones or with some other man about a bitch dog or a cow or mare"* (p. 168). This is what Miss Rosa cannot pass, the insult that subverts all the *"decorous ordering,"* all that might be left of *"the old lost enchantment of the heart"* (p. 150). Sutpen's proposal becomes the last and insurmountable barrier between Miss Rosa and truth, since to pass it would require her to give up the Calvinistic illusion that a devil has walked the earth in the figure of Sutpen, and that it is for the sake of his exorcism *" 'that Heaven saw fit to let us lose' "* (p. 20). To have intercourse with Sutpen, to *touch* him as she has touched nothing else alive, this would indeed be her awakening, her abandonment of dia‧bolical dreams and her coming to grips with the savage humanity of the Sutpen story. Having rejected Sutpen's lewd proposal, however, she remains on the other side of sleep; she has not known him in life, and her version of the story can go no deeper than the strategy that explains why she *could* not know him: because he was not human. Her tale is finally of shadows: the Satanic shape, the beautiful (unseen) murdered young man, a South in chaos and purgative flames—these are the form and substance of her stopped life. Having come to the edge of reality, both in her life and in her tale, Miss Rosa can now retreat, with *justification*, to her Coldfield world of illusion. She confines Sutpen once more to the shape of the black ogre still befouling the land: *"Because he was not articulated in this world. He was a walking shadow . . ."* (p. 171).

Her attempt to plunge to the meaning of murder in 1865 is no more than the symbolic repetition and defense of her own history. If Sutpen is the devil, then Rosa is justified in her fear of life. Having imagined this inhuman lust, this *"light-blinded bat-like image of his own torment"* (p. 171), she can, like her father, nail herself up in an attic of her own design: for who would traffic with the ogre once he has revealed himself, unequivocally, as such? And if Sutpen is the devil, then Rosa is justified as well in her puzzlement over the murder of Charles Bon, for this too must be the mad work of demonic forces.

She cannot conceive the tale in terms of human motive, the record of beings so immersed in life that dream requires irrevocable action. For her, *"the brain recalls just what the muscles grope for; no more, no less: and its resultant sum is usually incorrect and false and worthy only of the name of dream"* (p. 143).

III

Mr. Compson's narrative of the Sutpen history appears to stand in relationship to Miss Rosa's as a cool, rationalistic version to a near-hysterical one. Yet we must not infer from this a genuine objectivity or disinterest: just as much as Rosa, Compson creates his tale out of his own psychic and emotional needs. If he presents the characters, particularly Sutpen, as if they were the objective creations of a mind distant in time from the originals, eager only to see them with some kind of critical clarity, then this too is only a function of the personality of Compson. He sees this way because he must, not only because it is the habit of his mind but because he too must protect himself against what he suspects are the special implications of this story for him. The sense of detachment that we get from Mr. Compson's version is owing largely to his desire to rid the tale of its complexity: to see its remoteness as the result of the sheer simplicity of its actors.

". . . people too as we are, and victims too as we are, but victims of a different circumstance, simpler and therefore, integer for integer, larger, more heroic and the figures therefore more heroic too, not dwarfed and involved but distinct, uncomplex who had the gift of loving once or dying once instead of being diffused and scattered creatures drawn blindly limb from limb from a grab bag and assembled, author and victim too of a thousand homicides and a thousand copulations and divorcements." (P. 89)

Mr. Compson (at least until Quentin gives him additional information) is never able to understand why Henry murdered Bon or why Sutpen apparently refused to allow the marriage of Bon and Henry's sister, Judith; and this inability to understand (it is in part refusal) becomes itself the meaning of the story, the strategy of Mr. Compson's retelling: " 'It's just incredible. It just does not explain. Or perhaps that's it: they dont explain and we are not supposed to know' " (p. 100). That the whole conflict between Henry and Bon, Henry and Sutpen, should be over the question of bigamy, that Bon's "marriage" to an octaroon should so trouble the son of a slaveholder—this " 'is drawing honor a little fine even for the shadowy paragons which are our ancestors' " (p. 100). Finally this moral issue is not the issue at all for Compson. These actions of 1865 are hardly the result of principled commitments that we can understand, moral stances taken in the name of some concept of good and evil, justice and injustice. No, these characters can move to irrevocable action because there is no serious moral complexity here. Their concerns are "simpler" than our own, the choices "uncomplex"; and this is why they can know what is absolutely necessary and can *perform* it, without reservation or qualification, without the minute adjustments of those who live in more complex times.

In imagining this way, Mr. Compson is preparing his own retreat. By insisting that the inaccessibility of the tale is its very point, that its actions occur at such distance from us as to be incomprehensible, Mr. Compson begins the justification not only of his ignorance but of the static quality of his life. Miss Rosa exonerates her failure to engage herself with the human by her portrait of Sutpen as a demon and her world as torn with God's necessary vengeance. She accepts the irrationality of events on the Calvinistic grounds that the devil has been about his business. Mr. Compson, dispensing with religious imagery, sees only " 'a horrible and bloody mischancing of human affairs' " (p. 101). The Sutpen story for him is a sequence of gigantic actions, utterly without moral meaning. Sharply dividing human complexity and human action, Mr. Compson defends not his virginity but his cynicism: these people could act, but only because their world was so much simpler, so much freer of moral nicety than our own.

It is no wonder then that the characters in Mr. Compson's narrative should have at times the stark lineaments of Greek tragedy and epic, the heroes of which are frequently involved in allegiances and contexts—the capricious machinations of the gods—which free them from what we consider moral issues of right and wrong.[6] The Sutpens of Mr. Compson's imagination can act with a comparable boldness because they do not have to endure the terrible conflicts of inner argument, of the fine distinctions between what is right and what is to be done. Moreover, they are propelled by a controlling Fate, striking the sets even before the actors have completed a scene, a Fate of which some of them are even vaguely aware: " '[Henry] must have known, as he knew that what his father had told him was true, that he was doomed and destined to kill. He must have known that just as he knew that his hope was vain, what hope and what for he could not have said' " (p. 91). And so the upshot of all that Mr. Compson tells us, the purpose of the way he sees and the process by which he manages to bring Henry and Bon again to their rendezvous at the Sutpen gates, is to say that he, Mr. Compson, is not to be blamed for his own inactive and indecisive life.

Far more than Quentin, the Compson of *Absalom, Absalom!* reminds us of his characterization in *The Sound and the Fury*. That same tired cynicism with which he lectures to his troubled young son in the earlier novel is still present in this one. Quentin says in *The Sound and the Fury:* "Mother would cry and say that Father believed his people were better than hers . . . she couldnt see that Father was teaching us that all men are just accumulations dolls stuffed with sawdust swept up from the trash heaps where all previous dolls had been thrown away . . ." (p. 218). Quentin's need in the earlier novel is to *do something* that is significant, to save Caddy and himself from that "trash heap" where his father has confined them, to convert mundane promiscuity into heaven-defying incest. Faced with this need, Mr. Compson can only reiterate his pessimism, the sardonic view of all human effort which has caused Quentin's need in the first place.

> you wanted to sublimate a piece of natural human folly into a horror and then exorcise it with truth . . . you cannot bear to think that someday it will no longer hurt you like this . . . no man ever does that [commits suicide] under the first fury of despair or remorse or

bereavement he does it only when he has realised that even the
despair or remorse or bereavement is not particularly important
to the dark diceman . . . you will not do that until you come
to believe that even she was not quite worth despair perhaps . . .
then you will remember that for you to go to harvard has been
your mothers dream since you were born and no compson has
ever disappointed a lady. . . . (Pp. 220–21)

While comparisons of Faulkner novels dealing with the same characters can often be a misleading practice, the cynicism of the first Mr.
Compson seems implicit in everything the second says. He tells the tale
of Sutpen and his children in order to illustrate those truths he has
tried to instill in Quentin earlier.

"we have a few old mouth-to-mouth tales . . . we see dimly people,
the people in whose living blood and seed we ourselves lay dormant
and waiting, in this shadowy attenuation of time possessing now
heroic proportions, performing their acts of simple passion and simple
violence, impervious to time and inexplicable—Yes, Judith, Bon,
Henry, Sutpen: all of them. They are there, yet something is missing;
they are like a chemical formula exhumed along with the letters from
that forgotten chest . . . you bring them together in the proportions
called for, but nothing happens; you re-read, tedious and intent,
poring, making sure that you have forgotten nothing, made no mis-
calculation; you bring them together again and again nothing happens: just the words, the symbols, the shapes themselves, shadowy
inscrutable and serene, against that turgid background of a horrible
and bloody mischancing of human affairs." (Pp. 100–101)

Mr. Compson's insistence on his own ignorance must not be misin-
terpreted; it is, among other things, a confession of his superiority.
Naturally we cannot comprehend these people, even as we cannot imitate
their ability to act. Knowing what we know, seeing what we have seen,
how could we? The wise man, the twentieth-century intellectual man,
will simply contemplate this amusing and sometimes compelling, if
finally meaningless, history. He need not act and he will not know,
for the outcome of all effort is frustration and defeat.

The first part of Mr. Compson's narration is concerned with Sutpen.
Its pace is leisurely, the teller himself calm and controlled, producing
what is certainly one of the less dramatic portions of the novel. The rea-

son for this is simple enough. Sutpen is easy for Mr. Compson: he is
the blind titan of an earlier time, a near-barbarian whose capacity for
action and indifference to the assumptions of community Mr. Compson
finds amusing and easy to absorb. He admires Thomas Sutpen because
he does not understand him, and feels no need to. With sardonic humor
he presents the underbred stranger—come from where, whence, or why
Mr. Compson cannot wonder because it would be futile and probably
irrelevant anyway—who rapidly interests, intimidates, and at last dominates the entire community. Immune to the town's growing outrage,
Sutpen acquires land, house, furniture, and bride with dynamic speed,
while public opinion remains much of the time " 'in an acute state of
indigestion' " (p. 46). Dismayed not so much over what Sutpen does,
but at the candor of the way he does it, the members of community are
presented by Mr. Compson as gnats hovering impotently about a giant.
Sutpen is the larger-than-human who makes clear the insignificance of
the human.

Respectability may be one of Sutpen's self-determined requirements,
part of the necessary equipage, like furniture and a wife, but Mr.
Compson's admiration is owing to his sense that these are merely the
appurtenances of Sutpen: they neither reflect nor subjugate the man
himself: " 'anyone could look at him and say, *Given the occasion and
the need, this man can and will do anything*' " (p. 46). And for Mr.
Compson it is this potentiality for pure action unencumbered by customary social forms that throws all complexities, the innumerable duties
and conventions of society into a cocked hat: "He was not liked (which
he evidently did not want, anyway) but feared, which seemed to amuse,
if not actually please, him" (p. 72).

Given his conception of the size and simplicity of Sutpen, there is
no need for Mr. Compson to probe for motive and rationale. Obviously
there can be no motive which a man who is not a barbarian could de-
duce. Like the characters in a Greek tragedy, Sutpen is two dimen-
sional, the mask of a man, known to us by his chosen role and his
action. And his splendor is precisely his freedom from all the human
anguishes of inner conflict. There is no other way Mr. Compson can
dare to comprehend the dynamic and active man, and in the case of
Sutpen he scarcely need try. The historical evidence, handed down
largely from townspeople who knew almost nothing of him, and from
Miss Rosa, who cannot imagine him as human, easily permits the kind
of interpretation Mr. Compson makes here.

Mr. Compson can take pleasure in Sutpen because he is hardly conscious, an innocent savage with his children, dragging the Old South

to its inevitable, yet unforeseen destruction. His ability to act is only the function of his blindness—he doesn't know, is in fact outrageously ignorant that Fate is the real ruler here: "he was unaware that his flowering was a forced blooming too and that while he was still playing the scene to the audience, behind him Fate, destiny, retribution, irony—the stage manager, call him what you will—was already striking the set and dragging on the synthetic and spurious shadows and shapes of the next one" (pp. 72–73).

This is why Sutpen is easy for Mr. Compson, why he can admire Sutpen's bold dismissal of the community and the gods of necessity. Cynical, impotent, dryly amused, Mr. Compson tells the tale of the dynamic actor because it is clear that he, Compson, knows so much more. Perhaps jealous, perhaps regretful of his own status, he knows—and his whole narrative reveals this—that his passivity is a stance well taken. As he comments in the final sentence of his letter to Quentin describing Rosa Coldfield's funeral, *"The weather was beautiful though cold and they had to use picks to break the earth for the grave yet in one of the deeper clods I saw a redworm doubtless alive when the clod was thrown up though by afternoon it was frozen again"* (p. 377).

Turning to Sutpen's children, however, especially Charles Bon, Mr. Compson's narrative takes on a different cast. His intentions are still the same, but they are more difficult to achieve. A certain desperation makes its way into the telling, and thus its intensity increases; so, consequently, does our interest, as situation begins to compel strategy to more exacting tasks. As Sutpen is the barrier that Miss Rosa must pass, so Charles Bon is the crucial figure for Mr. Compson. " 'He is the curious one to me. He came into that isolated puritan country household almost like Sutpen himself came into Jefferson: apparently complete, without background or past or childhood . . . a mere spectator, passive, a little sardonic, and completely enigmatic' " (p. 93). It is perfectly in keeping with this novel's assumptions about the workings of imagination that Mr. Compson's narrative should quicken sharply when he begins to deal with the wealthy, handsome young man from New Orleans, who in some unfathomable way managed to end his life at Sutpen's Hundred, Mississippi.

For Charles Bon, unlike Sutpen, *knows*. He stands behind them all: " 'with an air of sardonic and indolent detachment like that of a youthful Roman consul making the Grand Tour of his day among the barbarian hordes . . . he knew at once that Sutpen had found out about the mistress and child and he now found Sutpen's action and Henry's reaction a fetish-ridden moral blundering . . . watching, contemplating them from behind that barrier of sophistication in comparison with which Henry and Sutpen were troglodytes'" (p. 93).

Bon is the second of the two ideal figures Mr. Compson presents in his narrative. Sutpen is the dynamic actor unburdened with knowledge, whose crudeness of mind and vision girds him with lethal power. Bon is his opposite, the epitome of a fin de siecle aesthete, premature as far as the Old South is concerned, but hardly for Mr. Compson. For him, Bon is "'an elegant and indolent esoteric hothouse bloom'" (p. 97), "'lounging before them in the outlandish and almost feminine garments of his sybaritic privacy'" (p. 96). His great insight, like Mr. Compson's, is the knowledge of human folly.

And yet this is the man, equipped with a cynicism that rivals Mr. Compson's own, who finds it necessary at last to die rather than give up his mistress or marriage to Judith Sutpen. The irony, of course is not merely that Bon would do such a thing, but that Mr. Compson, knowing from hindsight the way Bon will die, would *imagine* him the way he does. It is Mr. Compson's own ordering of things that makes Bon's personality what it is, and that devises the threat of bigamy as the cause of murder. The story he tells of Bon and Henry in New Orleans, their discussion of Bon's mistress and the marriage ceremony, their hope that the war will decide the conflict by doing away with at least one of them— this is all conjecture on Mr. Compson's part. In other words, Mr. Compson attributes to at least one of these characters a personality and values similar to his own, knowing full well that this figure is one who apparently *does* act, who chooses to die for a cause that Mr. Compson is at pains to describe as not being a very good one.

Mr. Compson's own task as a narrator becomes clear: to account for Bon's last action in such a way so as to keep intact his own fundamental attitude toward life, his insistence that action and commitment are impossible to the thinking, aware man. That this task will be especially difficult with the Charles Bon that Mr. Compson has himself created is exactly the point. If Mr. Compson is to enjoy the comforts of symbolic extrication from anxiety, if he is to force the fact of murder into a fiction consistent with his own attitudes, then he must strike the apparent opposition at its strongest link. The symbolic resolution will be effective only if it appears to be well tested.

Mr. Compson's strategy is to see Bon's "inflexible pessimism" (p. 94) as growing to an incurable fatalism, an awareness of doom that nothing transcends, and to see the lovers themselves (the brother Henry as well as Judith and Bon) as being guided and determined by psychological forces having little to do with love and choice. Mr. Compson will do away with the significance of action in the story of Sutpen's children by portraying it as hardly being action at all: rather it is the inevitable outcome of random meetings, conventional psychological forces, and the unfortunate clash of two diametrically opposed habits of vision, one belonging to Bon, the other to Sutpen. Mr. Compson reconciles his convictions with Bon's death by seeing the death not so much as the conclusion of a considered action, a climax of motives and commitments that thrust themselves against real obstacles, but as the result of Bon's passivity: his recognition of the poverty of motive and the imminence of destiny.

The love between Bon and Judith which might be seen as necessitating the murder is explained away by Mr. Compson. Since they saw each other only a few times in their lives—"'three times in two years, for a total period of seventeen days'" (p. 99)—it is preposterous to imagine that Judith and Charles Bon fell in love: "'You can not even imagine him and Judith together'" (p. 97). On the contrary it is Henry who is the lover here, incestuously attracted to Judith, homosexually attracted to Bon, resolving this psychological maze by uniting the two objects of his neurotic loves: "'it must have been Henry who seduced Judith, not Bon'" (p. 99).

This is not a love story, not a tale of death heroically endured or administered as the price of love, but rather a case book of more or less typical psychological responses. It is Mr. Compson who tightens the threads here, gradually depriving his characters of their freedom, with Charles Bon as the only one sophisticated enough to recognize and admit the truths that Mr. Compson demonstrates. Even the attachment of Henry to Judith is nothing more than what any modestly read man might easily imagine between brother and sister, the product of glands and conventional complexes: "between Henry and Judith there had been a relationship closer than the traditional loyalty of brother and sister even" (p. 79). So even this love was not chosen, it is "'such as might exist between two people who, regardless of sex or age or heritage of race or tongue, had been marooned at birth on a desert island'" (p. 99).

As for the friendship of Henry and Charles that leads to the engagement of Bon and Judith, even this can be interpreted as the predictable result of a meeting between the provincial and the New Orleans socialite, each a tantalizing product of another world. Overwhelmed with the sophistication, the dress, the bearing of Charles Bon, Henry chooses him as the agent of his own desire for Judith: " 'The brother . . . taking that virginity in the person of the brother-in-law, the man whom he would be if he could become, metamorphose into, the lover, the husband' " (p. 96).

The two young men, according to Mr. Compson, are as trapped in the structures of sex and social upbringing, the blood's attractions and the environment's demands, as Sutpen is in the schemes of the unseen fatality that rules him. Always quick to utilize a convenient typology, whether from Greek, Biblical, or Freudian sources, Mr. Compson sees Bon and Henry as the representatives of neatly opposed concepts: the Catholic and the Puritan; an extravagant and effete New Orleans and a spartan Sutpen's Hundred; a pessimistic and passive view of life that by-passes despair because it has never bothered with hope, and the active and aspiring view that wills realities it well knows are impossible. Although Mr. Compson is more engaged here than he has been with Sutpen, he is still too consciously in control, a puppeteer working cleverly formulated but still conventional behavior patterns as the proof of his particular attitudes. "[W]hat he describes," writes Olga Vickery, "is a battle of ideas or concepts and not a conflict of people."[7]

With the arrival of Henry and Bon in New Orleans, however, Mr. Compson's narrative picks up, as he becomes genuinely fascinated with the character of Bon and his attempts to argue Henry out of his puritan attitudes regarding a man's obligations to his future wife. Charles Bon at this point absorbs Mr. Compson's full attention and imaginative powers, appearing to the latter as a man marvelously shrewd, initiating Henry in the splendid sexual and social intricacies of New Orleans. Mr. Compson's interest here is not in the soundness of Bon's arguments—for he will eventually present these as specious and even callous—but with Bon's grace of maneuver, his ingenious undermining of Henry's provincialism: " 'I can imagine how he did it—the calculation, the surgeon's alertness and cold detachment' " (p. 111). Mr. Compson describes in detail the octoroon women, " 'a row of faces like a bazaar of flowers, the supreme apotheosis of chattelry' " (p. 112); the dueling that will be occasioned by those women; the place of love, " 'a place created for and by voluptuousness' " (p. 114), and at last the woman who lives in it, " 'raised and trained to fulfill a woman's sole end and purpose: to love, to be beautiful, to divert' " (p. 117). Mr. Compson attributes to Bon sophistic defences of his mistress, marriage, and child, but even in the sophistry he enjoys Bon's wit and elegance, every word and argument the signs of his worldliness.

Bon glibly attacks the easy targets of Anglo-Saxon repression and hypocrisy, justifying his own " 'normal human instinct' " (p. 116). He then shifts, in the midst of the Argument from Lust, to the Argument from Compassion: the bought woman as the sign of her new owner's sympathy!—" ' "But we do save that one, who but for us would have been sold to any brute who had the price, not sold to him for the night like a white prostitute, but body and soul for life . . . a sparrow which God himself neglected to mark" ' " (p. 116). And the woman herself, is she a whore? Rather " ' "the only true chaste women, not to say virgins, in America" ' " (p. 117). This is all part of the charm of Mr. Compson's Bon, cynical and world-weary like his creator. Gilded from mystery into an apogee of sophistication, Bon can argue brilliantly for morality or voluptuousness, for what-you-will: the whore he has bought becomes the sparrow he has saved, and her great gift is a knowledge of " ' "strange and ancient curious pleasures of the flesh (which is all: there is nothing else)" ' " (p. 116). Bon is the entertaining and agile skeptic, the con man with a role for every mood and situation, who can play each part to unscrupulous perfection.

Bon becomes in these passages a type of wish fulfillment for Mr. Compson, the possessor of a powerful sophistication derived from an utter nihilism. A comparable situation, oddly enough, exists between Miss Rosa and her imagined Sutpen, whose brutality is implicit in her frustrated desire. In both cases Sutpen and Bon are Miss Rosa and Mr. Compson writ large, the exponents of their creators. Because of this, Mr. Compson's narrative, like Miss Rosa's when she seems about to become Sutpen's wife, begins to exceed the intended limitations of the strategy that has shaped it up to this point. As readers we become aware of something here larger than alibi, a transformation from private explanation to public symbol, as Charles Bon's "sybaritic" pose becomes the essence of a worldliness we desire and fear, with its attendant pleasures and wisdom complicated by a gaping emptiness at the heart.

Mr. Compson's Bon, like Miss Rosa's Sutpen, begins moving toward autonomy, transcending fictional strategies of defense to embody a universal reality. The movement climaxes when Mr. Compson has Bon conclude his intricate arguments with the hole card that exposes their barrenness: " ' "Have you forgot that this woman, this child, are niggers? You, Henry Sutpen of Sutpen's Hundred in Mississippi? You, talking of marriage, a wedding, here?" ' " (p. 118). Sophistication is finally shorn of even the appearance of honor, of grace and decorousness. The sparrow saved, the chaste woman, the artist of the flesh, she is, when necessary, the nigger who cannot possibly *matter*. And Bon is Mr. Compson's man of the world, the consummate nihilist who will argue, love, kill, in the name of ends whose only purpose is to fill the time between birth and death.

Henry Sutpen, caught in all his diverse loves and obligations to father, friend, and sister, can only wait for Bon to act; and Bon simply submits himself to the necessity of whatever it is that is going to happen. Even Henry, whose father is the principle of vitality, the fate-defier, is drawn into Bon's fatalistic world: " 'Henry waited four years . . . waiting, hoping, for Bon to renounce the woman and dissolve the marriage which he (Henry) admitted was no marriage, and which he must have known as soon as he saw the woman and the child that Bon would not renounce' " (p. 119). And Judith, Mr. Compson says, means as little to him as she does to Bon: " 'just the blank shape, the empty vessel in which each of them strove to preserve . . . what each conceived the other to believe him to be' " (p. 119–20). Henry and Bon are both waiting for the war to determine the outcome of their hopelessly entangled lives. According to Mr. Compson, Henry saves Bon's life during the war, as if to help fate along a little by abandoning his friend on the battlefield would be more activity than the game permits: " 'waiting for something but not knowing what, what act of fate, destiny, what irrevocable sentence of what Judge or Arbiter between them since nothing less would do' " (p. 124).

Fate is the basis of Mr. Compson's understanding of the Sutpen story, and Charles Bon becomes the key to his narrative because Bon is the complete fatalist. He possesses that sophistication which Mr. Compson so well describes because he doesn't complicate it with the need or desire to act. His death at the end is seen by Mr. Compson as perfectly consistent with his worldliness: in fact it is the "act" that most confirms it. Even suicide is an action; what Bon does is more suitable: he *allows* himself to be murdered as the last necessary episode in this " 'horrible and bloody mischancing of human affairs' " (p. 101).

Mr. Compson imagines Bon's letters to Judith during the war as " 'gallant flowery indolent frequent and insincere . . . that metropolitan gallant's foppish posturing . . . the jackanape antics of a small boy' " (p. 128). One letter still exists, which Mr. Compson uses as evidence for his view of the story. It is not altogether appropriate for his purposes because it has nothing of "foppish posturing" in it, but it will, more or less, suffice: "gentle sardonic whimsical and incurably pessimistic, without date or salutation or signature" (p. 129). Bon has concluded it with the grim conviction that he and Judith *are, strangely enough, included among those who are doomed to live* (p. 132). Doomed to live: after four years of war, that is a way of putting it. For

Mr. Compson it is enough. At the gates of Sutpen's Hundred, Bon is
" 'the fatalist to the last' " (p. 132), riding calmly into Henry's bullets as
if there were simply no other space in which to move.

Bon has said to Henry, " *'I do not renounce'* " (p. 132), which may
echo later in the reader's mind when he learns how Sutpen put aside
his first wife, or how Judith informs Charles Etienne that he might put
aside his own, but here in Mr. Compson's version it has scarcely the
meaning of moral earnestness or fidelity. The octoroon mistress who,
according to Mr. Compson, commands Bon's loyalty is the voluptuous
maiden groomed for love, the sparrow whom God has ignored and Bon
has saved, or the nigger who should scarcely trouble Henry Sutpen—it
all depends on Bon's rhetorical purposes at the time. To imagine that
Bon would die for her is as unthinkable as that he would die for Judith
Sutpen. *Then why does he refuse to renounce her?* But the unanswer-
ability of that question is, of course, the whole point and substance of
Mr. Compson's narrative. The failure of all these bloody happenings to
mean, their failure to form a coherent, rational version of human affairs
—*this* is what Mr. Compson insists upon at the last.

Henry Sutpen does not murder Charles Bon to protect his sister's
honor or his own, does not drag the wounded Bon to safety for the
sake of a moral code. And Charles Bon, who does not woo Judith, who
loves her only " ' "after his fashion" ' " (p. 94), who becomes engaged
" 'without volition or desire . . . [and] took his dismissal in the same
passive and sardonic spirit' " (p. 100), does not suddenly discover either
love or honor. The photo of the mistress and child which, according to
Mr. Compson, Judith finds in his pocket, is for Mr. Compson probably not even a gesture of bitterness, any more than it is the gesture of
love which Quentin and Shreve stress in their later version. Like so
much in this narrative, it is idle, meaningless, for the simple reason
that, as Mr. Compson has said, we are not supposed to know. Henry
and Bon are there at the Sutpen gates because everything in their lives—
their blood, background, custom, vision—has merely conspired that they
should be nowhere else.

IV

In chapter 7 Thomas Sutpen, by means of a conversation with Quentin's
grandfather (repeated either to Mr. Compson, who told it to Quentin,
or directly to Quentin), tells his own history. It is the strangest tale of
all, eventful and yet oddly irrelevant, for there is no one in the novel less

capable than Sutpen of understanding what has happened to him. He is the imagination-less man, totally unequipped to answer the questions of meaning he does not even know how to ask: " ' "Whether it was a good or a bad design," Sutpen says to Grandfather," ' "is beside the point" (p. 263).

Free not only from the particular biases of Miss Rosa and Mr. Compson, Sutpen's version is free of distortion itself, and this makes it unique in the novel. Unlike the other narrators, he is trying to probe objectively his own past. Since symbolic consolations are meaningless to him, it never occurs to him to try to distort his story in order to persuade General Compson or anyone else of his own justification. The correctness or incorrectness of action, Sutpen will always believe, is part of that action, not a shifting abstraction to be colored and reversed by anyone with sufficient imagination to add a bias. It is the *facts* of the past, not its meaning or value, its why or worthiness, that dominate Sutpen's version of his life. He is trying to discover a "mistake," the thing done or the thing he failed to do, the error in calculation he might still rectify.

Sutpen is the man of action in this novel of meditating onlookers; and his ability to act is a direct corollary to his inability to imagine. He describes the crisis of a native uprising in Haiti: " 'on the eighth night the water gave out and something had to be done so he put the musket down and went out and subdued them. That was how he told it: he went out and subdued them, and when he returned he and the girl became engaged to marry' " (p. 254). The extent of Sutpen's imagination is his belief in the given social design he becomes part of when he moves from his mountain home to the lowlands. Scarcely an interpretation, it is merely a terribly naive man's self-imprisonment in a prevailing social system, and even this system is something he does not understand except for its visible apparatus: " ' "I had a design. To accomplish it I should require money, a house, a plantation, slaves, a family—incidentally of course, a wife" ' " (p. 263). His quest is not to create a design, but to accomplish an already existing one, a pattern he can neither understand nor modify to suit himself.

Sutpen's habit of vision reflects the conditions of his earlier mountain home and its distinction from the community to which he later journeys. In the former exists a unity of fact and meaning, of image and value, a unity prior to the mode of metaphor as a means of ordering reality. Sutpen's birthplace is a place of bare, brute deeds and simple objects: " 'Everybody had just what he was strong enough or energetic enough to take and keep, and only that crazy man would go to the trouble to take or even want more than he could eat or swap for powder or whiskey' " (p. 221). Nothing is "representative" in this world, or at least no meaning is detachable from things and deeds; nothing is symbolic, in our sense of the term, of something larger, more abstract, than itself. This is the place where the human imagination has no function, no need to provide meanings for what have become ambivalent images, or to create the syntheses that unify a broken world.

Like Vardaman's special vision in *As I Lay Dying*, the world of Sutpen's birthplace is intelligible in terms of Ernst Cassirer's version of the primitive world of mythic perception: "in this realm nothing has any significance or being save what is given in tangible reality. Here is no 'reference' and 'meaning'; every content of consciousness to which the mind is directed is immediately translated into terms of actual presence and effectiveness. . . . Such thinking . . . does not reach backward or forward from that vantage point to find 'causes' and 'effects,' but rests content with taking in the sheer existent."[8]

This primitive world is pervaded by an awareness of "a fundamental and indelible *solidarity of life* that bridges over the multiplicity and variety of its single forms"; "To mythical and religious feeling nature becomes one great society, the *society of life*. Man is not endowed with outstanding rank in this society. He is part of it but he is in no respect higher than any other member."[9] Raised in such a world, Sutpen is predictably baffled when he discovers in the lowlands the principles of distinction and hierarchy, and an evaluation of men that is not wholly relevant to what they can actually do. Sutpen " 'didn't even know there was a country all divided and fixed and neat with a people living on it all divided and fixed and neat because of what color their skins happened to be and what they happened to own' " (p. 221). Nor did he know that " 'there was a difference between white men and white men, not to be measured by lifting anvils or gouging eyes or how much whiskey you could drink then get up and walk out of the room' " (p. 226).

The difference between a world of solidarity and a world of hierarchic structure is the difference between meaning at one with action and meaning that fluctuates according to human imaginations. In the first world, Sutpen's world, "Whatever has been fixed by a name, henceforth is not only real, but is Reality. The potential between 'symbol' and 'meaning' is resolved; in place of a more or less adequate 'expression,' we find a relation of identity, of complete congruence between 'image' and 'object,' between the name and the thing."[10] But in the new world, words are never wholly reconciled to the things they name, and the possibility of such reconciliation lies not in the return to a mythic solidarity but in the power of metaphor to effect unities the mind can believe in.

From the unity of being in his mountains Sutpen falls into the elaborate social system of the South, into what Rosa Coldfield rightly calls the *"devious intricate channels of decorous ordering."* In this new world action has become symbolic, suggesting meanings, values, levels of status in a complex hierarchy that Sutpen finds bewildering. Gradually, not really knowing why—never knowing why—he comes to participate in the new system, learns to hit blacks not for what they are but for what they *represent:* " 'because they (the niggers) were not it, not what you wanted to hit' " (p. 230). He also suffers his climactic initiation into plantation society when he is made to see the abstract meanings of the front door and the back door, and how these foolish differences (why should a house have more than one door anyway?) result in differences in human value, his own and the landowner's.

Sutpen's failure to understand symbolic thinking is the innocence of which he often speaks. " 'He no more envied the man [who owned the white house] than he would have envied a mountain man who happened to own a fine rifle. . . . because he could not have conceived of the owner taking such crass advantage of the luck which gave the rifle to him rather than to another as to say to other men: *Because I own this rifle, my arms and legs and blood and bones are superior to yours* except as the victorious outcome of a fight with rifles' " (pp. 228–29). That a rifle might *mean* as well as shoot, and that its meaning would be larger than its accuracy or velocity, is something Sutpen painfully learns yet never really comprehends.

Sutpen's problem is that he is a literalist of the imagination, blind to the arbitrary nature of the symbols of society. To him the elements of social life—the house, the slaves, the wife, the son—have a magic power: phases of a ritual that is not symbolic but "real," incarnate with whatever gods such social gestures belong to. Olga Vickery writes: Sutpen believes "that the structure, the design, is itself the secret of its strength and its perpetuation, that he need only follow its ritual to grasp its substance and that he can do so with the same blunt honesty which was part of his mountain heritage."[11]

Human beings become subservient to whatever roles they must play. This is often characteristic of the plantation society as a whole, but in the mind of Thomas Sutpen it is an unbreakable law. He can see no woman, only a "wife"; no young man, only a "son." He moves these people about like counters on a game board. But in his innocence he simply does not know *how things mean* in a postprimitive world. A wife who is also a woman who will not accept the rules of the game Sutpen thinks he is playing is a puzzlement Sutpen cannot fathom. For despite the rigidity of the system, Sutpen's new society has suffered the discontinuity between word and fact, role and human spirit, that populates the world with fictions. Dreams as well as deeds are now part of the fabric. And the ordering of these problematic and fluctuating elements is impossible to the mind that sees words and roles as flesh rather than signs *to be made* into flesh through the discipline of the imagination. Even such tales as Miss Rosa's and Mr. Compson's are beyond his reach.

As a particular kind of consciousness Sutpen's function in the novel is comparable to Benjy's in *The Sound and The Fury* or Vardaman's in *As I Lay Dying*. He is Faulkner's reminder of an original apprehension of reality that cannot help but subvert the idea of the creative mind. The reality accessible to Sutpen, Benjy, and Vardaman is one that Faulkner is determined to surpass in richness and impact, but not without first acknowledging its special (anti-Faulknerian) power: a real rather than an invented world.

Faulkner's larger aim has to do with the possibilities of poetic, not primitive perception. He knows the costs of this aim, for as Cassirer has written, "If language is to grow into a vehicle of thought, an expression of concepts and judgments, this evolution can be achieved only at the price of forgoing the wealth and fullness of immediate experience." The meaning we crave must sacrifice the immediacy of a vision such as Benjy's or a literalism such as Sutpen's. In return there might be the achievement of a new reconciliation— unstable, precarious—a reality redefined as the meeting of a free creation and the irrevocable fact, embodied in *Absalom, Absalom!* in the murder of Charles Bon.

But there is one intellectual realm in which the word not only preserves its original creative power, but is ever renewing it; in which it undergoes a sort of constant palingenesis, at once a sensuous and a spiritual reincarnation. This regeneration is achieved as language becomes an avenue of artistic expression. Here it recovers the fullness of life; but it is no longer a life mythically bound and fettered, but an aesthetically liberated life.[12]

V

If there is truth in the narration of Quentin and Shreve, it does not depend on a closeness to historical fact, but on the vitality of the telling and the passionate involvement of the narrators with their subject and with each other. In terms of form, this part of *Absalom, Absalom!* is the climactic moment in Faulkner's career, for it is here that his essential style of fragmentation, of isolated narrators and actors placed at odd intervals on the rim of a single event, moves toward its most profound meaning.

Unlike the other narrators, Quentin and Shreve present what is largely a cooperative version of the Sutpen story. For Miss Rosa and Mr. Compson the listener of a tale is no more than a receptacle for the interpretation the teller is trying to press; for Quentin and Shreve listening and telling are identical actions: "It was Shreve speaking, though . . . it might have been either of them and was in a sense both: both thinking as one, the voice which happened to be speaking the thought only the thinking become audible, vocal; the two of them creating between them, out of the rag-tag and bob-ends of old tales and talking, people who perhaps had never existed at all anywhere" (p. 303). This engagement of the boys with each other is both metaphor and means of their engagement with the past, enabling them to pass beyond defense and self-justification to something we are prepared to call truth.

Imagining begins, however, in private need, and Quentin and Shreve, like Miss Rosa and Mr. Compson, must begin their narration of the Sutpen history in the shadow of their own personalities, coloring the tale with their youth, their distance from the past, their situation as freshmen at Harvard. The time is now January 1910. Shreve approaches the story with a heavy wit: " 'You mean she was no kin to you, no kin to you at all, that there was actually one Southern Bayard or Guinevere who was no kin to you? then what did she die for' " (p. 174). He quickly retells the story he has just heard in a few pages of parodic exaggeration: of " 'this old dame' " (p. 176) and " 'this Faustus, this demon, this Beelzebub . . . who appeared suddenly one Sunday with two pistols and twenty subsidiary demons' " (p. 178), who fiercely erected his minor kingdom and, just as fiercely, destroyed it. Shreve sees Sutpen as a " 'mad impotent old man' " (p. 180) who deliberately frustrates his own ambitions. And Quentin responds with his own device for keeping himself detached both from these matters and his

Canadian roommate: *"He sounds just like father. . . . Just exactly like father"* (p. 181).

Following, however, the story of Charles Etienne (mostly from Mr. Compson in chapter 6) and Sutpen's own version of his life (mostly from Grandfather in chapter 7), the two boys move into their own invention. They decide that Charles Bon must have been the older half-brother of Henry and Judith, determined either to marry his half-sister or to win recognition from his father, Thomas Sutpen, who, for some unknown reason, withholds it. The basis for their assumption that the threat of incest, not bigamy or the blind vengeances aroused by a demon, is the true cause of Henry's murder of Bon is never unequivocally explained, but it seems to be the result of Quentin's visit with Miss Rosa to Sutpen's Hundred in September 1909. Explaining to Shreve how Mr. Compson comes to know the incest motive, when in his own narrative he attributes all to bigamy and the " 'bloody mischancing of human affairs,' " Quentin says that he himself was the one who gave Compson the new information, " 'The day after we—after that night when we—' " (p. 266).

Regardless of this evidence, however, the important fact here is that Quentin and Shreve can expand and elaborate on the incest theme because it so richly suits the condition of their own youth: sons still seeking their maturity, potential lovers still dreaming of passions they cannot admit are usually confined to books. Whatever facts may exist here, the romantic tale of siblings and lovers which Quentin and Shreve evolve goes well beyond such facts. Their story is similar to the stories of Rosa and Compson in that this is the tale they can most afford to tell, a magnificent yet self-indulgent exploration of love and courage, of defiance and honor. The enigma of murder in 1865, which Rosa explains in terms of demonic powers and which Compson attributes to fatality, becomes with Quentin and Shreve a tale of star-crossed love and the quest for identity. It is the tale we would expect from two boys "who breathed not individuals now yet something both more and less than twins, the heart and blood of youth" (p. 294).[13]

Their story has all the trappings of a Byronic romance. First there is Charles Bon: the gallant, troubled young man isolated by his mother for some unknown reason; the lover torn with incestuous desires he is still prepared to restrain for the sake of honor; the son who demands from his mysterious father the nod of recognition that will send him on his way, a fugitive from his desire yet the owner at last of his identity. And there is Henry Sutpen: the younger brother, the acolyte trying desperately to catch up with his model. He is born into one world and follows his hero into another, attending him, even as he must guard their sister from him.

In the heat of this romantic re-creation it little matters, the objective narrator tells us, that the boys imagine Bon and Judith walking that Christmas in 1860 in a garden surrounded with "jasmine, spiraea, honeysuckle, perhaps myriad scentless unpickable Cherokee roses," despite the fact that it is winter and the garden devoid of bloom. "But that did not matter because it had been so long ago"; it does not matter "so long as the blood coursed—the blood, the immortal brief recent intransient blood which could hold honor above slothy unregret and love above fat and easy shame" (p. 295).

" 'And now,' Shreve said, 'we're going to talk about love' " (p. 316). This is the brunt of the first and longest phase of Quentin and Shreve's narration: a story of love and youthful heroism, intensified because it is also a story of potential incest. By interpreting the facts in this way, they free Charles Bon of the callousness and fatalism with which Compson has described him. But in doing so, the boys encounter the necessary crisis of their narration, the possibility that this is a story not so much of love as of exploitation. For if Bon is the half-brother of Judith and eventually realizes this fact, as the boys allow he does, then his actions toward Sutpen take on the quality of extortion. It could be charged that he is willing to use Judith as a human instrument in order to gain his recognition from the father.

Insofar as the boys are using this historical material for imaginative self-service, it is necessary for them to deal with this possibility of exploitation on Bon's part. If he is to be their Byronic hero, representing in the middle of the nineteenth-century values and possibilities attractive to the youths of 1910, then he can hardly be the callous rogue who uses the love of his sister to attack his father. Their problem here is again the requirement of symbolic resolution: if they are to enjoy the solace of symbolic form, then they must overcome some self-erected barrier, in this case the possible dishonor of Charles Bon. Shreve takes most of the initiative here. Charles Bon *did* want recognition from Sutpen, Shreve admits, but he *also* loved Judith.

Quentin resists Shreve's argument for much of their narrative, as if eager for a purer love than this. Yet Shreve gradually hammers home his point, emphasizing both the fervor of Bon's quest for recognition— " 'there would be that flash, that instant of indisputable recognition between them and he would know for sure and forever' " (p. 319)—*and* the growing intensity of his attraction to Judith: " 'It would be no question of choosing, having to choose between the champagne or whiskey and the sherbet, but all of a sudden . . . you find that you dont want anything but that sherbet and that you haven't been wanting anything else but that' " (p. 323). Shreve even uses the incest as evidence of the love of Bon for Judith—the impossibility of his being able to restrain it—and thus further excuses him from any possible charge of calculation. Finally, the love and the quest for recognition are involved with each other, for the measure of Bon's earnestness for the one is taken by his willingness to sacrifice the other: " *'Yes. Yes. I will renounce her; I will renounce love and all; that will be cheap, cheap, even though he say to me "never look upon my face again; take my love and my acknowledgment in secret, and go" I will do that' "* (p. 327).

The motive behind this retelling is the symbolic guarantee that adolescent notions of love and honor still operate in the world. By conceiving the story as they do, Quentin and Shreve conjure up a fiction in which these notions are not names but living factors. It is the *father,* not the young men caught up in this irresolvable dilemma, who is made to bear the deepest moral censure of the story. For it is he, according to the two boys, who withholds recognition from his eldest son, thus ensuring the final disaster.

But the motives of Quentin and Shreve are more personal and specific than this need to give fictional life to certain abstract values. For Quentin there is the additional problem of his complex relationship to the South. Proud of his heritage yet ashamed of its transgressions, Quentin participates in this retelling of the Sutpen story in the hope of ridding himself of his ambivalence. For despite the urgent cry with which he concludes the novel, it is clear that in certain ways Quentin *does* hate the South, finding in the Sutpen history a legacy of violence and hatred, of courage exacted in an unworthy cause, of grace and courtesy undermined by inhumanity.

Quentin's strategy here, aided by Shreve, is to shift the emphasis of the story to the sons, Henry and Bon, seeing them (as he must try to see himself) as the unwitting and faultless victims of the brutality of the father. By explaining the murder of Bon as a tragedy of incestuous love, Quentin can resolve his own and Henry's guilt in the necessary defense of honor and purity. Sutpen's refusal to recognize Bon, and thus prevent incest, gives Bon no choice: he *must* (for love and honor) insist on going through with the marriage. Henry Sutpen, Quentin's special alter ego, must then murder his friend and brother out of devotion to a code that transcends brotherhood. The actions of *both* sons are justified by Quentin and Shreve, and the concluding episode of violence is also justified by a difficult yet finally admirable allegiance to purity. Bon's love for Judith may be sincere enough, and Sutpen's rejection of him cruel and irrational, but Quentin's Henry Sutpen still has the larger responsibility of protecting his sister, even at the cost of his brother's life, against the violation of a universal, rather than a merely Southern, sanction against incest.

Both sons then, Henry especially, become the victims of circumstance, in whose wake they appear not only guiltless but brave. Through this strategy Quentin can see himself in a similar way, absolving himself of guilt for his own role and responsibilities as a Southerner.[14]

Shreve also has his special purpose in becoming actively involved with the Sutpen story. His personal investment will seem less to us than Quentin's, and yet the investment is real enough to allow him to participate fully in this retelling of the tale. For all his superficial cynicism, Shreve's growing interest in the story betrays his suspicion of the emptiness of his own life, a suspicion he makes explicit at the beginning of the last chapter of the novel: " 'Wait. Listen. I'm not trying to be funny, smart. I just want to understand it if I can and I dont know how to say it better. Because it's something my people haven't got. Or if we have got it, it all happened long ago across the water and so now there aint anything to look at every day to remind us of it.' " Shreve ponders a loss he can scarcely define—" 'What is it? something you live and breathe in like air?' "—and yet which he knows has something to do with " 'indomitable anger and pride and glory' " (p. 361). Almost as deeply as Quentin confronts his ambivalence toward the South, Shreve confronts an absence, something about love of land and heritage and community which, as a Canadian, he feels is no longer a living part of his character.

It is no wonder then that Shreve identifies so closely with Charles Bon, the one who, according to Shreve, is himself ruthlessly cut off from the heritage that is his, and is helpless to wrest from his father the sign that will return it to him. The complication of incest is able to provide Shreve, as it does Quentin, comfort for his inner grief, because it so romanticizes Bon's alien situation, transforming him into a giant Byronic figure. What better balm for the man without heritage than to see himself as *possessing* it, even as he is so hopelessly cut off from it? Shreve's Charles Bon is the man stripped of his past, yet *in actuality* the eldest son, the adored, the skillful, the brilliant hero of his own alienation, who rides to his death because he can neither have nor give up the woman he loves.

For Quentin and Shreve, then, as for Miss Rosa and Compson, this re-creation of the past becomes a source of symbolic consolation, a strategy with which to relieve the pressures of private anguish. Despite the intensity of all these tales and the investment being made, and despite the willingness to deal with some imagined crisis on which to test their aesthetic strength, the fact remains that they are all examples of imaginative manipulation for their creators' ends.

Nor can these interpretations be separated from the theme of exploitation that is so prominent everywhere in *Absalom, Absalom!* Depending, of course, on whose version of the story is operative, we see Thomas Sutpen exploiting a whole community, especially the Coldfield family, in order to gain his land and respectability; or we see Sutpen himself, along with other poor whites, exploited by a privileged class of landowners. Sutpen puts aside his first wife, not to mention his last mistress, and Charles Bon "uses" Judith to attack his father. Such exploitation, disregarding the integrity of another being, is also true of much of the narration in the book, involving an imaginative exploitation of people and facts long dead. And surely it is no accident that this exploitation fails to convince the reader of its validity.

But the scale of sensibility depicted in this novel does not end with art as manipulation. For the crucial fact of the Quentin-Shreve narration is that the boys eventually assert the *failure* of what they have created.

The italicized passages from pages 346 to 350 describe Henry Sutpen's agonized *acceptance* of the incestuous marriage of Bon and Judith. He accepts the fact that Bon has done all that honor demands in giving Sutpen the chance to recognize him and thus prevent the marriage. And this acceptance on Henry's part is also Quentin's, for this italicized section is the single voice of Quentin and Shreve, Henry and Bon: "two, four, now two again, according to Quentin and Shreve, the two the four the two still talking . . ." (p. 346). What we discover is that Henry does *not* murder Bon because of the threat of incest.

This reversal is the most extraordinary development in the novel. It is art breaking loose from the confines of calculation into a kind of freedom. The whole purpose of Quentin and Shreve's narration, up to this point, has been to establish incest as the basis for the act of murder in 1865. Just when they have succeeded in giving that motive a large measure of imaginative support—the lawyer, Charles's mother, the quest for recognition from Sutpen—and have also kept Bon and Henry morally unblemished, Quentin and Shreve cooperatively dismiss incest as the cause of the murder. They decide that Henry was willing to accept it. "'*Dont try to explain it,*'" Henry says, "'*Just do it.*' . . . '*Do I have your permission, Henry?' and Henry: 'Write Write,*'" (p. 349).

Henry's willingness to accept an incestuous marriage is a moment of temporary reconciliation, not only between Henry and Bon but between Quentin and Shreve, for it constitutes Quentin's acceptance of Shreve's argument that this *is* a story of love, not extortion. It is as if, for one moment, all the conflicts which Quentin and Shreve have imagined in the past and are actually living in 1910, have been eliminated. Henry will endure this social violation: "'"But kings have done it! Even dukes!"'" (p. 342); and Charles Bon will either marry Judith or force the father to kill him. He will have either his heritage or his recognition.

But this reconciliation is, of course, complete illusion. Whether Henry accepted incest or not, Charles Bon is in fact dead, at Henry's hands. For Quentin and Shreve to create this acceptance then, and still remain in the same world as the fact of murder in 1865, they must find another explanation. This moment of reconciliation, therefore, is not that at all; it is merely the boys' cooperative recognition that their tale must move on.

And with this sudden twist in the story the Byronic play and the manipulation come to an end. For the time has come now to move from an art that re-creates the past through the screens of present, personal need to an art of "becoming" the past, of transforming one's own life and the past into metaphors for each other.

Quentin and Shreve are striving for resolutions that so far are unknown in the various tales of *Absalom, Absalom!* These creations out of the past, these shadows called "Henry" and "Bon," are now being forced into a new arena, into an identification with Quentin and Shreve that is beyond the ordinary uses of metaphor, an identification of creator and created that must be the largest understanding of both: the candor of knowing the self through its perfect image in the imagined past. Henry and Bon are revealed to us as the incarnations of their creators. Invention becomes a repetition, a reenactment of imagined acts that confers upon them reality. The art product, strategy no longer, binds its creators to itself with the cords of their own creation.

The invention of Bon's Negro blood is the great imaginative leap of the novel, and it comes about primarily because of what has been happening to Quentin and Shreve during the bulk of their narration: the growing sense of communion, of the created tale as a cooperation of minds, the speakers giving themselves gradually up to each other as the only means of giving themselves to that past they are trying to comprehend. This is narrative as a marriage of minds: "it did not matter to either of them which one did the talking, since it was not the talking alone which did it . . . but some happy marriage of speaking and hearing wherein each before the demand, the requirement, forgave condoned and forgot the faulting of the other" (p. 316).

The coming together of the boys (there is nothing comparable to this in the other narratives) is the mirror of their imaginative engagement with the past, an engagement so profound as to give their meanings the status of facts in our minds. By this crossing into each other's lives, Quentin and Shreve emotionally propel themselves into communion with the lives of Bon and Henry as well: "the cold room where there was now not two of them but four, the two who breathed not individuals now yet something both more and less than twins, the heart and blood of youth" (p. 294). Out of their imaginative capacity for the one emerges the other; the one is the flesh of the other. The past is finally *known* in the dynamics of love, which becomes for Faulkner the power of the imagination to break down temporarily the fact of separation, of distance between knower and known.

Shreve's initial flippancy diminishes: " 'No . . . you wait. Let me play a while now'. . . . This was not flippancy either. It too was just that protective coloring of levity behind which the youthful shame of being moved hid itself" (p. 280). The boys begin alternating in the narration, "He did not even falter, taking Shreve up in stride without comma or colon or paragraph" (p. 280), until it is not a matter of alternation any more, but a single voice that speaks for both: "since for all the two of them knew he had never begun, since it did not matter (and possibly neither of them conscious of the distinction) which one had been doing the talking. So that now it was not two but four of them riding the two horses through the dark over the frozen December ruts of that Christmas Eve" (p. 334).

There has been much interest in how this climactic version of the Sutpen story comes about; how do Quentin and Shreve discover the blackness in Charles Bon? Cleanth Brooks has suggested that the boys by no means invent this story, but that Quentin discovered it the night he and Miss Rosa went out to Sutpen's Hundred.[15] There is some textual evidence, if ambiguous, to this effect, yet the implications of such a reading are rather disastrous for the novel, for it means that Quentin knows the full truth about Charles Bon *all the time* he and Shreve are having their passionate and absorbing conversation. This would not only make Quentin a hypocrite of psychotic proportions, but maneuvers Faulkner into the position of deceiving his reader for no good purpose. It is the objective narrator who says during the boys' retelling of the story that one speaks for the other and that finally they are *thinking* as one. Yet until its climax this cooperative re-creation is ignorant of Bon's part Negro blood, and consequently presents Bon as being also ignorant of it. On page 308 Bon, referring to his mistress, speaks lightly of a " ' "little matter like a spot of negro blood" ' "; on page 321 he refers to " '*whatever it was in mother's [blood] that he could not brook' ";* and on page 346, the chief obstacle to the marriage with Judith is still the problem of incest. Bon, of course, can be ignorant of his own blood only because Quentin and Shreve, who are telling his story, are themselves ignorant of it.

And yet there is some reason to think that Quentin *does* find out the secret in September 1909, before he ever meets Shreve. Brooks cites the passage in which Quentin tells Shreve that it was he who supplied Compson with information about Bon's paternity (see p. 266). That Quentin learns about Bon's Negro blood on the same night at Sutpen's Hundred seems at least possible. There is also an earlier passage, not mentioned by Brooks, when Quentin is relating Sutpen's conversation about his first wife with Grandfather: " 'He also told Grandfather, dropped this into the telling as you might flick the joker out of a pack of fresh cards without being able to remember later whether you had removed the joker or not, that the old man's wife had been a Spaniard' " (p. 252). Only someone who knows that Bon is part black could grasp the significance here—and Quentin is doing the talking.

If Quentin has known of Bon's black blood since September then why doesn't he simply give Shreve this information instead of going through the process of inventing what he already knows? The answer here is, I think, central to Faulkner's notions of the imagination and of the way truth is known. Between that italicized passage in which Henry accepts the incestuous marriage (p. 349)—thus sweeping away the basis of their whole explanation of the murder—and the italicized passage in which the fact of blackness first emerges clearly (p. 355), Shreve returns to that significant September night, 1909. For now he too knows the deepest truth of the Sutpen story and he knows how *Quentin* has come to know it: " 'And she didn't tell you in so many words how she had been in the room that day when they brought Bon's body in and Judith took from his pocket the metal case she had given him with her picture in it; she didn't tell you, it just came out of the terror and the fear . . . and she didn't tell you in the actual words because even in the terror she kept the secret; nevertheless she told you, or at least all of a sudden you knew' " (pp. 350–51).

Presumably, what Clytie is *not* telling Quentin at this point is that

Henry Sutpen is upstairs, but it is this kind of wordless communication, and the intuitive grasping of truth it necessitates, that must be the means by which Quentin has learned the secret of Bon's mixed blood. Yet this last truth is something that Quentin can really *know*, can possesss as a truth of the Sutpen family, only with the aid of Shreve and the communion that is created between them. Only then can he know what perhaps he has always known but could not admit to knowing, could not grasp except in the images of imaginatively realized truth.

The whole narrative of Quentin and Shreve, then, has been the process by which Quentin draws Shreve, the remote Northerner who exists a whole country apart from these Southern facts and legends, into the cooperative telling of truths Quentin cannot bear to face alone. Shreve, as his name denotes, is involved in an elaborate confession; he is the instrument through which Quentin comes into the full *imaginative* possession of what previously he has known only in fact. Quentin may be said to "use" Shreve, even as most of the characters in the Sutpen story have made use of other human beings. Shreve himself, it should be added, has been guilty of a similar act, since he is clearly using Quentin and the South not only to satisfy his curiosity—*"Tell about the South. What's it like there. What do they do there"* (p. 174)—but in order to indulge his own romantic notions of love and honor.

But "use" between the two boys is different from what it is elsewhere in the novel, even as one of the chief moral conclusions of their narration has to do with the special use Bon makes of Judith. Manipulation, according to Quentin and Shreve, has in that case been redeemed by love. Shreve insists, for example, that Bon's substitution of the octoroon's picture for Judith's is an act not of callousness or vengeance but of devotion: " ' "it will be the only way I will have to say to her, *I was no good; do not grieve for me*" ' " (p. 359). This is an interpretation Quentin and Shreve can believe in because it is true of themselves: their own exploitation of each other is redeemed by the depth of their communion. And the visible sign of *that* redemption is the tale that they have finally succeeded in telling.

The capacities of the imagination, in other words, are irrevocably rooted in our moral life. Quentin and Shreve can conceive of an enduring love because they have created it between themselves, and the reverse is also true. Still further, and what is most shocking and most moving of all, they have come to imagine the motives for the murder of a brother by thrusting themselves into brotherhood and then *experiencing* the resentment and regret that only this union can produce. The last chapter of the novel plays out, in the bitterness and mockery the boys express, the extraordinary love-hate implicit to the earlier, and completely imaginary, scene when Henry discovers that Charles Bon is part black (pp. 351–58). This is the scene which concludes with its invitation to murder: "—*You will have to stop me, Henry.*" The past yields up its truth only when the imagination propels the two boys into a repetition of the moral crises of Henry and Bon. Imagination imprisons Quentin and Shreve within the shapes of their imagining. They create those shapes in order to make grandly visible what they have become; they reenact an invented past in order to release it into meaning.

In making their momentous leap from the theme of incest to that of miscegenation, Quentin and Shreve separate themselves from Mr. Compson and Miss Rosa, for theirs is the only version of the story that has expanded itself just at the moment of its apparent completion. The tale as a rendering of the past into a stable unchanging artifact becomes the tale as organic flesh and blood, alive with the presence of change.

For Quentin the truth he has dared to imagine is the fullest truth of his ambivalent relationship to the South, the truth of human violation. Loving the South, conscious of its heritage, of a tradition in which one would die for one's land, Quentin yet forces himself to endure the dishonor and shame, the murderous denial of human responsibility. His despair is not over his hatred for the South, but over his love, for he cannot reconcile himself to its moral failures or to that moral superiority of Charles Bon with which Shreve has ended the tale. Quentin's agony becomes completely that of the Henry Sutpen he has imagined.

This last Henry is not the defender of a sister's chastity or a family's honor, but the murderer of the black man who is his brother. It is not incest now, the violation of an ancient taboo, but miscegenation that is the key to this history; and Quentin is much too candid to confuse Henry's resistance to it with a justifiable defense of honor and virtue. Henry's dismay at Bon's blackness is Quentin's own. For Quentin, trying to imagine truth in 1910, blackness rather than incest is the only adequate motive for murder. And this blackness becomes the fiction we believe in, for Quentin has not merely imagined its horror for Henry Sutpen; he has lived it.

The intense brotherhood of the tale of 1865 is the brotherhood in this freezing room in 1910. Shreve is the foreign intruder, the counterpart to Charles Bon, and Quentin is Henry Sutpen, the despair-ridden defender of his own shame. Together they create and live once more the brotherhood that attempts to defy the divisions of man. The symbolic form is not strategy but the visible contours of a young man's anguished soul; the only consolation is the tragic recognition of oneself.

Shreve, the co-creator of all this, endures the final separation of Charles Bon and *himself* from a heritage to which he has become imaginatively joined. No longer, however, can Bon face this separation as the Byronic hero glorious in his alienation; now he is only the lost being who horrifies the family whose acknowledgment he seeks: "*—He must not marry her, Henry*" (p. 354).

As victim, Shreve's Bon can own the last bravery: "'And he never slipped away,' Shreve said. 'He could have, but he never even tried'" (p. 358). His is the last gesture as well, the altruism of carrying the octoroon's picture in order to save Judith from grief. Shreve heatedly insists on this, and Quentin accepts. But for Charles Bon the gesture is death; and for Shreve it is the eternal distance between himself and these matters, these bloody affairs of "'anger and pride and glory.'" It is the distance, too, from the Southern stranger with whom he has reconstructed the tale, but who will at the end drive him, like any trespasser, from its boundaries.

The last pages of chapter 8 are the novel's climax, firing the unformable, unknowable heart of being human and the cold, enduring images of art into the violent oneness of a tragic form. Nineteen ten and 1865 are one, the two narrators and their completely realized shadows are one, the image is everything and everything is implicit to it: the creators and their creating and their creation all one in the realization of truth.

> Because now neither of them were there. They were both in Carolina and the time was forty-six years ago, and it was not even four now but compounded still further, since now both of them were Henry Sutpen and both of them were Bon, compounded each of both yet either neither, smelling the very smoke which had blown and faded away forty-six years ago from the *bivouac fires burning in a pine grove, the gaunt and ragged men sitting or lying about them, talking not about the war yet all curiously enough (or perhaps not curiously at all) facing the South. . . .*
> *—You are my brother.*
> *—No I'm not. I'm the nigger that's going to sleep with your sister. Unless you stop me, Henry.* (Pp. 351–58)

This is the novel's triumph of created image, measured by its ability to thrust its creators into a reality they have not anticipated. The tragedy of this triumph is that it can breed only the destruction of what gives it life: illusion becomes the voice of disorder and violence, love issues forth as fratricide, passionate communion devours itself in murder.

The fullness of form: communion shatters itself on the truth it utters. Its supreme victories are always its defeats.

VI

In the last chapter of the novel occurs the painful disintegration of the communion between Quentin and Shreve that has resulted in the most compelling version of the Sutpen history. The fiction realized, there is an inevitable wrenching apart by both Quentin and Shreve, as if in retreat from those truths of the self that their imaginative venture has revealed to them. Just after Shreve has offered to cover the shivering Quentin with overcoats, repeating Bon's act of covering Henry with his cloak (p. 346), they retreat into callousness and defensiveness. Shreve's confession that there is in the South " 'something my people haven't got,'" something that he would like to learn about, is answered by Quentin, " 'You cant understand it. You would have to be born there' " (p. 361), a statement that dismisses the meaning of everything they have done together. Shreve replies by summing up the whole story with a vicious insensitivity, calculated to detach himself completely from these matters in which he has obviously invested so much, *revealed* so much, of himself—as well as to punish Quentin for appearing to reject that investment: " 'So it took Charles Bon and his mother to get rid of old Tom, and Charles Bon and the octoroon to get rid of Judith, and Charles Bon and Clytie to get rid of Henry; and Charles Bon's mother and Charles Bon's grandmother got rid of Charles Bon. So it takes two niggers to get rid of one Sutpen, dont it?' " (pp. 377-78).

And he concludes with his comments on the mixed-blood Jim Bond: " 'I think that in time the Jim Bonds are going to conquer the western hemisphere. . . . and so in a few thousand years, I who regard you will also have sprung from the loins of African kings' " (p. 378). The lines may be read as a reflection of Faulkner's own racism, yet coming after the whole Sutpen story, and coming with such rednecked callousness, this would be an unfair indictment not only of Faulkner's morality but his artistry as well. The lines characterize Shreve, not Faulkner; their largest significance is hardly their sociology but the terrible impasse that has suddenly emerged between Shreve and Quentin. With a perversity that may reflect the awesome letdown from relationship to isolation, from communion to alienation, Shreve is taunting Quentin, building upon a fear of blackness the Northerner always assumes exists in the Southerner. He concludes with a question that surely pertains to a

"fact," an authentic aspect of Quentin, but is wholly absent of imagination, not to mention generosity: " 'Why do you hate the South?' "
(p. 378).

This is the working out of the divisions implicit to the images of
chapter 8, the return of the two boys, despite all that love and imagination can humanly perform, to those privacies of being where image
and meaning are lost in the soul's confusion and sorrow. The center of
chapter 9 is the literal confrontation between Quentin Compson and
Henry Sutpen. This is all truth; it contains no conjecture and, therefore, no metaphor:

And you are—?
Henry Sutpen.
And you have been here—?
Four years.
And you came home—?
To die. Yes.
To die?
Yes. To die.
And you have been here—?
Four years.
And you are—?
Henry Sutpen. (p. 373)

The scene is so grim and naked, so free of the imagination's insight,
that it seems the most factual but the least true of any scene in the
novel. This is fact stripped of art, the fusions of a supreme fiction now
dissolved, as is necessary, back into the reality that fails to mean. And
yet it *is* reality, what the eye has seen; and it colors everything that has
come before with the tint of irrelevance. Art, this wealth of words, is
disturbed, wrenched askew, by the shocking, disappointing revelation
of what is merely real. Present encounters past; but the voice, once so
rich and full, is now just this side of silence.

In chapter 9 reality, emptied of metaphor, of its Reality, is what is
left. Form and meaning have been achieved, and yet the creators themselves remain; except for Miss Rosa, they are still talking. The collective
illusion does not fully encompass the continuing history; we remember
now its origins in subjectivism, the conjectures piled one on the other.
But more than this we see that the meanings which have been won, the
total sympathy of creators and created, are now disintegrating into callousness, simplistic summary, the hysterical denial.

There is an anguish communicable only in the fullest achievement of form, the tragic form that draws its power from the fact of its impending destruction. The tragic art ultimately turns on itself, allowing once again to rise the dark knowledge—the original meaninglessness of murder—it has tried to illuminate. The words summon the very silence whose truth they would deny.

The fictional image survives, nevertheless, in memory. It is what we have: Henry and Bon brought to life by their identity with their creators, riding south in tattered gray to Sutpen's Hundred. Wearied with the years of war, still fumbling their way through the fragments of old dreams and old moralities—the sister's flesh Bon will give up for the word from the father, the incest Henry will condone—they find themselves at last at the gates of Bon's blackness, which can be neither given up nor condoned. The image, created in order to assuage, to resolve the inarticulate sorrow, again opens wide with murder in 1865 and its symbolic repetition in 1910.

At the bottom of this modern tragedy is the inability of one man to speak to another, some inviolable privacy at the center that imagination and love, feeding on absence, bring forth in the splendid contours of language and pattern, but which finally returns Bon and Henry, Quentin and Shreve, *Absalom, Absalom!*, to the wordless fact of a dumb and secret despair.

Three | *Mythos*

5 | *The Hamlet*

I

The Hamlet is a book of what Joseph Reed calls "plentitude": it "conveys a feeling of continuing surprise—not just to us but to the author."[1] Faulkner's last major novel, it is in some ways the best of all: the widest ranging, the funniest, the most varied in tone, subject matter, and style. The sureness of the writer's hand is evident everywhere, as he moves with ease from the light, anecdotal comedy of horse-swapping and job-hopping that opens the novel to the extravagant loves of Frenchman's Bend between man and woman, man and goddess, man and cow; from the violent hates of Mink Snopes, the murderer from ambush who is raised to tragic stature, to the wild farce of the sale of Flem's Texas ponies. And over the whole variegated panorama, sometimes subdued but never silent, is a sense of the land and the community of people who live on it—the first of Faulkner's novels to treat society, as Irving Howe has said, as something more than a "background against which a drama of isolation is enacted."[2]

To many readers the novel has seemed without structure, merely a composite of previously published stories, and certainly there are signs that the transition from story to novel is not always as graceful as it might have been. Yet I will argue in this chapter that it is in *The Hamlet* that Faulkner for the first time in his career turns to a genuine experiment with a mythic mode of writing. That is to say, structure is not only present in this novel; it is raised to the level of mythic force, controlling and defining the characters who live within it. This force is not, like the plot of *As I Lay Dying,* a contradiction to consciousness,

but the fitting if not quite leak-proof channel to the general flow of
event and motive.

The Hamlet, in other words, is the crucial shift in Faulkner's career,
the novel in which he moves from the description of struggles to formu-
late pattern to a new concern with the meaning of living in one already
intact. The primary source of this pattern is the hamlet itself: the
community of Frenchman's Bend and its indefinite surroundings. The
opening paragraph of the novel demonstrates clearly this shift in
Faulkner's method. Instead of beginning, as Faulkner novels usually do,
with a specialized point of view from a particular character—as if the
only reality we can be concerned with begins with the first word of this
book—*The Hamlet* begins with setting and an idea of real antecedence,
not fabricated history.

> Frenchman's Bend was a section of rich river-bottom country
> lying twenty miles southeast of Jefferson. Hill-cradled and remote,
> definite yet without boundaries, straddling into two counties and
> owning allegiance to neither, it had been the original grant and site
> of a tremendous pre-Civil War plantation, the ruins of which—the
> gutted shell of an enormous house with its fallen stables and slave
> quarters and overgrown gardens and brick terraces and promenades—
> were still known as the Old Frenchman's Place, although the original
> boundaries now existed only on old faded records in the Chancery
> Clerk's office in the county courthouse in Jefferson, and even some
> of the once-fertile fields had long since reverted to the cane-and-
> cypress jungle from which their first master had hewed them.[3]

The following pages describe the original Frenchman (if French he
was), the ancestors of present inhabitants ("from England and the Scot-
tish and Welsh Marches"), the cultural and political climate ("They were
Protestants and Democrats and prolific"), and Will Varner, the most
powerful man in the area.

This is more than just a framework in which Faulkner could set the
stories he had already written and published, such as "Spotted Horses,"
"The Hound," "Lizards in Jamshyd's Courtyard," "Fool About a
Horse," and "Barn Burning."[4] The world of Frenchman's Bend, including the natural surroundings of earth and recurrent seasons, becomes the generating power of *The Hamlet,* a structural pressure that
influences all the actions of the novel and by which they gain much
of their meaning.

Society and nature assume in *The Hamlet* a mythic status. This mythos may have little of the architectonic grace of the plot of *Tom Jones,* but it does provide a structural pressure, thereby creating in the reader a set of expectations—what R. S. Crane calls a "characteristic pattern"—which the novel eventually fulfills.[5] Mythos is a fundamentally conservative force; it implies service to powers independent of the foreground of content. And to suggest that such service exists in *The Hamlet* might seem to miss the obvious radicalism of a novel containing Ike and Mink Snopes, the sodomist and murderer who are blind to any social ethic. But unlike Faulkner's previous novels, and despite the antisocial rage and violence, *The Hamlet* is dominated by a community whose customs and codes are the impulse for human action in the novel. Village and land are what *The Hamlet* is about; and these make up a reality immune to the capricious imagination. The community outlasts and thus releases its individuals whose task is no longer to invent but rather to implement the necessary actions of a myth.

While *The Hamlet* may lack the schematic lines of a traditional novel, it embodies what novels often displace to the vanishing point, namely, the element of magic, of the preternatural. The community of Frenchman's Bend and its natural environment have what Richard Chase means by the term *mana:* some "impersonal magic force or potency" that brings significant order to an apparent chaos and violence.[6] This is most obviously true in Faulkner's treatment of nature, but it is part of the hamlet as well, part of the sense we have and never lose that this community is more than its physical identity, more than the sum of its members. It has a status of god-approval, as if touched with holy power. Its survival is assured, it is a given, something that exists before the rich paragraph that opens the novel and that is intact at the end as Flem Snopes rides calmly past the silent townspeople, fully united by their feelings of pity at the terrible fate of Henry Armstid.

Some readers have argued that *The Hamlet* is about the *destruction* of Frenchman's Bend, financially and morally, by Flem Snopes, but I believe this is not the case. Flem is more catalyst than character, and the effect of his machinations is to confirm rather than subvert the identity of Frenchman's Bend. At the end, Flem is gone, Houston is dead, Mink is in jail, and Armstid has gone mad—but the community has as vital a sense as ever of itself and its values. It has also acquired one significant addition to its population: V. K. Ratliff.

The Hamlet, then, contains a source of order that none of Faulkner's major works up to this point avails itself of: the unquestioned reality of an existing structure which the various events in the novel epitomize and confirm. This is a structure that is recognized but not invented by minds within the fiction. The mythic power within *The Hamlet* functions in the same way that, in *A Fable,* the narrative of Christ does: as a discovered structure which the Corporal confirms by his imitation of it. Such a formidable precedent in the novel, acting to organize the disparate strands, distinguishes *The Hamlet* from Faulkner's earlier work.

Both the conventions of Frenchman's Bend and, for example, the various explanations of the murder of Charles Bon are to some extent fictions, but *Absalom, Absalom!* is about the way in which each explanation is created and how this act of creation implies a moral as well as an aesthetic condition. The fictions of *The Hamlet,* on the other hand, are *collective* ones, inherited not invented, like a "still point of the turning world" from which meaning radiates. The issue of *The Hamlet* is a set of actions which, however violent at times, are rooted in a common understanding of what life and Frenchman's Bend mean; the issue of *Absalom, Absalom!* is a series of unique consciousnesses trying to create meaning where there has been none before: trying to explain the hitherto inexplicable murder of Charles Bon.

The imaginative life of Frenchman's Bend is a shared one. The histories and fantasies (the difference is not always clear) that circulate constantly about trades, women, the discovery of the old Frenchman's buried money, are part of a communal rhetoric. Even the most extreme acts in the novel—Armstid's mad persistence in his search for buried treasure, Ike Snopes's infatuation with Houston's cow, Mink's brutal murder of Houston—are outrageous variations on the conventional concerns of Frenchman's Bend: the desire to pull off a successful deal, especially with an acknowledged champion like Flem Snopes; the pursuit and seduction of a woman; the insistence that one's dignity be inviolate.

In using the idea of a community as a basis for order in fiction, Faulkner first begins to take advantage of an imaginary Yoknapatawpha County and history as a formal strategy, a way of tying things together.[7] The Jefferson of *The Sound and the Fury, Light in August,* or *Absalom, Absalom!* has nothing of this formal function; its place in these novels is tangential to the exploration of consciousness. But "the subject of [*The Hamlet*]," Melvin Backman has written, "is the hamlet—the people of Frenchman's Bend. Their creation is Faulkner's great achievement in this novel. . . . *The Hamlet* is their story—the story of their passions, rancors, greed and violence; the story of their decency, kindliness, shrewdness, and wry humor."[8]

Viola Hopkins provides a fine sense of the quality of this community, demonstrating how its pace and habits and concerns are at the center of the novel.

Not accidentally is it entitled *The Hamlet;* we might say that its outer limits extend beyond the boundaries of Frenchman's Bend only as far as Jefferson, and the core, in the community and the novel, is Varner's crossroads store. The pace of a rural community in the 1890's is reflected in the slow, discursive movement of the novel. There is time to spend a Saturday whittling and chatting on the gallery of the village emporium. Amusements are simple and usually communal—church picnics and socials, hunting and fishing, horse trading—but most of all, talk is the staple of entertainment. The land and the seasons are the great facts; the speech, manners, and habits of the hard-working, independent farmers determine the pitch and provide a richness of texture, a concreteness, and a fullness of life which acts as a framework to sustain the numerous sub-structures, variety of styles, and themes, which in a sparser work would seem gratuitous. It is this closeness to the "folk" . . . though most difficult to define specifically, which is perhaps the key to the particular individual quality and unity of this novel, if any one "key" can be isolated.[9]

The hamlet is linked irrevocably to the land, and this too is part of the controlling force in the novel. T. Y. Greet has written: "A sense of the richness and inviolability of the land pervades much of Faulkner's earlier work, especially the Indian stories, *Absalom, Absalom!* and *Old Man,* but not until *The Hamlet* does it become the dominant interest." Seeing the chaotic activities of the men of Frenchman's Bend as "the pursuit of a bootless freedom," Greet writes: "The earth endures and in man's acknowledgment of this lies his hope for restoration."[10]

The community of Frenchman's Bend and the land to which it is tied becomes in *The Hamlet* an unusual but still palpable structure. From it emerges every action in the book, for the community has a code or custom for every form of activity, from business dealing to fruitful fornication. Freed from the obligation to discover the Real, *The Hamlet* unfolds an enduring pattern whose truth is never questioned. Life begins to look like a life remembered, a store-porch anecdote lived with unfailing energy again and again.

What makes *The Hamlet* such a rich novel, however, is not its mythic underpinning alone but the fact that Faulkner is able to combine with it such diversity and freedom. The danger of the kind of mythic pressure I have been describing is that it may decline into ritual: a sense of character moving in such obedience to a narrative or moral precedent that the work is less fiction than ceremony, a somnambulistic service to design. This is the danger Faulkner all too often falls victim to in his fiction of the 1940s and 1950s, the period of "The Bear," *A Fable,* and the concluding testaments of Yoknapatawpha County. *The Hamlet* is a brilliant exception, for Faulkner has built an anarchy, indeed a madness, into the structure of Frenchman's Bend. There are codes in the hamlet to which everyone subscribes, hence the mythic force of the novel. But, paradoxically, they are codes of radical individualism, of a trading ethic in which practically anything goes, of an impulsiveness (at least among the men) that repeatedly issues in violence.

Frenchman's Bend is a community of real, yet loose, definition: "Hill-cradled and remote, definite yet without boundaries, straddling into two counties and owning allegiance to neither." The geographical ambivalence of the community is analogous to the combination of structural pressure and vitality that Faulkner seeks in the form of *The Hamlet;* and both are the mirror of the community's own mores, its sense of communal identity *as* an insistent individualism. Even in their condition as near-vassals to Will Varner, the people of the hamlet come to Varner, "not in the attitude of *What must I do* but *What do you think you would like for me to do if you was able to make me do it"* (p. 5).

Florence Leaver has correctly observed that although there is "a fine sense of comradeship" among the members of the hamlet, their code of individualism transcends that communal sense.[11] Minding one's own business is the most rigid law, particularly when it comes to interference "in another man's trade" (p. 83). The virtue of neighborliness must yield to that of self-reliance if the two are in conflict. It is this respect for individualism, rather than callousness or indifference, that allows the community to stand by while Henry Armstid and his wife are being taken advantage of by Flem; and it forces Tull and Bookwright, ordinarily compassionate men, to observe passively an earlier example of unethical conduct.

> "Aint none of you folks out there done nothing about it?" [Ratliff] said.
> "What could we do?" Tull said. "It aint right. But it aint none of our business." (P. 72)

A further aspect of this individualism, evidenced primarily by the men, is the impractical attachment to objects either worthless or out of reach. To be "a fool about a horse" is the way Ratliff sums it up, and

the whole evolution of *The Hamlet* is the gradually growing membership of those who can be numbered among such "fools." The novel
ends only when the list includes every male character but Flem. Commenting once on the "Spotted Horses" episode in *The Hamlet*, Faulkner
linked this capacity for irrational behavior with the individualism central to the life of Frenchman's Bend.

> [The horses] symbolized the hope, the aspiration of the masculine
> part of society that is capable of doing, of committing puerile folly
> for some gewgaw that has drawn him, as juxtaposed to the cold
> practicality of the women whose spokesman Mrs. Littlejohn was
> when she said "Them men!" or "What fools men are!" That the
> man even in a society where there's a constant pressure to conform
> can still be taken off by the chance to buy a horse for three dollars.
> Which to me is a good sign, I think. I hope that man can always
> be tolled off that way, to buy a horse for three dollars.[12]

This male irrationality is a vital part of the flexibility of the mythos
of Frenchman's Bend, for all the embarrassment and suffering it can
cause. In "committing puerile folly" these characters are in fact con-
forming to the largest design in the novel. While Faulkner's comment
suggests that this behavior is antisocial, in *The Hamlet* it is absolutely
consistent with the community's fundamental spirit. Only through
such behavior are the authentic members of the community able to define themselves, in a real sense *defend* themselves, and to fulfill the
mythos that presides over Frenchman's Bend and *The Hamlet*.

II

The Hamlet is a series of rhetorics as well as a series of stories, and the
first of these is the tall-tale style of Book One, dominated by the voice
of V. K. Ratliff. While the rise of Flem Snopes from sharecropper's
cabin to the flour-barrel chair in front of the Old Frenchman's place is
the major action of this section, it is Ratliff who controls its atmos-
phere and style, transforming the story of Flem into what is the most
elaborate of the several tall tales that make up Book One. The four
principal anecdotes are the two narrated by Ratliff about Ab Snopes,
the goat trade Ratliff engages in, and the central one in which Flem
is the chief character, and they are of a single fabric: comic narratives of
trade in the Old Southwest tradition, man pitted against man in the
"science and pastime of skullduggery" (p. 83).

Ratliff's Frenchman's Bend is the community in its most customary guise, prior to the explosions in Books Two, Three and Four. For Ratliff, the essential spirit of Frenchman's Bend lies in its traditions of trade: not only the dickering itself but even more the *talk*, the telling and retelling of stories that are really the principal fruits of trade. A serious change in economic status is rarely the result of Ratliff's tales of negotiation. What is important is the complexity of the transaction, and even this takes a back seat to the subsequent hours of talk with which men lovingly decorate even the most inconsequential bits of dealing. Ratliff's story of "a fool about a horse" presents the legendary Pat Stamper in a demonstration of championship horse swapping, but the real triumph belongs to the teller himself. Ratliff provides the necessary suspense (as to how, not whether, Ab Snopes will be defeated by Stamper), some portentous invocations of "fate," a graphic account of the precise means by which Stamper finally gets the best of Ab (inflated horse indeed!), and a perfect joke denouement: Viney Snopes as the contented owner of a milk separator for which she has just sold her only cow.[13]

Behind this piece of foolery lie the style and values of the Frenchman's Bend that V. K. Ratliff believes in: the frame setting at Varner's store, with the men quietly gathered at dusk, undoubtedly waiting for just such a prize yarn as this; Ratliff's unhurried, soft-spoken narrative style; the focus of the tale on a contest of champions, its attention to certain motives such as the defense of the honor of Yoknapatawpha County. Implicit to the tale and its telling is a community fascinated with the machinations of trading, responsive to the exaggerations to which a teller is entitled and to the comic possibilities of violence—most of all a community, "Hill-cradled and remote," geared to the leisurely pace of seasons, always willing to consume an hour or two in dealing and talking.

The wages of dealing are hardly the mule, the clerk's job, the burnt barn, the goats, or the correct change from Jody Varner—these are merely the currency, the language of competition. The true prize is the verdict that concludes each contest, announcing to the world exactly who is the *taker* and who the *taken*.

Ratliff's version of the short story "Barn Burning" (published separately in June 1939) makes this hierarchy of values clear. The themes of social inequality and of the conflicts of family loyalty vs. abstract justice, idealism vs. realism, that create the tragic overtones of "Barn Burning," are transposed by Ratliff into a battle of wits between Ab Snopes and DeSpain. The young boy of "Barn Burning," Colonel

Sartoris Snopes, is now missing, leaving a contest of traders rather than a conflict of father and son. The frame of the story in *The Hamlet,* with Ratliff's quiet and patient telling punctuated by Jody Varner's choric "Hell fire!"—Ratliff, "pleasant and drawling and anecdotal, while Varner's suffused swollen face glared down at him" (pp. 15–16)—begins its transformation into a tale of entertaining, no-holds-barred competition. The frame also supplies a traditional tall-tale dramatic situation of the knowing raconteur and the baffled listener who unwittingly supplies the straight man's responses.

In the conclusion of Ratliff's story the burnt barn is no longer, as it was in "Barn Burning," the symbol of Ab's integrity, of his defiance of the economic system that has created such a gap between him and De-Spain. Now it is the occasion of Ab's triumph over DeSpain, a victory of wit and timing. The morning after the fire Ab announces: " 'It looks like me and you aint going to get along together . . . so I reckon we better quit trying before we have a misunderstanding over something. I'm moving this morning.' And DeSpain says, 'What about your contract?' And Ab says, 'I done cancelled it' " (p. 18).

The humor is completely a factor of this new telling of the tale, for there is none in "Barn Burning"; and the defeat of DeSpain by Ab is not Ab's successful arson but the fact that the concluding scene so obviously belongs to him: burn the barn and *then* cancel the contract so as to avoid "misunderstanding"! "Barn Burning" is now a story about that quickwittedness and brashness that the men of the hamlet so much admire and enjoy. That this should be the upshot of the barn-burning episode, even as it is the upshot of Ab's horsetrading with Stamper and Flem's bargaining with Jody Varner, is part of the spirit of Book One. Largely owing to the presence of Ratliff—this shrewd yet humane and dignified man—the tales of Ab and Jody and Flem are coated with a sheen of comic delight, with most of the brutal possibilities of competitiveness buried beneath an illusion of harmless gamesmanship.

These possibilities come to the surface in the rest of the novel. We have glimpses of them in Flem's rise, and in the fact that Jody Varner's original intention was to take advantage of Ab Snopes. It is true that the tactics of Flem seem to be in keeping with the trading ethic of Frenchman's Bend, involving, as Michael Millgate has written, "principles of respect for the most skillful, of unconcern for the defeated, and, at all times, of noninterference in other men's trading."[14] But *The Hamlet,* as Cleanth Brooks has pointed out, is not an attack on skullduggery, and Frenchman's Bend is not simply getting its just deserts for being a place where horsetrading is serious business.[15] *The Hamlet* is about how Frenchman's Bend becomes a *community* of the *taken,* confirming in the process its trade ethic, its individualism, and its literary staple—the tall-tale tradition. The unity of the book emerges from the coherence of all the strands of Frenchman's Bend into the renewed sense of its identity: an entire community "tolled off," and by that very act committing itself once again to the structure and the mythos of the hamlet and *The Hamlet.*

Ratliff is the key here, for his development in the novel is its most vivid figure for the workings of a mythic fiction. His progress is to lock himself into the mythos of Frenchman's Bend. He moves from his role as community poet, passively telling its comic history from his perch just outside it, to his final role as active defender of the community, challenging Flem Snopes.

This challenge begins with the goat trade that ends Book One, in which Ratliff realizes that the trading code of Frenchman's Bend has found an entirely new kind of practitioner in Flem, whose competitive sense does not rule out exploitation of his idiot cousin Ike. In Book Three Ratliff's awareness of the dangers of Snopesism grows, as he finds Lump Snopes charging admission to the scene of sodomy between Ike and the cow. Ratliff's eventual defeat is foreshadowed here in the anger he allows to come over him, the moral and emotional responses which have no chance against the passionless Flem Snopes. Ratliff succeeds in putting a stop to Lump's sideshow profits, as he violates the community code of noninterference for the sake of another, the code of pure individual conviction and power: " 'because I am strong enough to keep him from it. I am stronger than him. Not righter. Not any better, maybe. But just stronger' " (p. 201). But in his success he has already revealed the emotional levels that make him vulnerable to Flem and will allow him to be defeated soundly by him in Book Four.

The outcome of the challenge to Flem, with Ratliff purchasing the Old Frenchman's Place in return for his share of a restaurant in Jefferson, paves the way for Flem's departure for Jefferson and brings Ratliff fully into the orbit of the hamlet, as property owner and leading name on the list of Flem's victims. Ratliff's development describes the arc of the novel: the coming together of the poet-outsider and the community, the independent fragment and the mythic core of *The Hamlet.* No one, not even Ratliff and Will Varner, "can risk fooling with them folks" (p. 28).

III

The violences of the rest of *The Hamlet* are counterpoint to the pleasant and complacent calm of Book One. Patrons of this violence, fueling its flames, are the two people who are completely untouched by it: Flem Snopes and Eula Varner. Like Thomas Sutpen, Flem has made the visible codes of a society part of his instinctive response, but he understands nothing of their underlying value. He shows no interest in sex, trades not for honor or pride but solely for gain, and most important of all, he has little interest in talk. Similarly, Eula is the champion of sexuality, the object of every man's desire; yet she herself is largely passionless and immune to the lust she inspires.

Free of those desires with which the other townspeople run willingly to their undoing, Flem and Eula are, as Backman writes, symbols rather than people. They are embodiments of pure acquisitiveness, but indifferent to acquisitions, and of pure lust, but without desire.[16] They have no real place in Frenchman's Bend; their function is to serve as static images of the codes to which they are impervious: the devil of barter and the goddess of love.

They arouse the rest of the male community, however, to violent action. In the case of Eula this effect is related to the effect of nature: "[Eula's] presence," Viola Hopkins writes, "arouses bright dreams and passions. . . . The association of the female with the land as the procreative force which condemns man to servitude is a pattern which recurs throughout the novel."[17] Like nature, Eula is the embodiment of a vital chaos: the warm rains "washing out of the earth the iron enduring frost, the belated spring hard on its bright heels and all coming at once, pell-mell and disordered, fruit and bloom and leaf, pied meadow and blossoming wood and the long fields shearing dark out of winter's slumber, to the shearing plow" (p. 269). And like the nature whose appearance as chaos can only provoke the need to shape this disordered awakening into the structure of planted fields and the cultivated rows of cotton, so Eula Varner must arouse in men—all of them but Flem— the urge to control her, to possess her sexually or, like her brother Jody, at least to harness her in corsets.

The dual strands of desire and trade reach their climax in the characters of Ike and Mink Snopes. Ike is the most devoted lover in the novel, raising lust to such elevation that he displaces it into love. Mink is the most committed trader, the one who responds to a three dollar defeat at the hands of Houston with the unanswerable shrewdness of a shotgun blast. Enraged at this defeat and its reminder of all his other defeats, Mink distills from this particular deal its essential ingredient: pride. Like the single-minded lust of Ike, Mink's desire for successful trade transcends the whole idea of economic profit. Mink does not even care to search Houston's body for the fifty dollars he has probably been carrying. If Flem and Eula are the symbols of acquisitiveness and desire, then Ike and Mink are their fiercest acolytes: moving manifestations, in human form, of the universal emotions of love and pride.

In Books Two and Three, *The Hamlet* moves from more or less traditional tall-tale humor into other narrative conventions. That the stories of Eula and Ike at least would be suitable for Ratliff's pleasant humor is unquestionable; instead Faulkner pulls out all the stops and calls upon older and loftier fictional traditions to tell these tales, abruptly putting aside Ratliff as the poet of Frenchman's Bend.

The self-conscious and ostentatious prose styles of Eula and "The Long Summer," despite their brilliance, have raised acute objections from readers. Irving Howe writes:

> Yet for all its brilliance, this very mixture of tones occasionally seems gratuitous, a surplus of splendor. That Ike Snopes's affair with Houston's cow should be celebrated in a style both the extreme and parody of romantic prose, that this prose should nevertheless convey the moral superiority of poor befuddled Ike over the ice-blooded Flem, is all very fine; we realize that the section is meant as an ironic fantasia, the high romantic lyricism blended to a subject matter poor and pathetic, and soon we learn to respond to both elements, keeping one in a firm relation to the other; yet, as it goes on and on, page after dazzling page, it defeats its own end, the parody by its very excess parodying itself. . . . Such excesses—for all that we know they are meant to be excesses and to amuse and dismay us as excesses— seem too wilful, too completely mere displays of virtuosity.[18]

This seems to me very much to the point; such passages, and they exist not only in the Ike section, *are* "mere displays." But that, I believe, is their function: an extreme stylistic equivalent to what is going on in the action of the novel, a pushing back of the apparent boundaries of order and decorum.

In each of the episodes involving Eula, Ike, and Mink, Faulkner sets up a deliberate gap between style and event, pressing the most mundane and even base material into stylistic contexts usually reserved for more elevated subjects. At least one of the results of this gap is to call attention to the author himself, for these are clearly "performances," an outrageous coupling of form and content that parades the writer's mastery

both of his craft and his material. In *Light in August,* in the intricate
web of echoes and cross references that imposes a certain order on that
fragmented novel, the result is a reinforcement of the book's fatalism,
a sense of characters imprisoned in externally controlled events. The
mirror images suggest the practice of the puppeteer, who marches his
characters through patterns of which they themselves are unaware. But
the authorial ostentatiousness in *The Hamlet* has quite a different quality: it does not reduce the characters but raises them; it does not so
much mock them as supply them with a grandeur that, whatever our
awareness of its inappropriateness, we cannot deny them.[19]

In "Eula," the least excessive of the stylistic experiments, Faulkner
tells the story of the overdeveloped, undermotivated, cold-potato-eating
young girl partially in the language of a pre-Hellenistic, Dionysian
Greece. Eula's appearance suggests "honey in sunlight and bursting
grapes, the writhen bleeding of the crushed fecundated vine beneath the
hard rapacious trampling goat-hoof" (p. 95). She is imaged as "a moist
blast of spring's liquorish corruption," "the supreme primal uterus,"
who transforms Labove's schoolroom into "a grove of Venus" in which
the male students battle each other "for precedence in immolation"
(pp. 114–15). In contrast to Labove, the man of order, hierarchy, and
language—"of invincible conviction in the power of words as a principle worth dying for if necessary" (p. 106)—Eula becomes the patroness
of chaos, shattering the designs of his classroom and curriculum like
some Dionysian force shattering parodies of Apollonian structures.

The love story of Ike and Houston's cow is the most famous of these
episodes. In embellishing what is little more than a farmer's dirty joke,
Faulkner makes use of the conventions of comedy and romance, adorn-
ing Ike with honored stylistic formulas that rescue him from his pathetic state, but that never fail to remind us that the laurels here are
not only Ike's but the author's. The movement from a civilized, fallen
world to a green Edenic one; the heroic rescue of the maiden, who re-
wards the hero by defecating all over him; the successful trickery
practiced on the *senex iratus* (the farmer from whom Ike steals feed);
the formation of a new society around Ike and the cow as they move in
harmony, immune to the "shibboleths" of Ike's "upright kind" (p. 185);
the miraculous meeting of man with both the animal and natural
worlds—these are all part of the Ike story, scandalously borrowed from
conventions appropriate to perfect love and a redeemed world. Through
it all there is the language of a unity of elements, man and beast, reality
and reflection: "each face to its own shattered image wedded and an-
nealed" (p. 186); the rain-dripping earth and the sky "which glint by

glint of fallen gold and blue, the falling drops had prisoned" (p. 187); man, cow, and sun descend "into the bowl of evening and are extinguished" (p. 188).

Less frequently noted in terms of stylistic excess is the story of Mink, which, in its adoption of a classical tragic mode, performs a comparable elevation, transforming the snakelike sharecropper who murders from the safety of ambush into a character of genuine tragic dimension. Faulkner achieves tragic effects not only by the language and manipulation of content but by the contrasts he sets up between Mink and Ike, emphasizing their place in opposing literary modes. Ike's romance with the cow is characterized by a harmony achieved between man and natural forces: "from now until evening they will advance only as the day advances, no faster" (p. 186). Mink's attempt to conceal the rotting body of Houston is a battle against those forces: Houston's hound, the corpse, the night, and time are all transformed by his single action into the unbeatable structure of his defeat and his tragic definition.

While Ike moves in unison with the moving day, Mink is always in conflict with a racing night that will not allow him to complete his task. Ike is wedded to a beast in whom he sees love and the fulfillment of his devotion, with whom he lies down, while Mink is in conflict with the hound who is the cause and image of his anguish. Ike is permitted to undermine with ease the human enemies of his enterprise—the old farmer and Houston—whereas Mink is unable to escape the badgering Lump. Ike witnesses the miracle of day breathed into existence by an awakening earth: "frond by frond, from whose escaping tips like gas it rises and disseminates and stains the sleep-fast earth with drowsy insect-murmur . . . it upward bursts and fills night's globed negation with jonquil thunder" (p. 184). Mink must watch the forming night, "the darkness, emerge from the bottom and herd, drive, the sun gradually up the slope of the cornpatch . . . and at last take the house itself" (p. 231).

As in conventional tragedy, there is a clear sense in Mink's story of the consequences of action becoming immediately apparent to the actor, however much he may try to conceal from himself that knowledge. As soon as the shot that kills Houston is fired, like a switch innocently flicked by one who acts in what he believes is freedom, the whole sequence of days to follow suddenly looms up: "He must rise and quit the thicket and do what he had next to do, not to finish it but merely to complete the first step of what he had started, put into motion, who realised now that he had known already, before he heard the horse and raised the gun, that that would happen which had happened: that he had pulled the trigger on an enemy but had only slain a corpse to be hidden" (p. 222). The hound's first cry from the bottom is not merely heard but *recognized* by Mink as part of the logic of his action: "It was as though he had been expecting it, waiting for it; had lain down and composed and emptied himself, not for sleep but to gather strength and will as distance runners and swimmers do, before assuming the phase of harried and furious endeavor which his life was about to enter . . . as if he knew that those ten minutes were to be the last of peace" (p. 227). It is this recognition, as well as the endurance and affirmation of himself and what he has done, that identifies Mink as the central actor in a tragic narrative.

The fatality of events is clear, the inevitable completion of a pattern whose beginning always seems less than what it will ultimately require. Yet, and this is common to tragedy, the hero's action belongs to him, and Mink well knows that there was an "irremediable instant when the barrels had come level and true and his will had told his finger to contract, which nothing but his own death would ever efface from his memory" (p. 227). In the aftermath of murder Mink defines the nature of his integrity; he *acts* even in the grim knowledge of the end of action— "by then he realised it could have but one ending" (pp. 230–31)—pitting himself against forces more formidable than himself, yet all the time growing into a stature which, in the light of his lowly origins, is the most remarkable development in the novel. The fruit of his suffering is a tragic wisdom. It is a knowledge which only he, for having pursued the anguish of his action, can come to own: "It began to seem to him now that that puny and lonely beacon [the light in Mrs. Littlejohn's kitchen] not only marked no ultimate point for even desperate election but was the period to hope itself, and that all which remained to him of freedom lay in the shortening space between it and his advancing foot. I thought that when you killed a man, that finished it, he told himself. But it dont. It just starts then" (p. 247).

The wisdom this particular hero puts on is the customary one of the implacable structure of events, of the meaning of cause and effect that allows him to see the end implicit in what he can now identify as the beginning. Mink's knowledge is his insight into the tragic nature of the plot he has created and in which he is imprisoned. And this knowledge is at once the recognition of destiny and the affirmation of himself as its source. Knowing what is inevitable now, he continues unswervingly in the single action whose doom is its only possible meaning.

The economic factors, which are so dominant in *The Hamlet* and which are the initial motive of Mink's rage, are reduced in "The Long

Summer" to trivia: petty intrusions into concerns of infinitely greater weight. The fifty cents Houston gives Ike, the fifty dollars Lump swears must be on the person of the dead Houston, are parallel instances that the heroes of romance and tragedy can scarcely be concerned with. Although the money would make possible his successful escape, Mink cannot consider the advantages of Lump's proposal, even as he has willfully refused to consider *any* of the pragmatic aspects of his action: " 'you had no money to get away on if you ran, and nothing to eat if you stayed' " (p. 244). It is as if he knows that escape must alter the meaning of what he has done, transforming it from an action that confers upon him a stature he has never had and could hardly articulate, to a simple murder for vengeance and profit. And this escape never figures in his mind as an alternative, for he is totally involved and identified with the action that is defining him.

The stories of Eula, Ike, and Mink are the most extreme episodes of the novel's freedom, the expansion of the human into the furthest ranges of action, feeling, courage, endurance, hate, and love. And this is also the *writer's* lark, his own deliverance from the protocols of fiction—not only from the particular comic tradition he works with in Book One, but from the whole concept that a literary form must be commensurate with, and therefore limited by, its chosen material. These episodes are the writer's insistence on his independence, his defiance of the meaning of stylistic decorum.

Ultimately one violence echoes the other, and stylistic extravagance becomes, in fact, appropriate to the extreme actions that Eula, Ike, and Mink carry out. The anarchy of style which the succession of Dionysian, romantic, and tragic modes suggests is finally not an anarchy at all because it *is* suitable to what is going on in the novel. The style has become decorous in its very freedom from the apparent requirements of content. The paradox applies as well to the general development of *The Hamlet:* the apparent violations of community and order are actually consistent with the codes of Frenchman's Bend.

From a larger perspective we can see that this stylistic release in *The Hamlet,* resulting in some of Faulkner's most brilliant writing, is made possible by the existence of that vague but nevertheless presiding order I have tried to define: the mythos of community and nature that controls, however loosely, even the actions of those characters and events that seem the least circumscribed by external forces. In his earlier fiction Faulkner employs a succession of voices and styles (although never with such radical differences as here) not so much in the interests of freedom, but in quest of some adequate definition of reality; freedom is the painful given, requiring a quest for order. The juxtaposition of voices does not suggest the bravura performance but the search for forms that will suffice. In *The Hamlet,* however, this illusion of style as the author's desperate attempt to embrace an ever shifting reality is reversed and becomes the illusion of an author so assured of the direction and shape of his material that he can afford every stylistic excess available to him. In "Eula" and "The Long Summer" the writer displays his own artistry without apology or the pretense of invisibility. The novel's status as mythos makes the performance possible. Like Frenchman's Bend *The Hamlet* is "definite yet without boundaries," sprawling into a number of stylistic traditions and "owning allegiance" to none. The structure externally imposed becomes in this novel the opportunity for freedom. Because reality is immune to human invention, style escapes into an indulgence that is indeed excessive. So too the people of Frenchman's Bend are delivered by their profound sense of place and community into a wild and exuberant freedom.

Between the two figures of Ike and Mink stands Houston. Free of the stylistic embellishments bestowed on the idiot and the murderer, he is tied to both of them, not only because he must suffer the triumphs of each, but because he shares their qualities: the love, the pride, and the rage when that pride is crossed with humiliation. Like Mink, as Backman points out, Houston has searched for a freedom he has never found, imprisoning himself at last to the land and woman who have been waiting for him all his life.[20] He encounters Lucy Pate as a man longing "for that fetterless immobility called freedom" (p. 209) would encounter the figure of his enslavement; as Mink Snopes, believing that "there was reserved one virgin, at least for him to marry" (p. 242), encounters the nymphomaniac forever "surrounded by the loud soundless invisible shades of the nameless and numberless men" (p. 225). Houston's frustration at the limits he has been unable to escape survives Lucy's death. Insofar as the stallion who kills her is indeed "that polygamous and bitless masculinity which he had relinquished" (p 218), then Houston too is guilty of a murderous act.

But Houston is also devoted to principles of love and fertility: "sooner or later that silver and blanched rectangle of window would fall once more . . . as it had used to fall across the two of them while they observed the old country belief that the full moon of April guaranteed the fertilising act" (p. 220). In this respect he is closer to the meaning of Ike, not Mink. The cow Ike adores is Houston's, and his giving it to Ike is his implicit recognition and sanction of the love that Ike represents.

Houston's place then in "The Long Summer" is to reveal to us the meanings of human love and human rage in a less extreme form. Ike's total attachment to the cow is the exaggerated image of Houston's commitment to love and the desire to have a child; Mink is the epitome of Houston's anger against the limitations of freedom that are the other name for love. The comic antagonist of the one, the tragic antagonist of the other, Houston yet shares in the impulses Ike and Mink represent. He even helps to draw the links between those extreme manifestations of human desire and the community from which they seem so remote.

The stylistic extravagance of the Ike and Mink episodes constitutes a most elaborate tour de force, which Faulkner later defined, speaking of *As I Lay Dying,* as the art that results when "technique charges in and takes command of the dream before the writer himself can get his hands on it."[21] For Faulkner tour de force is the pressure of preconceived structure; content does not create the shape it will assume but rather conforms to a shape already determined. Clearly this is what is going on in the Ike and Mink sections, and in the Eula episode to a lesser degree: arbitrary literary conventions are forced on material inappropriate to those conventions. Yet the result here is scarcely an inferior form of fiction—although Faulkner is suggesting that in his comments on *As I Lay Dying*—but a rich example of stylistic fireworks which the presence of an unquestioned structure can allow.

I V

"The Peasants" returns us to the tall tale, although underlining the light comedy of Book One with some of the violence of Books Two and Three. Horse swapping again takes center stage as the scene is set for the total capitulation of Frenchman's Bend to the new champion, Flem Snopes. The very sight of Flem's ponies is enough to goad most of the men into the joyous surrender of whatever shrewdness they may possess. No one is really fooled here; the auction is like a ceremony in which men cheerfully acknowledge their own vulnerability to the temptation of wild horses. As Eck Snopes says, " 'Me buy one of them things? . . . When I can go to the river anytime and catch me a snapping turtle or a moccasin for nothing?' " (p. 286). Yet tempted they are, and the uproarious playing out of their victimization is a concluding summary of the community ethos. If Faulkner's comment can be taken as a sound interpretation of the values of *The Hamlet*—"I hope that

man can always be tolled off that way, to buy a horse for three dollars"—
then this victimization is the evidence that Frenchman's Bend is intact,
its conventions as rich and as operative as ever.

The wild desire to own a wild horse is paralleled here by a sensitivity
to spring, for it is one of the functions of "The Peasants" to bring together the two mythoi of the hamlet and nature, the progress of whose
seasons is also a structural principle in the novel. The horses and spring
are clearly linked: "the tremulous April night murmurous with the
moving of sap and the wet bursting of burgeoning leaf and bud and
constant with the thin and urgent cries and the brief and fading bursts
of galloping hooves" (p. 310). In the midst of their bargaining and the
pursuit of the animals, the men remain aware of the land's changes.

A bird, a shadow, fleet and dark and swift, curved across the moon-
light, upward into the pear tree and began to sing; a mockingbird.
"First one I've noticed this year," Freeman said.
"You can hear them along Whiteleaf every night," the first man
said. "I heard one in February. In that snow. Singing in a gum."
"Gum is the first tree to put out," the third said. "That was why.
It made it feel like singing, fixing to put out that way. That was why
it taken a gum." (P. 282)[22]

While there is embarrassment over still another victimization by
Flem, and pity for the anguish of Henry Armstid, Will Varner's comments on the whole episode are a recognition that in this further instance of foolishness there is embedded the health and vitality of the
community: " 'They'll get the money back in exercise and relaxation.
You take a man that aint got no other relaxation all year long except
dodging mule-dung up and down a field furrow. And a night like this
one, when a man aint old enough yet to lay still and sleep, and yet he
aint young enough anymore to be tomcatting in and out of other folks'
back windows, something like this is good for him. It'll make him
sleep tomorrow night anyhow, provided he gets back home by then' "
(p. 313).

Opposed to the men and their behavior are the women, whose leading
representative is Mrs. Littlejohn. The sale of the horses is broadly juxtaposed to the domestic chores of Mrs. Littlejohn, who carries wood,
washes and cooks, all the time heaping scorn on male foolishness: " 'I'll
declare,' she said. 'You men' " (p. 310). Excepting Eula, the women in
this novel—Lucy Pate, Mrs. Armstid, even Mink's wife, who cannot
comprehend his total impracticality—are the enemies of freedom and

of that "puerile folly" which seems in Faulkner to be indigenous only to men. Even the horses recognize the distinction: "'He went through that house quick,' Ratliff said. 'He must have found another woman at home'" (p. 310). Unlike other communities in Faulkner, however, Frenchman's Bend remains essentially male in its codes and values, and it is these codes that are being fulfilled in "The Peasants."

In the concluding episode of the novel, V. K. Ratliff, too wary for wild horses, succumbs to the most irrational hope of all, that he will be the one who discovers the long-buried treasure of the Old Frenchman. This last triumph of Flem's completes the community by making Ratliff one of its members: he becomes the largest on the list of the taken. Yet this addition of Ratliff is not only a further demoralization, but a reaffirmation of Frenchman's Bend. The hamlet is intact, its members drawn together not so much despite as because of Flem Snopes.

At the end the people of Frenchman's Bend stand quietly in front of the Old Frenchman's place, watching the crazed Henry Armstid still digging for treasure. Somewhere else this might be construed as a kind of heartless curiosity, but in the hamlet it is the simple recognition that something terrible, something worthy of consideration, even respect, has happened. They are not there to mock but to bear witness, for Henry Armstid is a part of their community: "Armstid continued to run until he stumbled and fell headlong and lay there for a time, while beyond the fence the people watched him in a silence so complete that they could hear the dry whisper of his panting breath" (p. 373).

Flem passes by on the way to Jefferson, his time in Frenchman's Bend now over. The hamlet is still somewhat in shock at his whirlwind progress from sharecropper to economic champion, a development that will surely be the basis of subsequent anecdotes, with Flem replacing Pat Stamper in their tales of trade. The people are not so much defeated, however, as deeply awed by what they have seen.

> "That's a fact. Wouldn't no other man have done it."
> "Couldn't no other man have done it. Anybody might have fooled Henry Armstid. But couldn't nobody but Flem Snopes have fooled Ratliff." (P. 372)

Frenchman's Bend remains the embodiment of a structure of conventions and codes that, in the course of the novel, it has fulfilled perfectly. Its characters have gradually conformed to the mythos implicit from the beginning, and in doing so they have confirmed and deepened it, as is always the case in a mythos-controlled fiction.

For Faulkner it is a unique achievement: the merger of a provided structural principle with a creative energy that neither dislocates nor creates it. Rather energy *serves* that structure, and without sacrifice in vitality. It is the only absolutely first-rate novel he wrote in which he describes a genuine meeting of the community and the individual.

6 | *The Last Novels*

The last twenty years of Faulkner's creative life, from the writing of
Go Down, Moses to *The Reivers,* are ones of uneven yet unquestionable
decline. This decline begins, I think, with a book that contains one of
Faulkner's most highly esteemed stories, "The Bear," and continues
through *Intruder in the Dust, Requiem for a Nun, A Fable, The Town,
The Mansion,* and *The Reivers*—lifted only by occasional flashes of
power—as in "Pantaloon in Black" and the Mink section of *The Mansion*—or humor as in "Was" and parts of *The Reivers*. The comparatively minor quality of these works has a great deal to do with Faulkner's increasing dependence on the mythic mode he used with such
originality and success in *The Hamlet*. What is so different from *The
Hamlet* is the tedium of much of this late writing. The exuberance
and vitality of Faulkner's first "community" novel all but disappear,
a most costly sacrifice to a coherent framework.

Like *The Hamlet,* there is in each of these books a structure independent of human invention, a structure beyond consciousness, possessing an unchallenged priority. The determining contexts of the later
novels, however, are far more formidable and less flexible than the
rural ethic of Frenchman's Bend. Hovering over the minds and actions
of characters like Ike McCaslin, the Corporal, Chick Mallison, and
Nancy Mannigoe are the laws of the wilderness, the hunter and the
hunted; or the pattern of human sin and the Christ who completes and
redeems it; or the saga of Yoknapatawpha County, its history, its traditions, and the numerous characters whose interrelations and genealo-
gies Faulkner tries to keep up with, as if he were less the "sole

proprietor" than the badly overworked clerk of his "postage stamp of native soil."

Along with these more inflated contexts is a developed mythic consciousness in the central characters, what Thomas Mann calls a "subjective . . . mythical point of view," in which the ego becomes aware "of its recurrence and its typicality," aware that "it [is]a fresh incarnation of the traditional upon earth."[1] That is to say, characters have a knowledge of the patterns that anticipate their own lives, and they see those lives in terms of service to that pattern. This is not the primitive mythic consciousness Ernst Cassirer describes, in which the mind senses the divine in the inanimate, the solidity of self and nonself, but a sophisticated sense of repetition: the conviction that one is duplicating a role in an earlier narrative. The chaos of what Mann calls "the unique and the present," in which one is "confused, helpless, unstable," is replaced by the awareness of a controlling pattern. Right action is the consciousness and enactment of prior things.

A good example of this kind of vision is Ike McCaslin in "The Bear." Ike believes in the existence of a total plan, created by God, suspended above actual human experience yet destined at some point in time to close with it. This plan consists of man's necessary exploitation of man and nature, the penance for that crime in war and suffering, and the eventual redemption through relinquishment: the return of the land and its people to their freedom. Ike identifies himself as one chosen by God to perform the Christ-like act of expiation for sin. As a result he models his life, not without a sense of the disparity, after Christ's: "because if the Nazarene had found carpentering good for the life and ends He had assumed and elected to serve, it would be all right too for Isaac McCaslin."[2] The passivity of Ike's choice is evident; as Eric Jensen has observed, Ike is convinced "not that he has chosen Christ but that Christ has chosen him."[3]

Ike's role, as he sees it, is to become the link between the two worlds of the potential and the actual, the ideal and the real. These worlds are manifest in the big woods where the annual hunt and the pursuit of Old Ben take place, and in the community, "the tamed land" (p. 254) where ordinary life must be lived. The actions within the woods become a metaphor, an aesthetic repetition of the events occurring outside the woods and a means of understanding those events. The hunting down and killing of animals repeats the actions of the world of time, but it also reaches out to the world of timelessness, to the completed pattern of redemption, through the discipline and knowledge that cleanse the hunter at the very moment he commits his crime. In the ritualized hunt, killing is metamorphosed into ceremony. In the same way, human history—when seen correctly, through metaphor—is not the endless folly it appears to be, but is also a comprehensible sequence that concludes with redemption. History is the working out of God's plan: a ritual as determined and exact as the hunt. The discovery of the New World, the hope of recovered Eden, the rape of the earth and the coming of slavery, the catastrophic war: " 'He permitted it, not impotent and not condoning and not blind because He ordered and watched it' " (p. 258).[4]

In the woods the acquisition of Lion and the subsequent killing of Old Ben signify the end of the wilderness, yet, mythically viewed, it is also a necessary step in the ascent of Old Ben and Lion and Sam Fathers and Boon and Ike to their fullest meanings: "It was like the last act on a set stage. It was the beginning of the end of something, he didn't know what except that he would not grieve. He would be humble and proud that he had been found worthy to be a part of it too or even just to see it too" (p. 226).

Trained by his wilderness experience, Ike can see the world of time as the reflection of timelessness; he can see that the Civil War is really the incarnation of God's love for the South: " '*Apparently they can learn nothing save through suffering, remember nothing save when underlined in blood*' " (p. 286). Through this kind of mythic sense linking the woods to the community, Ike translates the tragedies of his life and his region into phases of a unified pattern of sin and atonement.

Lucas Beauchamp, in "The Fire and the Hearth," from *Go Down, Moses,* also thinks mythically, although he lacks Ike's ability to see himself in the full sweep of Southern and American history. Lucas's own ancestry is all the context he needs, finding in it the meaning of his life and a guide to his behavior. That he is the oldest McCaslin on the Edmonds plantation is a fact Lucas never forgets, "almost as old as Isaac, almost, as old Isaac was, coeval with old Buck and Buddy McCaslin who had been alive when their father, Carothers McCaslin, got the land from the Indians back in the old time when men black and white were men" (pp. 36–37).

McCaslin blood, particularly that of the founder, Old Carothers, is running in Lucas's veins, guiding, justifying, occasionally thwarting his actions. When the Indian mound in which he is digging collapses on Lucas, throwing into his face an earthenware fragment, it was "a blow not vicious so much as merely heavy-handed, a sort of final admonitory pat from the spirit of darkness and solitude, the old earth, perhaps the old ancestors themselves" (p. 38).

The chief example of Lucas's attention to such forces is the scene with

Zack Edmonds when Lucas asserts his manhood in the face of Zack's having kept Lucas's wife Molly with him for six months. Throughout, Lucas is thinking not so much of Zack as he is of Old Carothers, of " 'what Carothers McCaslin would have wanted me to do' " (p. 53). In retrospect, he sees the dead man as instrumental, who caused the pistol to misfire: *"Old Carothers,* he thought. *I needed him and he come and spoke for me"* (p. 58).

At the end of "The Fire and the Hearth," when Lucas finally gives up his quest for buried money, he understands his act as simply a further submission to given laws: one from the Bible, the other from that destiny, already existent somewhere, which belongs to Lucas Beauchamp: " 'Man has got three score and ten years on this earth, the Book says. . . . But I am near to the end of my three score and ten, and I reckon to find that money aint for me' " (p. 131).

The center of *Go Down, Moses* is, of course, "The Bear," and its action is a model for much of what goes on in the other stories.[5] In four of the five parts of "The Bear," as in "The Old People," Faulkner gives us a moving portrait of the wilderness and the hunt in terms of a participation in ancient patterns. The descriptions of Ike's experiences in the woods conform completely to the idea of a mythic fiction, for all is lived as if it were the fulfillment of a prophecy: "He had experienced it all before, and not merely in dreams. He saw the camp . . . and he knew already how it was going to look. . . . even his motions were familiar to him, foreknown" (pp. 195–96). The bear is a presence to Ike long before he sees it, visible to him as if in the origins of time, their fate already marked out: "It seemed to him that he could see them, the two of them, shadowy in the limbo from which time emerged and became time" (p. 204).[6]

What Sam Fathers sees in the tracks of the "wolf" who will prove to be Lion, the dog to hold Old Ben, is the fulfilled pattern, the end of Old Ben, of the hunt, of Sam himself. Sam's ability to comprehend in its midst life's totality, and to participate in that pattern by training the animal who will bring an end to all he loves and has lived for, by *serving* that which is necessary, is as much a model to young Ike as is his dedication to the wilderness.

What prevents the whole story from being no more than a presentation of ritual, of service without conflict or contradiction, is part 4, in which Ike attempts to transfer the life and lessons of the wilderness to "the community." At this point Ike is trying to find in the rules of the hunt the clue to his responsibilities as farmer, husband, and citizen. He decides, on the basis of his wilderness education, to give up the property he has inherited.

There has been considerable debate among readers about the merits of Ike's decision, whether in the context of the story and *Go Down, Moses* it is a good decision. Moral evaluation of Ike, however, does not seem to me quite relevant, even as moral questions in the later novels in general do not seem as relevant as many have thought. Ike believes himself to be "chosen" for this role: "if he could have helped himself, not being the Nazarene, he would not have chosen it" (p. 310). Cass Edmonds, his apparent antagonist but actually his complement, also sees himself as without choice: "I would deny even if I knew it were true. I would have to. Even you can see that I could do no else. I am what I am; I will be always what I was born and have always been" (pp. 299–300).

"The Bear" and, to some extent, *Go Down, Moses* are *about* the debate between Ike and Cass, and the reader's task is not to arbitrate it but to understand its meaning as a whole, to learn to see as Ike sees: mythically, that is to say, "doubly." Cass and Ike, possession and relinquishment, town and woods, are each necessary steps of a single process. They are reflections of each other, a single melody in minor and major keys. The apparent conflict between Ike and Cass is a version of the conflict within Ike himself, between wilderness rituals and the problems of actual human living. For Ike there can be no question of choosing between what his vision persuades him are the inseparable modes of time and eternity. He wishes to serve them simultaneously in a life in the available community. This choice creates great hardship for Ike and his wife, and misunderstanding among his friends and relatives, for Ike's mythic vision is one the others do not share. The hunt is a well-plotted novel, in which each act clearly serves the whole, whereas outside the woods life seems fragmentary and fallen, necessarily unredeemed. Ike's appointed task is to see the two as one, life as art, fact as metaphor, aimless time as completed, intelligible history.

The problem of "The Bear" can also be expressed as the problem of evil: How can one reconcile the realities of human sin and suffering with a faith in God and in the existence of a plan which He is working out through history? Within the staged ritual of the hunt the problem is resolved: murder is performed, then atoned for in the total pattern of *"honor and pride and pity and justice and courage and love"* (p. 297). The buck is killed, yet (in "The Old People") it "still and forever leaped, the shaking gunbarrels coming constantly and forever steady at last, crashing, and still out of his instant of immortality the buck sprang, forever immortal" (p. 178). There are moments of relinquishment in the woods, followed by moments of grace. Ike abandons his gun, watch, and compass; "all the ancient rules and balances of hunter and hunted [are] abrogated" (p. 207)—and he is rewarded with his first look at Old Ben.

In the community, in the stream of time, Ike tries to duplicate the rituals of the woods: through relinquishment to redefine sin into a necessary stage of a larger pattern. But now his actions are weighed according to different criteria. In the woods *not* shooting the bear can be sublime. In the community Ike's putting aside his patrimony has symbolic value, but at the pragmatic level it is pointless. To some extent Ike knows this: he has no illusions about the speed of redemption: " 'It will be long. I have never said otherwise' " (p. 299). Moreover, the act is complicated with the evil it is intended to erase. Ike's slight hesitation when praising the black race to Cass indicates that "even in escaping he was taking with him more of that evil and unregenerate old man [Carothers McCaslin] . . . than even he had feared" (p. 294).

That there is a distance here between symbolic and pragmatic value is the condition of "the tamed land." Ike is not to be judged harshly for this, certainly not by us. Faulkner is describing an act that has mythic meaning, larger than its literal meaning, and significant in this story and *Go Down, Moses* as a whole as the image of a redemption that is immanent. Ike's act of repudiation is both the futile gesture that only consigns Ike to childlessness, and the act that symbolically completes God's pattern.

Ike's giving up of his land lives partially at the level of potential: a visible image that, although deprived of pragmatic power, represents the possible meeting of the real and the ideal. Repudiation becomes for Ike time's version of timelessness: a dream that he envisions as a destiny, drawing fact toward truth.

The point of "The Bear," then, is the complex relationship between human life and certain fixed patterns and the need to recognize them as much as possible. The story is a religious one in that it suggests a faith that those patterns effectively preside over our lives whether their presence is evident or not. The story makes clear the difficulty of translating faith into action, but it never challenges the accuracy of the particular historical pattern Ike sets up or the idea of a single truth which is the theoretical basis of what he does. Ike says, " 'And I know what you will say now: That if truth is one thing to me and another thing to you, how will we choose which is truth? You dont need to choose. The heart already knows. . . . Because the men who wrote his Book for Him were writing about truth and there is only one truth and it covers all things that touch the heart'" (p. 260).

This is a faith that is largely missing from the world of Faulkner's earlier novels, in which truth may well "touch the heart," but is not one, and is hardly unchanging. Among the old ledgers which hold the history of the McCaslin plantation, Ike is able to discern the truth of his grandfather's incestuous relations with his slave-daughter Tomasina, and to determine as well the clear path of his own atonement for the crime of which this act is the most horrifying image. In *Absalom, Absalom!*, by way of contrast, Quentin and Shreve can discover, "out of the rag-tag and bob-ends of old tales and talking," only a dark history that can never be judged as unquestionable fact, and the deep moral complexity of themselves and their strange complicity with the shadows they have created.

As for Ike McCaslin's faith in the oneness of truth, it is not even challenged by Cass Edmonds, who deplores Ike's act of relinquishment: *" 'Truth is one. It doesn't change. It covers all things which touch the heart' "* (p. 297).

This faith is the subject of the last two stories of *Go Down, Moses* ("Delta Autumn" and the title story). In the first of these, Ike still endures the consequences of the imperfect manner in which his repudiation echoes the truths of the wilderness. The sons and grandsons of the men Ike once hunted with can comprehend even less than their fathers the meaning of his life. But his mythic sense of an operative pattern is as secure as ever, and so, therefore, is his faith: the United States " 'will cope with one Austrian paper-hanger, no matter what he will be calling himself' " (p. 339); and " 'There are good men everywhere, at all times. Most men are' " (p. 345); and " 'I still believe. I see proof everywhere' " (p. 347). Despite the appearances of chaos, God is the creator of the world: " '[He] created man and . . . the world for him to live in and I reckon He created the kind of world He would have wanted to live in if He had been a man. . . . And maybe He didn't put the desire to hunt and kill game in man but I reckon He knew it was going to be there' " (p. 348). As for the repudiation which, at fourteen, he dreamed would end all wrong, he knew at twenty-one when he performed it that it would not, except "in principle" (p. 351). Yet, throughout this first part of the story, Ike McCaslin speaks "in that peaceful and still untroubled voice" (p. 347).

For Ike's faith to be meaningful, however, and for the pattern he has believed in to be substantiated again, the old crimes must be repeated. Wood is cut and the fires stoked by Negroes, who do not hunt; and at the end, the granddaughter of "Tenny's Jim" reveals to Ike that incest, miscegenation, and exploitation have been perpetrated again by the white McCaslin line. Ike must again confront his own complicity in evil, which he recognized in "The Bear," and sees coming now: "he knew that his voice was running away with him and he had neither intended it nor could stop it: 'That's right. Go back North. Marry: a man in your own race. . . . Marry a black man . . .' until he could stop it at last and did" (p. 363). Again he makes a symbolic gesture, as he had when he gave up his land for "principle," this time offering the old hunting horn he received from General Compson. And again it is misunderstood, as it must be, this token in time, even as his words, the heritage of "that evil and unregenerate old man," invoke from the girl a bitter response: " 'Old Man,' she said, 'have you lived so long and forgotten so much that you dont remember anything you ever knew or felt or even heard about love?' " (p. 363).

The anger is appropriate, but the contemptuous question is not, for Ike remembers love very well. He has spoken of it the evening before to the young men: " 'I think that every man and woman, at the instant when it dont even matter whether they marry or not, I think that whether they marry then or afterward or dont never, at that instant the two of them together were God' " (p. 348). But he must receive the insult and the misunderstanding because the pattern and his own presence in it are embedded in history and in human nature. This is his faith as well as his sorrow: the order will complete itself as it has been willed. Beyond this realization, as the story amply demonstrates, lies Ike's faith in the direction toward which everything moves, and it is that also to which he submits himself.

The same fundamental acceptance of the evil that God permits, and the faith in the redemption that can emerge *only* as a consequence to evil, are at the core of the brief story that concludes the book. The Negro murderer's body is sent home from Chicago to Jefferson. For his grandmother his death is the result of white exploitation: " 'Roth Edmonds sold my Benjamin. Sold him in Egypt' " (p. 371). Molly Worsham's view, like Ike's, is a mythic view, although stronger because rooted more substantially in that Bible whose stories provide a constant shape and meaning to her own life: " 'Sold him to Pharaoh and now he dead' " (p. 380).

Gradually Gavin Stevens and the newspaper editor come to understand the kind of vision Molly has: her sense of life as that which is destined to be, of an order prior to herself to which she belongs: " 'Is you gonter put hit in de paper? I wants hit all in de paper. All of hit' " (p. 383).

Stevens thinks, in the last paragraph of the story: *"Since it had to be and she couldn't stop it, and now that it's all over and done and finished, she doesn't care how he died. She just wanted him home, but she wanted him to come home right"* (p. 383). The meaning of *Go Down, Moses* is that "it had to be." Awareness of that meaning is seen by Faulkner as the beginning of faith and perhaps the end of guilt.

Two stories in this collection I have not mentioned: "Was" and "Pantaloon in Black," possibly the two best pieces in the book and, significantly enough, the two that depart most seriously from the book's prevailing tone and its mythic dimensions. "Was" has its own mythos, but it is primarily a "Sir Walter Scott gentility affected by some members of the planter caste" that the story ridicules.[7] In "Was," myth is something to be played with, as the characters at once adhere to it and manage to shake themselves loose from its most severe requirements. Uncle Buck dutifully puts on his necktie when he must approach the domain of Miss Sophonsiba Beauchamp, yet he is perfectly willing to be rescued from his commitment to her by Uncle Buddy's card prowess (which does not even pretend to gentility).

Given structure exists in the story, for example, in the pattern of black-white relations that even the participants recognize as archaic. But it is deprived of most of its weight through comic presentation. The characters submit, to some extent, yet they clearly retain the right to modify when necessary. The result is a fine comic story rather than the kind of religious, at times sententious, writing we find elsewhere in the book.

"Pantaloon in Black" is a powerful story of the impotence of various patterns to save Rider from an overwhelming grief over his dead wife. Rider has lived with Mannie a life of rich and satisfying order: their home (its fire on the hearth), his work schedule, the Saturday bath and shopping, the ample weekend meal. When she dies, he is suddenly thrown violently on himself, stripped of everything that has sustained him, and nothing he inserts in its place, not physical labor, religion, whiskey, gambling, or fighting, can help him.

Rider can submit to nothing but his grief, and thus becomes the man too large, too hopelessly *man* to absorb himself in the available structures. For a moment Faulkner has returned, at least partially, to a world centered in the existential problem of creation rather than in the various patterns or laws in which one can discern one's identity and obligations. Rider can neither discover nor create what he requires. His own body is "the insuperable barrier" (p. 141) between himself and Mannie. He submits to the white lynch mob that alone can end his sorrow. In comparison with Rider, the fundamental values and beliefs of Ike Mc-Caslin, of Lucas Beauchamp, of Molly in "Go Down, Moses," are part of an entirely different fictional world.

II

A Fable is the novel Faulkner plotted on the walls of his office, as if to work literally "inside" it. In this book the mythos form grows from regional and national history to cosmic pattern. Both the Corporal and the Old General of *A Fable* are fully aware of the drama they are re-enacting. The Corporal, more role than man, is surprised at nothing. His life is the ritual repetition of the son who must endure his sacrifice by the father in order to provide an image of man's potential honor and love. In his first appearance in the novel, carried with his twelve compatriots in a lorry through crowds howling for his blood, the Corporal knows the outcome in advance.

> looking down at the fleeing sea of eyes and gaped mouths and fists with the same watchfulness as the other twelve, but with neither the bafflement nor the concern—a face merely interested, attentive, and calm, with something else in it which none of the others had: a comprehension, understanding, utterly free of compassion, as if he had already anticipated without censure or pity the uproar which rose and paced and followed the lorry as it sped on.[8]

The Corporal's understanding is equalled, perhaps surpassed, by the Old General's, who presides over the whole as an embodiment of all experience, for he has committed every act in the allegory of human possibility which is the novel. He is both the father who sacrifices his son and the Father who accepts the sacrifice; he has given up a man in order to prevent a war, and he has given up himself in order to save France, perhaps the world; at one time he has even repudiated that whole structure of civilization of which he is now the chief defender.

Between them, the Corporal and Old General possess a perfect awareness of the ancient ceremony of human folly and glory which they perform. Reactions to this inevitable pattern vary in the novel: perfect acceptance, the inability to accept, attempts to modify. But this mythos of the quest, of betrayal, of the sacrifice of others and the self, of the complicity in evil, of death, of rebirth and the beginning again of quest—this is the essential pattern of *A Fable*. It is presented and known by the Corporal and Old General as an unfailing, unalterable history.

All the characters live the same pattern: each sacrifices and is sacrificed; each corrupts his quest with what seems to be evil, yet each also demonstrates a principled selflessness that, however flawed by stupidity, immaturity, pride, or even self-interest, becomes a link to the self-sacrifice of Christ. General Gragnon, the Runner, Sutterfield, Levine, Marthe—they are all exploited and they exploit others. They are the pawns of plans that transcend their own small lives, and they create abstract patterns in which others are pawns. They must all endure a voluntary going under, sometimes in the form of suicide. In the largest sense, they are all the Father, sacrificing someone or something—a regiment, a son, a husband—in the interests of a foreseen destiny, and they are all the Son, who goes willingly to the cross in order to redeem the evil that requires his life.

The key scene (only because it repeats in the clearest terms what is performed everywhere else in the novel) is the one between the Corporal and the Old General on the mountain. The Old General is in the position of trying to tempt his son into giving up the sacrifice which he himself knows is built into the logic of the total pattern, the act whose eternal possibility provides direction and shape to the whole. Yet the temptation is necessary to the significance of the gesture; in fact the whole iron sequence of exploitation and inhumanity are necessary to it. As the Old General says to the Quartermaster General: " 'By destroying his life tomorrow morning, I will establish forever that he didn't even live in vain, let alone die so' " (p. 332).[9]

R. P. Adams has commented perceptively on this scene between the Old General and his son.

> The two seem usually to be engaged not so much in conflict as in an indirect kind of cooperation, and they both seem to know it. Throughout the temptation scene the Old General acts as if he were offering his inducements more as tests than as persuasions, in the expectation and even the hope they will be rejected. When they are rejected, he acts as if he were more pleased than disappointed, as if the result were what he had set out to prove, rather than a defeat for his side of an argument.[10]

The man of fact, of " 'this mundane earth' " (p. 348), and the
man of hope, committed to " 'unfact,' " combine to complete what is
necessary. The Corporal, in all his hope, can admit that " 'man and his
folly' " will endure, that the sacrifice of man, which his own death is
designed to redeem, will continue endlessly. *Because* of that admission
the Old General can dare believe that man " 'will prevail' " (p. 354),
that the erected crosses will always have their victims, that hope is secure because it is implicit in the very futility of hope.

III

Intruder in the Dust is a good example of Faulkner's use of mythos at
the level of a social fiction. At first glance the novel seems to present a
typically Faulknerian situation of the defiance of the existing standards
of a community by several people somewhere on its periphery: Lucas,
the independent black man, Chick Mallison and Aleck Sander, youths
white and black, highly dubious about social efficiency, and Miss Haber-
sham, the old white spinster who aids the boys in digging up a freshly
buried corpse.

As things turn out the novel is not about defiance but about the acceptance and revitalization of a community. Chick is the central consciousness who gradually discovers that his purposes, if not his methods,
are consistent with that social ethic which, whatever his impatience
with it, has in fact shaped him into what he believes and what he has
become. Chick eventually realizes that he is being driven not by hatred
but by love, not by rejection of his community but by a hope for it so
strong that it becomes a standard of excellence almost too difficult for
community to bear:

> that fierce desire that they should be perfect because they were his and
> he was theirs, that furious intolerance of any one single jot or tittle
> less than absolute perfection—that furious almost instinctive leap and
> spring to defend them from anyone anywhere so that he might excori-
> ate them himself without mercy since they were his own and he
> wanted no more save to stand with them unalterable and impreg-
> nable: one shame if shame must be, one expiation since expiation must
> surely be but above all one unalterable durable impregnable one: one
> people one heart one land.[11]

Intruder in the Dust is a novel dominated by traditions which, like any
mythos principle, provide a predictability to life. Virtually every event

and example of behavior in the book is in some respect a characteristic one, anticipated, prophesied, by the existence of certain customs, certain expectations established through long usage.

Lucas Beauchamp's assertion of his superiority to most men, white or black, is more or less the spring-board of the main action, and is related in his own mind to that side of his blood that goes back to the founder of the present Edmonds plantation. Once, when verbally accosted by a white man—"'You goddamn biggity stiff-necked stinking burrheaded Edmonds sonofabitch,'"—Lucas replies, "'I aint a Edmonds. I dont belong to these new folks. I belongs to the old lot. I'm a McCaslin'" (p. 19).

The Gowries and all they do in the novel are also part of an established tradition, one which, like Lucas's pride, everyone in Jefferson recognizes and can usually anticipate:

> a race a species which before now had made their hill stronghold good against the county and the federal government too, which did not even simply inhabit nor had merely corrupted but had translated and transmogrified that whole region of lonely pine hills dotted meagrely with small tilted farms and peripatetic sawmills and contraband whiskey-kettles where peace officers from town didn't even go unless they were sent for and strange white men didn't wander far from the highway after dark and no Negro at any time—where as a local wit said once the only stranger ever to enter with impunity was God and He only by daylight and on Sunday—into a synonym for independence and violence: an idea with physical boundaries like a quarantine for plague so that solitary unique and alone out of all the county it was known to the rest of the county by the number of its survey co-ordinate—Beat Four. (Pp. 35–36)

There are the traditions of racial inequality, which Faulkner does not hesitate to point out—"Aleck Sander and Edmonds' boy with tapsticks and he with the gun" (p. 5); or, "They left Aleck Sander with his breakfast at the kitchen table and carried theirs into the dining-room" (p. 114). There is the tradition of the shiftless young men "who did nothing at all that anyone knew . . . the men who his uncle said were in every little Southern town, who never really led mobs nor even instigated them but were always the nucleus of them because of their mass availability" (p. 43). And there is the fundamental belief in the necessity of law expressed by the jailer, Mr. Tubbs, even after he has muttered that Lucas isn't worth defending against a lynch mob: "'Don't mind me. I'm going to do the best I can; I taken an oath of office too'" (p. 54). Over and above all this there is the largest tradition of all, "the land's living symbol—a formal group of ritual almost mystic significance identical and monotonous as milestones tying the county-seat to the county's ultimate rim as milestones would: the beast the plow and the man" (p. 147).

Chick believes, for much of the novel, that he is violating society, yet he invariably understands what is happening in terms of its traditions, and his progress in the book is to become fully conscious of, and to defend, their fundamental basis. Ultimately, a tradition exists even for the violation of custom which the two boys and the old woman have perpetrated: "'In fact, you mought bear this in yo mind; someday you mought need it. If you ever needs to get anything done outside the common run, dont waste yo time on the menfolks; get the womens and children to working at it'" (pp. 71–72).

The traditions of Yoknapatawpha County, including those that Chick and Gavin Stevens agree must eventually be eliminated, are those that make up what Gavin calls the "'homogeneity'" (p. 153) of the South, the only thing from which "'comes anything of a people or for a people of durable and lasting value'" (p. 154). These traditions are the essential ingredient in the shaping of Chick Mallison. They are responsible for his initial insult to Lucas, his attempted payment for a meal he would certainly have accepted as normal hospitality from a white man, but they are also responsible for his efforts to save Lucas's life:

> and now he seemed to see his whole native land, his home—the dirt, the earth which had bred his bones and those of his fathers for six generations and was still shaping him into not just a man but a specific man . . . even among a kind and race specific and unique . . . since it had also integrated into him whatever it was that had compelled him to stop and listen to a damned highnosed impudent Negro who even if he wasn't a murderer had been about to get if not about what he deserved at least exactly what he had spent the sixty-odd years of his life asking for—. (P. 151)

The evil of intolerance, like human sin in "The Bear," is both real and illusory; it is an expression of human violation yet it ends in justice and in a larger understanding of the total structure.

The pressure of these traditions, which breed, cajole, and use even his rebellion to force the boy into his present form, is a social version of Ike McCaslin's woods, compelling the hunters and beasts "according to the ancient and immitigable rules" (p. 192), providing men with a complete narrative in which to move. The context of *Intruder in the*

Dust is less idealistic and mysterious; it is not a symbolic story, but an attempt to describe realistically the living context of an actual society. The chief purpose of the novel is to demonstrate that the end product of all those traditions is the emerging Chick Mallison, the effective and just young man.

IV

Faulkner's efforts in creating a mythos fiction constitute a major effort on his part; his last seven novels belong more or less to this mode, and one of them *(A Fable)* took ten years to complete. In several late interviews and speeches he spoke of the "old verities," "the old universal truths," and their existence to him seems comparable to those laws of wilderness, history, and society that he was trying to give fictional life to in the novels of this period. According to his Nobel Prize speech, the writer himself, if he works without adequate sense of such truths, "labors under a curse," as if only by possessing the sense of what exists *before* and *after* can a writer be significant.

Despite some twenty years of creative effort, however, the fact remains that almost all of these last novels have seemed to most critics to be minor in importance. I think this is true of *Go Down, Moses* as well, although it is superior to the others, and although "The Bear" has been generally held in high esteem.

The reason for this comparative lack of success is, I believe, the fundamental inappropriateness of Faulkner's special fictional talents for the mythos form. Or, to put it another way, there is a gap between the "beliefs" of this period, a hope of order in heaven and on earth, and the fictional vision, the special way of seeing experience, which was naturally his. As a result there is a definite reduction in that vitality and energy, both in prose style and characterization, which are the hallmark of his best work. Part of the difficulty for Faulkner is an inability to combine in his characters a mythic consciousness with a necessary creativity, with an independence that might make a character into a recognizable human being as well as the agent of a myth. The ritual of the feast becomes in the last books exactly that, the result being a string of characters who are little more than servants to their assumed roles.

In an early review of *A Fable,* V. S. Pritchett makes an important observation on this essential problem of characterization: "In the novels of his generation, like *Ulysses* or *Finnegan's Wake,* which have influenced Faulkner (novels which had worked back through the chaos of the mind's associations toward archetypal myth), the human representative figures, like Mr. and Mrs. Bloom, for example, have been more powerful than their myth. Mr. Faulkner's are weaker.[12]

The Corporal in *A Fable* belongs so completely to the role he sees as his own that he has no identity apart from it. He is not a *man,* conscious of some paradigm out of the past which he decides is his own destiny, but the incarnate shape of destiny itself. The crucial events of Jesus' life are only mechanical incrustations on a figure of whom we know almost nothing. This is not a re-telling of the tale, a repetition or celebration in Mann's sense, but the tale twice-told. As a result, all the energy of the Corporal's having to enter consciously an awaiting history, to fit it to his own life, is diminished until he is nothing but the shape of his progenitor. The potential drama of Mann's "life in the myth" is dissipated by a total submission of life *to* myth. As Andrew Lytle has written, the Corporal "is no Son of Man. He is begot of the sound of the author's voice upon an idea."[13]

The Old General is a more interesting figure, but that is only because he is a mixture of so many roles: God, Christ, Satan, the creator of the pattern as well as a principal actor in it. Precisely because he is supposed to have experienced all the available roles, he can be passive to events; he recognizes that all that occurs is what *has* occurred and *must* occur. He does not put his son to death, but rather accepts that life which completes the necessary pattern. Part of his passivity may be explained by his cynicism: "who no longer believed in anything but his disillusion and his intelligence and his limitless power" (p. 13), but his acquiescence to events is no greater than that of the Corporal, who also knows the necessary end of all action, and must have known it even on that day when he persuaded a regiment to mutiny in the interests of a peace which he also knew would not be forthcoming.

Elsewhere in *A Fable* there is an apparent creativeness, inasmuch as each of the other characters invents a rationale for his life in the form of a particular narrative that always has at its center a sacrificial victim. For Gragnon, with narrower vision than most, the purpose of the mutiny has been "to bring him to attention here before the table on which lay in its furled scabbard the corpse of his career" (p. 233); for Marthe, the Corporal's sister, the Old General's seduction and abandonment of her mother is necessary in order " 'to create a son . . . to condemn to death as though to save the earth, save the world, save man's history, save mankind' " (p. 287).

But it is clear that encompassing these variations is the single pattern to which the Corporal and Old General submit themselves; and their submission is so complete that it transforms this pattern into a rigid and unchallengeable structure. The result is an enormous stasis, as if the book were halted in the very tracks of its conception. All known, all foretold, each event merely part of the endless chain of sacrifice and martyrdom, the novel searches frantically for a place to go. The prose struggles to break loose, to combat its constricting narrative with incessant qualification and hair-splitting modification: "to notice, see, remark" (p. 17), "to precede, guide, conduct" (p. 149), "the old habit or mantle or aura or affinity" (p. 21). The simplest notions are elaborated as if they were heroic deeds, as if words alone could deepen the iron simplicity of the pattern.

[In which General Gragnon leaves the Old General's room, accompanied by the chief-of-staff and the Old General's aide]: The chief-of-staff saluted. But the division commander [Gragnon] did not wait for him, already about-facing, leaving the chief-of-staff once more the split of a second late since he had to perform his own maneuver which even a crack drill-sergeant could not have done smoothly with no more warning than this, having in fact to take two long extra steps to get himself again on the division commander's right hand and failing—or almost—here too, so that it was the old marshal's personal aide who flanked the division commander, the chief-of-staff himself still half a pace behind, as they trod the white rug once more back to the now open door just outside which a provost marshal's officer correct with sidearms waited, though before they reached him, the division commander was even in front of the aide. . . . So the aide was flanking, not the division commander but the chief-of-staff, pacing him correctly on the left, back to the open door beyond which the provost officer waited while the division commander passed through it. (P. 234)[14]

Qualification, of course, has always been part of Faulkner's prose ("From a little after two oclock until almost sundown of the long still hot weary dead September afternoon they sat in what Miss Coldfield still called the office because her father had called it that") but what was once a genuine creative vigor, suggesting a perpetual assault on clarity, gives way here to a mere affectation of energy. For all its forced and painful struggling, the prose is empty; the narrative is known and cannot be invented. The prose is made sterile by the fact that Faulkner has stripped it of anything it might do.

The passivity of Ike McCaslin in part 4 of "The Bear," his submission to a pattern he does not fully understand, for ends which "were and

would be always incomprehensible to him" (p. 310), also results in a
tired and highly mannered prose. The other parts of "The Bear," though
ritualized, at least ground that ritual in the concreteness of Ike's education: a fully realized portrayal of the novitiate in his mastery of the
skills of obedience. In part 4 there is only the pathos of words trying to
conjure substance from faith alone. The prose has the quality of a
learned chant, a litany from which consciousness is absent:

> 'I cant repudiate it. It was never mine to repudiate. It was never
> Father's and Uncle Buddy's to bequeath me to repudiate because it
> was never Grandfather's to bequeath them to bequeath me to repudi-
> ate because it was never old Ikkemotubbe's to sell to Grandfather for
> bequeathment and repudiation. Because it was never Ikkemotubbe's
> fathers' fathers' to bequeath Ikkemotubbe to sell to Grandfather or
> any man because on the instant when Ikkemotubbe discovered, rea-
> lised, that he could sell it for money, on that instant it ceased ever to
> have been his forever, father to father to father, and the man who
> bought it bought nothing.' (Pp. 256–57)

> 'He made the earth first and peopled it with dumb creatures, and
> then He created man to be His overseer on the earth and to hold
> suzerainty over the earth and the animals on it in His name, not to
> hold for himself and his descendants inviolable title forever, genera-
> tion after generation, to the oblongs and squares of the earth, but to
> hold the earth mutual and intact in the communal anonymity of
> brotherhood, and all the fee He asked was pity and humility and
> sufferance and endurance and the sweat of his face for bread.' (P. 257)

At times the passivity of character becomes a literal mindlessness in
those who recognize and serve the patterns best. Nancy Mannigoe, in
Requiem for a Nun, replies to the judge's sentence of death, "Yes,
Lord."[15] She is listening, not to the judge, but to her own awareness of
a cosmic order. As Lucas Beauchamp, in the midst of his struggle with
Zack Edmonds, is thinking only of his ancestor Carothers McCaslin,
Nancy, about to murder the infant child of Temple, addresses herself
only to God: "I've tried. I've tried everything I know. You can see
that" (p. 187).

Later, when Temple Drake questions the nature of her faith and its
object—"Is there a heaven, Nancy?"—she answers, "I don't know. I
believes." "Believe what?" Temple asks; "I don't know. But I believes"
(p. 281). She can offer no explanation for her belief that sin and suffering lead irrevocably to salvation; it is as if faith, the commitment to a

Christian mythos, must not be complicated even with thought. In his earlier fiction Faulkner's less intellectual characters, such as Lena Grove, are also given certain privileges of insight; but the particular patterns in which they believe (this is true of Dilsey's Christianity too) never receive the kind of authorization which the faith of Nancy receives.

The various mythoi of the last novels are no longer questionable; creativity is now the distance between ourselves and truth. It is only by submission, by an obedience apparently born of the rejection of thought, that we can understand and accept the patterns in which we move.

Opposed to all this is the Faulkner I have described in the bulk of this book: the writer obsessed with the need to create, convinced that the struggle for proper words must be the center of any fiction. Implicit to that view is a world chaotic enough to require and challenge creation. In the later novels Faulkner tries to escape that obsession and that conviction; but they are the core not only of his vision but of his talent, and the result is a considerable decline in energy and power.[16]

V

How might he have done it better? The question is important partly because it forces us to see that Faulkner's problems in writing a mythic literature are not necessarily inherent to the form. Mann's *Joseph and His Brothers*, the tetralogy in which he discovered and best illustrated the meaning of the modern mythic consciousness, brilliantly resolves the opposition of service to a prior structure and a necessary vitality of consciousness and movement. What in Ike McCaslin and the Corporal is rote action becomes in Mann's Joseph an impassioned pursuit of an inescapable destiny.

Joseph is fully aware that his life is in part a repetition of the lives of Abraham, Isaac, and Jacob. In fact it is that awareness which is partially responsible for the close similarity his actions have to theirs. Whatever his condition, momentarily cast down or elevated, Joseph strains to surmise the outlines of his ancestors; the eventual coincidences are at least partially the product of his own imagination.

This is the central difference between Mann and Faulkner in their mythos fiction. For Mann the awareness is an *active* principle, not the passive acceptance of fated events but a creating of those events out of some strange hindsight, a recollection of that which on one level has not yet occurred, but which, on another, has always occurred. Mann's knowledge of Freud is central here. In his lecture "Freud and the Future," he points to an essay of Schopenhauer as "the most profound and mysterious point of contact between Freud's natural-scientific world and Schopenhauer's philosophic one": "precisely as in a dream it is our own will that unconsciously appears as inexorable objective destiny, everything in it proceeding out of ourselves and each of us being the secret theatre-manager of our own dreams, so also in reality the great dream that a single essence, the will itself, dreams with us all, our fate, may be the product of our inmost selves, of our wills, and we are actually ourselves bringing about what seems to be happening to us."[17]

Joseph, like all the others in this novel, wills *out of his own character* the destiny that we believe has always been his. *Joseph* may be about that "higher reality" without which "nothing in the lower world would know how to happen or be thought of,"[18] but it is also about one's freedom to live fully the life that is inescapably his. The famous scene of the hoaxing of Esau illustrates Mann's superiority to Faulkner in this mode of writing. Like Jacob and Isaac, Esau knows which son is meant to receive the father's blessing. Like Cain and Ishmael before him, like Joseph's brothers after him, he vaguely anticipates the myth of the preferred younger son. But he comes to the great hour of his life, when this knowledge is to be dramatically enacted before all, not with the studied inertness of the character giving himself up to his doom, but with the determination to play his part rightly: to possess completely for the first time the necessary definition of his life.

Thus he went on, with mouth and hand, with ha, ha! and ho, ho! and bombast and braggadocio, with windy boasting of his father's preference and the great day come to the red skin; so that the folk of the household bent double and writhed with laughter and wept and held their sides. He went off with his dish, holding it high before him like the tabernacle, and throwing out his legs and prancing up to his father's tent; and they shrieked aloud, clapping and stamping their feet—and then were suddenly still. For Esau, at the door of the tent, was saying:

"Here am I, my father. Let my father arise and eat of his son's venison that thy soul may bless me. Is it his will that I come in?"

Isaac's voice came forth:

"Who is it that sayest I and will come in to the blind man?"

"Esau, thy hairy-skin," answered he, "hath hunted and cooked for the strengthening, as thou commandest."

"Thou fool and robber!" the voice said. "Why speakest thou falsehood in my sight? For Esau, my eldest, he was here long since and gave me to eat and drink, and I have blessed him."

Then Esau was so startled that he almost let everything fall and he gave such a jump that he spilled the sour cream sauce all over him. His auditors roared with laughter. They wagged their heads feebly and wiped the water out of their eyes and shook it off. But Esau rushed into the tent, without more asking, and there came a silence, while those outside covered their mouths with their hands and thrust their elbows into each other's ribs. But presently came a roar from inside, a perfectly incredible roar, and Esau burst out again, no longer red, but purple in the face, with uplifted arms. "Curse it, curse it, curse it," he shrieked, at the top of his lungs—words we might use to-day on occasion of some trifling vexation. But at that time, and from the lips of Esau the shaggy, it was a new cry, full of the original meaning, for he himself had really been cursed, instead of blessed, solemnly betrayed and made a mock of like no one before him, in the eyes of the people. "Curse it," he shrieked. "Betrayed, betrayed, betrayed!" And he sat himself down on the ground and howled with his tongue hanging out, his tears rolled down the size of hazel nuts, while the crowd stood round and laughed until they cried at this tremendous sell, the story of the hoaxing of Esau the red. (Pp. 139-40)

The pain, the humiliation of this passage are real, but they have little to do with surprise. For the rage of Esau, like the loss of his blessing, is "the role he had to play; he knew and accepted the fact that all events are a fulfillment, and that what had happened had happened because it must, according to archetype" (p. 132).

Compared with Mann's comedy of conscious repetitions, Faulkner's mythic writing is a ponderous, nearly lifeless form of fiction. There is, moreover, a decline in serious moral interest. For many literary critics, the last period of Faulkner's career is the explicitly "moral" one, when he deliberately takes up questions of value supposedly implicit in the earlier work but less accessible. Olga Vickery, discussing *A Fable,* writes, "In the interest of universality, he restates abstractly most of the ideas developed in dramatic fashion in his preceding novels."[19] And R. P. Adams observes that, after 1940, "the moral implications which were always present are brought out more explicitly."[20]

Such a point of view minimizes too much the thematic dimensions of Faulkner's interest in form. The ideas of *Absalom, Absalom!* and "The Bear," the tragedy of an unfaltering creativeness and the passive acceptance of a structure scarcely understood, are remote from each other in virtually every respect. Moreover, I would argue that the late novels are not merely different in moral implication, but that they are nearly empty of *any* significant moral content. Granted that these books frequently allow characters to speak certain notions about the wilderness, the South, and the world which are almost extractable as moral essays, and which may indeed reflect William Faulkner's own opinion on such matters. But this is not the same thing as serious moral concern in fiction, which I take to be an evaluation of human conduct embedded in the nature and presentation of character and action.

The effect of works like "The Bear" and *A Fable* is to strip from fiction the possibility of moral evaluation because they emphasize the absolute necessity of events and our subservience to them. When we see characters too much chosen, too much the possession of their roles, then moral problems can no longer be an issue. In fact, one of the underlying motives of this later work seems to be that moral discriminations *should not* be an issue. The Corporal and the Old General, for example, have little to do with the complexities of good and evil; they fill the roles which a turning world requires, and they make clear the narrowness of vision of those who cannot accept or understand the nature of those requirements.

A presiding order is always intact and every character, whether aware, as the Corporal and Old General, Nancy and Ike McCaslin are aware, or whether still remote from such knowledge, as are Temple and the Runner, must still contribute to the ruling context. They are all Christs, delivered up to a pattern that depends upon their service in order to complete itself. To them all one might say, as in *A Fable* General Gragnon's superior remarks, " 'Call yours martyrdom for the world; you will have saved it' " (p. 54). Even Flem Snopes, no longer the indefinable force that pervades *The Hamlet*, is swept up, in *The Town* and *The Mansion*, into the necessities of community tradition: less lofty than the laws of the wilderness and history, but still unchallengeable. In none of these characters can there be an evaluation of human experience; what happens is only what *must* happen. Peter Swiggart's comment on the moral aspects of "The Bear" is much to the point: "What is unfortunately missing in this fusion of Yoknapatawpha mythology with Southern history is the moral analysis usually present in Faulkner's novels. The Civil War is described neither as a symbol of the South's moral sin nor as the consequence of its refusal to accept responsibility, but as the destiny of the land 'whirling into the plunge of its precipice.' "[21]

Temple Drake and Nancy Mannigoe in *Requiem for a Nun* are not identical, yet there are no grounds for *moral* distinction between them. What impresses us at last is their membership in the same pattern, alternates in a twice-told play. Nancy murders a child, but the moral weight of the act is greatly reduced by her conversation with God before she commits it, even as Ike McCaslin's repudiation of his property is carried out in a spirit of his selection by God for that act. Temple is also a whore, Nancy's echo in disgrace, and she also sees herself as the murderer of her child: "I destroyed mine myself when I slipped out the back end of that train that day five years ago" (p. 280). Her distinction from Nancy is not a moral one; it is her inability, as yet, to give herself freely to the pattern of suffering and salvation that she has already begun to act out. For all their self-probing, these characters are presented not as the inventors of their lives but as the inhabitants of them. Whatever else is here, moral concern is not.

Although Mann is working in a similar fictional mode, his *Joseph* is rich in moral matter because its characters are creative as well as prescient. They recognize not only what is necessary but their own responsibility to live fully the terms of their feast, to force the bonds of what awaits them to their fullest expansion. Potiphar, another of Joseph's "fathers," knows that the time of his betrayal by his wife and Joseph is implicit in the nature of himself (a eunuch) and his household. That betrayal (the accusation will be enough) is the great testing of his worthiness, the moment when he defines not the destiny but the *quality* of the destiny.

> So now: we are come to Petepre's [Potiphar's] feast-hour, the most painful in his life, and at all times inwardly anticipated by him: when he hunted birds, or the hippopotamus, or followed the desert chase; even when he read his good old books, always that hour abode in the background of his thoughts, always he vaguely looked forward to it, ignorant only of its details—though these, when it came, were largely in his hands. And as we shall see, he shaped them nobly.
> (P. 438)

As indeed he does: this just and mild ruler, brutally consigned by his parents to a sexless existence of "pure form, adornment without purpose" (p. 688), is compelled to stand at the center of a violent sexuality and judge it with discretion.

Dudu, Potiphar's dwarf steward, has the role of pimp, the go-between who dictates the love letters which the inexperienced Mut-em-enet sends to Joseph, and who becomes the serpent, tempting the woman into a forbidden lust: " 'I was able not only to know all the treacherous dealings of the couple but to lead them on and blow up the fire, that I might see how high it would blaze, to what extreme of guilt they would be led, in which I might trap them' " (p. 790). More than the passive servant of the tempter's role, he is the name of baseness; in his pride he even boasts to Potiphar of how he has skillfully brought the lovers to the peak of lust, precisely so that he may expose them. The demands of myth do not prevent Mann from portraying in his character an awful depravity, the responsibility for which the Satan archetype does not spare him. Dudu knowingly, even enthusiastically, repeats the crime that has always condemned him.

It should be clear that by moral concern in a work I am not speaking of its susceptibility to a ranking of characters and events into easy categories of the good and the bad. To render such judgments is only to erect a barrier between oneself and the genuine moral content of the work. The great value of literature is that it rescues us momentarily from just that day-to-day need to judge, to evaluate quickly and simplistically while still under the pressures of necessary action. Literature absolves us of these pressures—these words won't really bleed, these people are not alive—and allows us to come close to the fictions of the imagination so that we may explore human depths rarely visible to us in life.

Freed from the world by entering into a reflection of it, we begin to understand the richness of what it means to be alive in that world. From the vantage point of art we come to an awareness of life that is larger, less rigid, than the codes we erect and live by. To bring us to such awareness is what I take to be the function of literature.[22]

When we put a book aside, we return to a world that in certain ways must disappoint us in the superficiality of its condition, for it is somehow less real than that fullness of life we have found in the work of art. So too, the moral situation is more binding than we had remembered, and just a shade less relevant to what life is than we had thought prior to our reading of the book. The value of literature is realized not when we introduce the necessarily narrow moral strictures of life into the reading of it, but when we bring back to life something of the expansions and moral subtleties of literature.

In those works of Faulkner's that are unquestionably major, there is a deep moral presence. Invariably that presence is a function of his de-

liberate study of the creative consciousness: the aesthetic process of conceiving and understanding the real. In the desperate attempts of a figure
like Quentin in *Absalom, Absalom!* to create a truth about the history
of Sutpen and the South, we are made to see extraordinary possibilities
of perception and love at the moment of their greatest triumph. In the
same novel, there is in Miss Rosa and Mr. Compson a similar need, and
a similar courage too, yet finally we are aware of a lesser vision, a lesser
compassion. Their egoism and their fear make impossible for them
the tragic breakthrough that Quentin achieves. In *The Sound and the
Fury* we see another Quentin, a young man of rare sensibility who
nevertheless is strangling in an infatuation with his own purity, and
whose remoteness from the world is a condition of his ignorance of
love.

That portraits like Quentin and the coldly vicious Mink Snopes
should belong to the same canon is sufficient testimony to Faulkner's
scope as well as to his moral perception. The moral dimensions of Mink,
in *The Hamlet,* compel us to expand our notions of what moral behavior is nearly to the breaking point. Unlike Nancy Mannigoe, Mink
does not confer with God before he shoots Houston with a shotgun
from ambush; nor, significantly enough, does he have anything like
the kind of surface justification Faulkner later allows him in *The Mansion*. Yet his act and what follows make for more powerful fiction.
Faulkner works into the story not only the values implicit to a tragic
convention, those having to do with human worth and the consequences of excessive pride, but the more complex values that emerge
from the fact that this particular tragedy has been invented out of such
unlikely materials. Mink is not a demigod but a pitiful and hate-ridden
sharecropper who yet redefines for us the nature of courage and honor.
After reading his story we know more about what moral action means
than we knew before.

It is this kind of moral concern that is absent from the so-called moral
period of Faulkner's career. Faced with Faulkner's increasing tendency
to emphasize unalterable patterns of existence, to strip his characters of
creative energy, one gets the impression not of optimism or of faith in
traditional structures, but of fear: a despair over our power to destroy
ourselves unless creativity be restrained. There was a time when Faulkner's faith, both in the possibilities of literature and the possibilities of
human conduct, founded itself wholly on the creative imagination. He
preferred a literature that took chances, "trying to put the whole history
of the human heart on the head of the pin,"[23] a literature that would
risk flaunting the muses of decorum and good taste for a shot at sub-

limity. And he seemed to admire human beings most at the peak of their struggle against what is long established, whether a tale more consoling than true or a convention more comfortable than just. Locked within impossible conflict, their courage seems indistinguishable from desperation, their pride akin to madness. Yet they draw forth from us the tragic assent: we did not know men could do or bear so much.

Four | *Faulkner*
and Modernism

The attempt to identify the idea of literary modernism continues. If every period sees itself as modern, then ours may distinguish itself at least by the intensity of the effort: the obsession we have with establishing our novelty, our uniqueness. The modernity of our texts is not so much a set of concerns or a style but the preoccupation with their struggle to be. The process of making comes to the foreground, seeking to liberate itself from any content that could exist prior to the event of form: to free itself from plot, from extractable meaning, from referentiality, above all from the past—from everything that would limit the action of this present making to an imitation of what is conceivable apart from or prior to that action.

The completely original text would be the autonomous text, empty of all we mean by antecedence, all that prefigures and thus limits an original expression. The text seeks the originality of the system that fathers itself, that *means* not through convention, through comparison and contrast, through context, but through its own uniqueness. The only relaxation from originality that the text admits is the minimal convention necessary to dramatize a breakthrough. There can be just so much pressure from existing generic forms, so much narrative line or lyric development, so much of what J. Hillis Miller refers to as "the familiar models of order—organic unity, dialectical progression, or genealogical series"[1]—to expose the impotency of such models and to evolve the new that would forget everything. The purpose is to force us as readers to act out a similar process of forgetting, to follow each bridge into the work, each familiar feature, only to see it dissolve behind us in flames. The original text can exist only to the original reading that permits its own conventions of entrance to burn.

Paul de Man, working from Nietzsche's essay "The Use and Abuse of History" (1874), writes: "Modernity exists in the form of a desire to wipe out whatever came earlier, in the hope of reaching at last a point that could be called a true present, a point of origin that marks a new departure. This combined interplay of deliberate forgetting with an action that is also a new origin reaches the full power of the idea of modernity."[2] De Man knows, as he makes clear later in his essay, that the desire for modernity must always confront the tools of its expression. "The discovery of his inability to be modern leads [the writer] back to the fold, within the autonomous domain of literature, but never with genuine appeasement. As soon as he can feel appeased in this situation he ceases to be a writer. . . . The continuous appeal of modernity, the desire to break out of literature toward the reality of the moment, prevails and, in its turn, folding back upon itself, engenders the repetition and the continuation of literature."[3]

What is clear from de Man's version of the modern project is both its universality and the impossibility of its completion. Could there ever be a fully modern text? Could there be a nonmodern text worth the reading? For what important text is it, contemporary or classic, that accedes comfortably to its paternal sources in the world of established meaning, that robes itself in received convention without a touch of vengeance: a forgetting of the father that is both the triumph of will and the origin of an eternal remembering in the form of guilt? Or, for that matter, what text is it, however urgent to be its own progenitor, the self-originating father, that does not fold back into cultural and communal gifts —the boon of all the remembered texts—that enable it to speak to us? The modern seems everywhere in living literature, if only as an impossible yearning: an affinity for "the unmediated, free act that knows no past"[4] yet can never escape the armor of its own expression.

In Harold Bloom's discussions of the anxiety of influence, or in Edward Said's *Beginnings,* we find this desire to be fatherless considered roughly within the historical range we usually accept under the blanket of the term "modernism." Bloom focuses on the period from the late eighteenth century to the present; Said confines himself more severely to the half-century of 1875–1925. Whatever the chronological difference in locating the modern, what links these approaches is the sense of modernism as a dynamic activity of freedom and grudging appeasement, the text as torn by necessarily opposed tendencies: the urge to break form, to step outside received structure into a freedom of direct presentation; the contrary urge to enfold presence into communicable, hence recognizable form, reshaping freedom into an eloquent yet compromised dependency. The text becomes, paradoxically, a calculated free-play; it is a self-reflexive discourse on the impossibility of *being* a self-reflexive discourse.

In the preceding pages I have discussed some of Faulkner's novels in ways designed to invoke their modernism, to see them as versions of the struggle for a form consistent with freedom, a structure of changes; and to understand the extent to which this dynamic can generate a unique and coherent vision. At this point I want to describe in some detail the theoretical attitudes implicit to the novels as well as the theoretical path by which I have come to read them the way I have. I must acknowledge at the outset that, while Faulkner was more widely read than has sometimes been thought and probably more concerned with literary theory than he was usually willing to admit, there is no reason to think that he brought to the writing of fiction anything like the conceptual outline I am about to describe. Nevertheless, his books are major documents of modernity, regardless of how limited or universal we may find that phenomenon. An attempt to trace in a more abstract form their implicit aesthetics, their understanding of the nature and intentions of fiction, should prove valuable to our interpretation of Faulkner and the place he occupies in twentieth-century literature.

The Dislocation of Form

On at least two occasions Faulkner acknowledged an indebtedness to the philosophy of Henri Bergson. Once, in an interview with Loïc Bouvard, he said, "I was influenced by Flaubert and by Balzac. . . . And by Bergson, obviously."[5] Talking with Joan Williams about *Creative Evolution* in 1950, he said " 'Read it . . . it helped me.' "[6] What Faulkner learned from Bergson or, perhaps more accurately, what he found in Bergson that confirmed what he already knew is something we can guess at only from the evidence of the novels themselves. What we find there is an understanding of the fundamental nature of reality that squares well with Bergson's, as well as a similar sense of the philosophic (or aesthetic) method through which that reality might be perceived.[7]

Bergson understands reality as a creative and constant movement in time: a "bottomless bankless river" that eludes all conceptual frameworks that try to define or categorize it.[8] This temporal reality is a "continuous creation of unforeseeable form" (CE, p. 35), an evolution initiated and sustained by something called a vital impulse. The negative side of this notion of reality, and the side that constitutes Bergson's most important contribution to philosophy, is his powerful critique of the attempts of human intellect to deal with it: "against this idea of the absolute originality and unforeseeability of forms our whole intellect rises in revolt" (CE, p. 34). Dominated by the intellect and its need and ability to encase the real in various kinds of organization, we find that we are made uncomfortable by the idea of reality as flow, of time as duration that collapses every organization into irrelevance. In fact, Bergson writes, "We are at ease only in the discontinuous, in the immobile, in the dead" (CE, p. 182).

Bergson's critique of the intellect and its characteristic activity of conceptualization echoes the thrust of literary modernism, the drive of texts to rid themselves of forms and modes as irrelevant to a present reality as the patterns of intellect Bergson describes. The challenge raised by the early twentieth-century writers to such forms as the classical novel and its habits of plot and characterization or, more significantly, to the fundamental idea of continuity that makes any literary form into an organization of progressive states building to a coherent, unified end—this challenge finds a strong philosophical basis in the writings of Bergson. His work, like their own, is a celebration of creativity and its resistance to everything that seeks to curb it.

The intellect, according to Bergson, encounters reality not as a continuous stream but as "a series of positions" (CM, p. 127). Having thus broken reality into particles, intellect "is obliged next to reunite them by an artificial bond" (CE, p. 5). In this way intellect "substitutes for the continuous the discontinuous, for motion stability, for tendency in process of change, fixed points marking a direction of change and tendency. This substitution is necessary to common sense, to language, to practical life, and even, in a certain sense, which we shall endeavor to determine, to positive science" (IM, p. 50).

The intellect imposes one of two possible theories of order on reality. Bergson calls one, "mechanism," the other, "finalism." The mechanistic explanation of reality "regard[s] the future and the past as calculable functions of the present, and thus . . . claim[s] that *all is given*" (CE, p. 43). It views reality as "the gradual building-up of [a] . . . machine under the influence of external circumstances" (CE, p. 99). The doctrine of finalism is an extreme teleology, implying "that things and beings merely realize a program previously arranged" (CE, p. 45). What unites both theories, stamping them clearly as modes of intellect, is that "both doctrines are reluctant to see in the course of things generally, or even simply in the development of life, an unforeseeable creation of form" (CE, p. 51).

To the twentieth-century novelist, the techniques of traditional fiction were just such a conceptualization of reality as Bergson attributed to the intellect. Conventional narrative repeats the error of intellect in that, beginning with a sense of time as "an infinity of particles, pulverized so to speak" (CM, p. 126), rather than a sense of duration, it can do no more than organize these particles into false systems. That is, it "starts from immobility . . . and by an ingenious arrangement of immobilities it recomposes an imitation of movement which it substitutes for movement itself" (CM, p. 127).

Bergson thought a truthful novel must create some sense of the incessant motion of reality. It must present a character not as if he were being *lived* by a preconceived scheme, but in the act of creating the scheme itself.

> Consider, again, a character whose adventures are related to me in a novel. The author may multiply the traits of his hero's character, may make him speak and act as much as he pleases, but all this can never be equivalent to the simple and indivisible feeling which I should experience if I were able for an instant to identify myself with the person of the hero himself. . . . All the things I am told about the man provide me with so many points of view from which I can observe him. All the traits which describe him, and which can make him known to me only by so many comparisons with persons or things I know already, are signs by which he is expressed more or less symbolically. Symbols and points of view, therefore, place me outside him; they give me only what he has in common with others, and not what belongs to him and to him alone. But that which is properly himself, that which constitutes his essence, cannot be perceived from without, being internal by definition, nor be expressed by symbols, being incommensurable with everything else. Description, history, and analysis leave me here in the relative. Coincidence with the person himself would alone give me the absolute. (IM, p. 22)

This prescription for fictional characterization is also a prescription for a modern text. The presentation of original character is the effort to break through every kind of description or analysis that originates "outside"—everything, that is, that allows the work to mean by virtue of what it "has in common with others": what it receives from the past. Emphasis on the continuities of literature, like those of character, can only make the work into a traceable, "predictable" stage in this or that tradition. The thrust of Bergson is toward the "essence," "that which is [in character] properly himself," and like no one else.

163

Such a sense of novelty can be achieved only by placing the reader within the process of formation, within the creating movement which is the source and center of character. Analogously, as writers came to see, the whole literary work must explore its generation, its materialization into form. The text is original when its revealed process unfolds like the process of durational time, as a "creation of unforeseeable form." The work is no longer being built up like a machine, a static imitation of movement, but is a flowering as time flowers—not formless, yet not arranged in advance.

This conception of the work as process (far more inclusive than the limited stream-of-consciousness technique of characterization) is the common denominator of much of the most important twentieth-century writing, bringing together such diverse, novelists and poets as Proust, Gide, Conrad, Joyce, Woolf, Pound, Eliot, Stevens, Williams, and of course Faulkner. In its fragmentation, its self-questioning, its break-up of traditional means of continuity, the mode of process exemplifies Bergson's impatience with "description, history, and analysis." It also exemplifies his solution to the problem of the dominating intellect, namely, the need of mind to engage in an act of self-destruction.

In order to free itself for a more authentic encounter with reality, Bergson writes, "The mind has to do violence to itself, has to reverse the direction of the operation by which it habitually thinks, has perpetually to revise, or rather to recast, all its categories" (IM, p. 51). This violence against the intellect is the indispensable step toward an awareness of reality: "You must take things by storm: you must thrust intelligence outside itself by an act of will" (CE, p. 212). The natural tendency of intellect is to "transform matter into an instrument of action"; and it is only by "reversing its natural direction and twisting about on itself" that it can "think true continuity, real mobility, reciprocal penetration—in a word, that creative evolution which is life" (CE, p. 178).

The turn of mind against itself, like the turn of originality against the "domain of literature," is the basic action of *The Sound and the Fury*. As I tried to show in my first chapter, this novel is a brilliantly negative assault on the possibilities of narrative, including the interior monologue: the constructing consciousness either entangles itself hopelessly in fantasy or gives rise to the most simplistic and thus implausible moral stance. As for the classic fiction of the last section, it is like a narrative from another novel, as remote from the conception of fluid reality implicit to the first three sections as Dilsey's faith in a Christian order is from the confusion of Compson consciousness.

Like Eliot's "The Waste Land," in some ways its most important formal precursor, *The Sound and the Fury* turns against the tools of expression. Herein lies the vigor of the novel as well: the pain of self-mutilation is also the creative mind making room for itself. The limbs it lops off are the barriers to true speech.

The fragmentation of works like "The Waste Land" and *The Sound and the Fury,* however, still retains one quality of Bergson's intellect: it represents reality as a "series of separate acts" (CE, p. 5). What is important is that these works present this fragmentation *prior* to its re-consitution into an "artificial bond." Their fragmentariness, then, is the necessary initial step by which literature opens itself to a chaos freed of the falsifications of system.

But Bergson's critique of intellect, like the modernist critique of received forms, is only the first stage of his philosophy. Following the violence to intellect, Bergson writes, the mind must "attain to fluid concepts, capable of following reality in all its sinuosities and of adopting the very movement of the inward life of things" (IM, p. 51). The intuition must replace the intellect in the perception of reality. Beyond the knowledge of reality-as-states (unified *or* fragmented) is the knowledge of reality-as-flow: the intuitive awareness of the form that "life must create . . . for itself" (CE, p. 65). This awareness differs from intellect in that it "carves the animal without breaking its bones, by following the articulations marked out by nature" (CE, p. 172). By focusing on its mental activity, observing the processes of its awareness, the intuition comes to a recognition of reality as a fully creative, changing and growing form.

Bergson is aware of the contradiction of "change" and "form"; he realizes that duration can be visible, even to intuition, only as a materialization. The life force is always "at the mercy of the materiality which it has had to assume. . . . The most living thought becomes frigid in the formula that expresses it. The word turns against the idea" (CE, p. 141). Duration is knowable only in the context of matter, "the movement that is the inverse of its own" (CE, p. 274). The real, then, is not a mechanical organization; nor—the intellect reversed—is it a series of discontinuous moments. Visible at last to the intuition, reality becomes a dynamic activity in form: *"a reality which is making itself in a reality which is unmaking itself"* (CE, p. 270). It is a "continuity of shooting out. . . . unceasing life, action, freedom" (CE, p. 271) coming into being as the impulse to the contrary movement of matter: "we catch a glimpse of a simple process, an action which is making itself across an action of the same kind which is unmaking itself, like the fiery path torn by the last rocket of a fireworks display through the black cinders of the spent rockets that are falling dead" (CE, pp. 273–74).

The philosophy of Bergson is a clear presence in Faulkner's fiction, whether there by design or a common understanding. The poles of intellect and intuition, as Bergson defines them, are crucial in Faulkner's best novels. In *Absalom, Absalom!*, for example, we see these poles in the different possibilities of narration. There is, on the one hand, the tendency of Miss Rosa, Mr. Compson, and especially Sutpen to force the facts of history into preconceived patterns. Opposed to this, although not completely free from vested calculation, is the ability of Quentin and Shreve to live in a reality of change, to submit themselves to the right of their *narration* to change. Thus they escape the confines of the strategy of incest and expand into the unwanted and unprepared-for theme of miscegenation. The Sutpen history achieves in their hands a life of its own. It is narration gone inward: it is not directed by an imperious will so much as it follows from within the shape of its own realizing form.

In *Light in August* Joe Christmas is the character who, despite the aura of fatality that surrounds him, experiences his life as an endless process of growth. Born into a tight, restrictive narrative that is, however, without weight or conviction, Christmas fills that narrative to overflowing with his determination to accede neither to a "black" nor a "white" characterization. He opens his life to a constant creativity that community, ever on the side of intellect and its unreal orders, finds intolerable. As Bergson writes: "We are at ease only in the discontinuous, in the immobile, in the dead" (CE, p. 182). Gavin Stevens—"the District Attorney, a Harvard graduate, a Phi Beta Kappa"—typifies the Bergsonian intellect, as Panthea Broughton points out, in his attempts to define retrospectively the fluid reality of Christmas.[9] From the vantage point of the present he composes the past into intelligible, discrete moments: " 'Because the black blood drove him first to the negro cabin. And then the white blood drove him out of there, as it was the black blood which snatched up the pistol and the white blood which would not let him fire it.' "

Stevens demonstrates the fatalism of so much of *Light in August*, which sees the present as locked into the structure of the past. All that happens is "reserved." The life that looks forward, that views the past as a series of possibilities whose achievement of full form is unforeseeable—this is the awareness of Joe Christmas. The black-white unity he tries to live out is, to him, a reality of growth, a motion whose meaning and end lie only in the process of its unfolding. To the community of Jefferson, momentarily torn from the security and complacency of its divisions, this reality is visible, but only as an image: "black blood" rushing from his "pale body like the rush of sparks from a rising rocket." An image of death, it is still "serene" and "triumphant," catching the inexpressible, alternating rhythm of Christmas's life, even as it freezes and ends it.

These particular examples of Bergsonian attitudes at work in Faulkner lead finally to the whole concept of literary form implicit to his major novels. Behind the historical re-creation by Quentin and Shreve, or the characterization of Christmas as the pursuit rather than the completion of a pattern, is the idea of a fiction that seeks the status of "a continuous creation of unforeseeable form." Written in words, made visible by the systems of literature, the fiction tries to break through into the present— becoming, as Bergson puts it, *"a reality which is making itself in a reality which is unmaking itself."*

Toward a Supreme Fiction

In Bergson's description of a reality of making and unmaking there are tragic possibilities as well as aesthetic complexities he chooses not to emphasize. These are aspects of time-as-duration that give Faulkner's novels, more specifically his sentences, their characteristic movement and tension: on the one hand, the hope that out of the rush of words, clauses, paragraphs, there will appear the place where language becomes sufficient, where it will intersect with duration; on the other hand, the fear of that sufficiency. Motion that is always toward a crucial *end* risks destroying itself on its own success; and yet, unsuccessful, it falls back into that chaos where words and aesthetic forms are meaningless. But if Bergson refused to see the tragic potential in the idea of the materialization of time, of the adequacy of form to motion, Nietzsche saw little else. Bergson's materializing force is Nietzsche's Apollonian force, "the fair illusion of the dream sphere," molding unorganized life into visible forms; and Bergson's duration is Nietzsche's more sinister Dionysian power, the chaotic flow of reality. Viewed in this way, these forces make up a tragic dynamic of opposed commitments—one to motion and the other to form—that comes closer than Bergson to the special quality of modern literature.

Authentic tragedy for Nietzsche rises from an interaction: illusion and the breaking of illusion, form and the annihilation of form, image and music: each is driven by its opposite to the richest expression of itself. Like Blake's Los enchaining Urizen in the limits of body and earth, the Apollonian force solidifies Dionysian sound into visible image. The Dionysian, in turn, "endows that symbolic image with supreme significance" by disclosing and finally descending back into—along with the now dissolving image of itself—"the heart of original Oneness."[10] For Nietzsche, tragedy is the greatest of art forms because it contains, in their fullest power, our two most basic needs: "It shares with the Apollonian the strong delight in illusion and contemplation, and yet it denies that delight, finding an even higher satisfaction in the annihilation of concrete semblances" (BT, p. 142).

The great insight into the idea of modernity that *The Birth of Tragedy* gives us comes from its graphic demonstration of how a text—that which, according to Edward Said, commonly "hold(s) back a far more fluid poetry than words can convey"[11]—can be an open dynamic of forces simultaneously hostile to and generative of each other. The core of that dynamic is the special candor with which Apollonian image, the principal embodiment of literature and history, concedes the stability of its own existence: that is, it admits its fundamental illusoriness. Inspired by its Dionysian enemy to the furthest reaches of image-making power, the Apollonian force builds "individual forms" as solid and impressive as they are in Homeric epic; yet (unlike the figures in epic) they expose themselves as "merely a symbolic image." This image possesses a "luminous concreteness" that both arrests us with its absolute adequacy and, at the same time, "fail(s) to satisfy us, for it seem(s) to hide as much as it reveal(s)" (BT, p. 141).

The result is a conception of tragedy opposite to that developed by Aristotle in the *Poetics*. Tragedy for Aristotle is the achievement of an ending, of a wholeness that presides over the stubborn but at last submissive characters of the play. The characters of Aeschylean and Sophoclean tragedy are the large embodiments of specific roles—king, queen, messenger, prophet, defender of a city, avenger of a wrong—and in their duty to role they also serve, half blindly, the evolving clarity that is the action of the total form. "For Tragedy," writes Aristotle, "is an imitation, not of men, but of an action and of life. . . . The Plot, then, is the first principle, and, as it were, the soul of a tragedy: Character holds the second place." The irony of the form is that the central character commits himself so completely to a role whose resolution in action requires his own catastrophe. From this condition emerges the special beauty of the form as well, the beauty of design that is both served by, yet separate from, the influences of human character. We witness design methodically composing a most formidable, yet finally subservient will.

Nietzsche, writing on the same plays, sees an open form: the destruction of pattern, the failure of design. The culmination of the tragedy is the revelation of an "eternal life continuing beyond all appearance and in spite of destruction." The drama escapes denouement and meaning, and delivers itself over to possibility, "the turbulent flux of appearances" (BT, pp. 101–2). Yet crucial to Nietzsche is his insistence that the image destroyed has equalled if not surpassed the Apollonian strength of Homeric epic.

This paradoxical situation of image gathering energy from the imminence of its collapse is closely related to the critique of forms so prominent in modern literature. For this critique is not only destructive; it is also an attempt to regain for form a lost power, the power of the fictive that has been abandoned in the fascination with mimesis. The struggle with representation, with form as a series of canonical structures that contain truth, is comparable to what Thomas Hanna calls Nietzsche's struggle against "external authority": the triumph of the phenomenal world, as opposed to the individual vision, which Nietzsche attributed to Socrates.[12] Despite the Kantian challenge to external authority at the end of the eighteenth century, the modern writer's originating act as artist must still be to break loose from it.

In the deconstruction of the Apollonian that Nietzsche describes we can see the modernist urge to expose the illusoriness of language by freeing it from referentiality, from the "things" it seems to exist only to name. This effort to gain autonomy for language is not necessarily a quest for irrelevance, for structures empty of the inconvenience of life, but a desire to alter the conditions of significance for language: to justify language, like form, on fictive rather than scientific grounds. The modernist project for language is to achieve that power basic to Nietzsche's tragedy, a power that depends entirely on the willingness of language to give up representation for creation. The irony, of course, is that it is giving up a privilege it has never had the right to claim.

In Nietzsche's capsule history of ancient Greek art he sees two periods of remarkable achievement—the ages of Homeric epic and Aeschylean and Sophoclean tragedy—and two periods of comparatively lesser achievement—the ages of Doric art and Euripidean tragedy. The Homeric age is the triumph of "naive" expression, a deliberate giving over of the self—despite, or rather *because* of a deep awareness of "the terrors and horrors of existence" (BT, p. 29)—to the consolations of illusion. The Homeric epic is "the ripest fruit of Apollonian culture," the triumph over suffering and despair "by means of illusions strenuously and zestfully entertained." It is a "true naiveté," doubtless unrepeatable, in the sight of which the conquering, imagined Olympians become the "mirror images" of the Greeks (BT, pp. 31–32).

The more sophisticated art of the Doric period that follows finds it impossible to dispense with Dionysos, yet its recognition is partial and cautious. To Nietzsche, Doric art is like "a perpetual military encampment of the Apollonian forces. . . . so defiantly austere . . . [that it] could endure only in a continual state of resistance against the titanic and barbaric menace of Dionysos" (BT, p. 35). The Doric period is of less interest to Nietzsche than either the Homeric or the Attic period because it lacks the splendid naiveté of the former, an ability to make a "complete identification with the beauty of appearance" (BT, p. 31); and lacks as well the candor and self-knowledge of tragedy. Having passed beyond Homeric naiveté, the Doric knows the inadequacy of the Apollonian yet still clings to it, garnering consolations it does not properly earn.

In the tragedies of Aeschylus and Sophocles lies Nietzsche's version of our modernity. There is a clear breaking forth from history, from art and illusion, from everything that carries over from the past, including image: those Homeric figures inherited from a traditional epic art. At the same time, this Dionysian presence, "the newborn genius of Dionysiac music," arouses the Apollonian to "its profoundest content, its most expressive form" (BT, p. 68). Image in Nietzschean tragedy is both emptied and rejuvenated; it achieves its grandest manifestation just as it uncovers its condition as irrelevant "literature." The result is that form endures a climax of critique that paradoxically restores to it an original Homeric strength.

With Socrates and Euripides, according to Nietzsche, comes the decline, as well as the attitudes that prevailed from the fifth century B.C. to the second half of the nineteenth century. Euripides' quest for a new realism in tragedy, his desire to bring the Apollonian figures closer to the size and concerns of his audience—and thus to have the aesthetic image truly *represent* recognizable realities—is the abandonment of not only Dionysian but Apollonian truths: "And because you had deserted Dionysos, you were in turn *deserted by Apollo*" (BT, p. 69, my emphasis). The aesthetic form, that is, as well as fundamental reality, becomes trivial in its very claim to representational completeness.

The modern struggle against literature and history, against the subjection to reference, is the struggle for an eloquence that slices precariously between chaos and decadence: between, say, the determined artlessness of the Dadaists and the proud irrelevance of the Symbolists. The difficulty is the idea of an autonomy, a celebration of illusion, that feeds on the reality of its unmaking.

In one of his diary entries, Franz Kafka alludes to the frustration of the writer who wishes that his creations could transcend the world: "Writing's lack of independence of the world, its dependence on the maid who tends the fire, on the cat warming itself by the stove; it is even dependent on the poor old human being warming himself by the stove. All these are independent activities ruled by their own laws; only writing is helpless, cannot live in itself, is a joke and a despair."[13]

More recently Sigurd Burkhardt has described the fundamental aim of poetry as a desire to achieve for language "corporeality": "to release words in some measure from their bondage to meaning, their purely referential role, and to give or restore to them the corporeality which a true medium needs." The apogee of a poem, according to Burkhardt, is the creation of "a word no longer a sign; a word removed from the mutability of things, the infinitely greater mutability of feelings, of which ordinary words are the signs. This kind of word does not *have* meanings but rather *gives* them."[14]

Attitudes like those of Kafka and Burkhardt become truly reflective of the modern when the flight of the word from reference couples itself with the Nietzschean recognition that the climax of autonomy combines a complete Homeric adequacy, a fullness of illusion in which appearance subsumes reality, with the sudden opening of the Dionysian, exposing the poverty of image. The word, glorying in a "luminous concreteness," at the same time "denies itself and seeks to escape back into the world of primordial reality" (BT, p. 132). It is the tightrope walker's final trick: to wave aside not only the net and balancing pole but the rope itself. He becomes the purely fictive, poised like a mortal angel on the lip of his fall. The height of his ascendancy marks the exact moment of his unmaking, as the word becomes the voice of a wordless chaos. The end of this autonomy is the evocation of the real.

In the final effect of tragedy the Dionysiac element triumphs once again: its closing sounds are such as were never heard in the Apollonian realm. The Apollonian illusion reveals its identity as the veil thrown over the Dionysiac meanings for the duration of the play, and yet the illusion is so potent that at its close the Apollonian drama is projected into a sphere where it begins to speak wih Dionysiac wisdom, thereby denying itself and its Apollonian concreteness. The difficult relations between the two elements in tragedy may be symbolized by a fraternal union between the two deities: Dionysos speaks the language of Apollo, but Apollo, finally, the language of Dionysos; thereby the highest goal of tragedy and of art in general is reached. (BT, p. 131)

The modernist attack on literature is rooted in a frustration with forms that claim a reality they cannot have, display too little of the fragility which, as forms, they *must* have, and, as a result, are empty of that reality—Nietzsche's Dionysian flow—whose presentation is their largest excuse for being. The most impressive achievement of that attack is a modern literature of genuine tragic dimensions, epitomized in works like *Lord Jim, Nostromo, The Castle, Ulysses, Women in Love, Doctor Faustus, Light in August, Absalom, Absalom!,* and the mature poems of Yeats and Stevens. This is not, of course, an Aristotelian tragic art of completed action, bearing and being borne by a grand heroic agent, but Nietzschean tragedy—open, lyric, self-reflexive—of design articulating the darkness of its own collapse.

Of all twentieth-century writers, Wallace Stevens has perhaps responded to the Nietzschean aesthetic most directly and enthusiastically. In an early poem, "Domination of Black," he shows how it is chiefly the black background, the absence of image, that illuminates the flames of fire, leaves, peacock tails, and planets into a purely metaphoric yet brilliant unity. Into this illusory order "the night came, / Came striding like the color of the heavy hemlocks." Yet the flames—what more visible in autumn darkness?—mount their very frailty as if it were a Pegasus.

In its most significant accomplishments the modern imagination is what Stevens describes in his *Esthetique du Mal:* it has defeat implicit in it, for it lives on, and therefore requires, the death of what it im- agined yesterday. It is that "evil" in the self from which "fault / Falls out on everything." Content with nothing, it lives on the wreckage of its own creations: "Like hunger that feeds on its own hungriness."

Let there be "Clear water in a brilliant bowl, / Pink and white car- nations," he writes in "Poems of Our Climate." Let there be the per- fectly defined image, "Still one would want more, one would need more." There remains "the never-resting mind" that drives us "back / To what had been so long composed." The exquisite image triumphs, and falters in its triumph. For there is a mind that cannot bear to be bereft of its image-making power. This evil in the self, "The evilly com- pounded vital I," is Nietzsche's modern urge, knowing itself in the images that become its instant past and therefore the necessary victims of its continuing existence. It is the Dionysian as human hunger, feeding on its own hungriness.

We can move easily from here to Faulkner's most comprehensive versions of a "supreme fiction," the modern tragic form, *Light in August* and *Absalom, Absalom!* The latter novel is a series of powerful images climbing to a moment of complete adequacy, "the massive impact of image, concept, ethical doctrine, and sympathy" (BT, pp. 128–29) within the Apollonian: the union of Quentin and Shreve with each other, and the sublimation of the real lives of Henry Sutpen and Charles Bon into the created versions of history. Yet that adequacy, like the momentary conviction that attends even the stories of Miss Rosa and Mr. Compson, dissolves in the racial fratricide that explains and explodes explanation; as their *words* return to the condition of conjecture where we know they originate; as the two "brothers" Quentin and Shreve, making and mirroring the brothers Henry and Bon, recede into the two strangers they were at the beginning. Reality sounds its Dionysian music, but of course it has been there all along: filling the images from within, bestowing on them a power they can possess only in the secret awareness of their weakness. The tragic art of the novel sustains, as Nietzsche said it would, our need for "illusion," for the power of the word to articulate and thus momentarily vanquish the horror of chaos and death; and our *equal* need to see image give way: "the Apollonian illusion . . . broken through and destroyed" (BT, p. 130). The grand house of Sutpen is in flames, accompanied by the screams of the last of the line, Jim Bond. Quentin and Shreve, echoing in 1910 the love they imagine in 1865, sink back into resentment and rage: *"I dont hate it! I dont hate it!"*

In Faulkner, of course, there is little of that gaiety we find in Stevens. Stevens well knows the terror of night that consumes in "Domination of Black" all the artful combinations of color and motion, or that "fatal, dominant X" from which we flee to metaphor. And yet, with Nietzsche, he can delight in "the annihilation of the individual," in that "spirit which playfully shatters and rebuilds the teeming world of individuals— much as, in Heraclitus, the plastic power of the universe is compared to a child tossing pebbles or building in a sand pile and then destroying what he has built" (BT, pp. 143–44).

Faulkner comes to his modernity more painfully. Closer in this respect to Conrad than to Stevens or Joyce, Faulkner retains a nostalgia for stability, for what in later years he would call the "old verities," that prevents him from a too unequivocal acceptance of a condition of perpetual making. His Southern heritage here is doubtless crucial. Yet *Light in August* and *Absalom, Absalom!* remain Nietzschean in their fundamental commitments. That is, they affirm the condition of the modern imagination: the conviction that only in courting chaos, only in meeting and interacting with the shapes of its own subversion, does imagination achieve its most brilliant form.

The Sound and the Fury and *As I Lay Dying,* despite their obvious achievement, do not have quite the power of these two novels, because they do not bring together, with the same resonance and richness, the dual forces from which they spring. In one the modern thrust is too clear, in the other, too compromised.

In *As I Lay Dying* the Dionysian is finally encased in a coffin, as madness is confined to an asylum. Death, in other words, is dealt with, whatever the ironies Faulkner lavishes on the Bundrens and their strange doings. Form is like the armed camp of Nietzsche's Doric art, thrusting Addie's body backwards into a box, Cash's broken leg into a sleeve of solid cement, the self-interested Bundrens into the ancient narrative of the journey to Jefferson. In *The Sound and the Fury,* on the other hand, the Dionysian is too powerful, while the images that the various narratives offer are too remote from what seem to be the realities of Compson suffering. In the willful autonomy of Quentin's dream of incest, the paranoia of Jason, or the ordered plot of a Christian-centered world in the last section of the novel, we discover images that only partially tempt us with their adequacy. Their collapse is not touched with tragedy because reality speaks not so much *through* the mouth of image as outside and around it. As for the first section, Benjy's considerable image-making power is clearly the product of his idiocy, not his artfulness. He tempts us only into conceptual simplifications the rest of the novel effectively subverts. In the not quite relevant image-making of *The Sound and the Fury,* in the emphatic domination by image in *As I Lay Dying,* we have versions of dislocation that have yet to rise to a fully developed tragic aesthetic.

In *Light in August* and *Absalom, Absalom!* Faulkner builds his most powerful examples of the modern dynamic: literature and denial fuel each other, like angry halves of a single being. Image comes forth in all the richness of Homeric outline even as the terror of the Dionysian presence "endows that symbolic image with supreme significance" and dissolves it.

Mythos

At one point in Sartre's *Nausea* Roquentin ponders the shapelessness of his existence, in which things become intelligible only in the recounting, in the telling. In the living all is present and formless: "Nothing happens while you live. The scenery changes, people come in and go out, that's all. There are no beginnings. Days are tacked on to days without rhyme or reason, an interminable, monotonous addition. . . . Neither is there any end."[15] This is life completely deconceptualized. Everything once considered bounded and defined, the appearance of nature as well as human history, leaks through the seams of order: "existence had suddenly unveiled itself. It had lost the harmless look of an abstract category: it was the very paste of things, this root was kneaded into existence. Or rather the root, the park gates, the bench, the sparse grass, all that had vanished: the diversity of things, their individuality, were only an appearance, a veneer. This veneer had melted, leaving soft, monstrous masses, all in disorder—naked, in a frightful, obscene nakedness." The world has become pure presence, denuded of what Frank Kermode, commenting on the novel, calls "the absurd dishonesty of all prefabricated patterns."[16] The result for Roquentin is nausea.

The only redemption he can imagine to this vision of presence is to fictionalize his life, to make it into a text:

> But everything changes when you tell about life; it's a change no one notices: the proof is that people talk about true stories. As if there could possibly be true stories; things happen one way and we tell about them in the opposite sense. You seem to start at the beginning: "It was a fine autumn evening in 1922. I was a notary's clerk in Marommes." And in reality you have started at the end. It was there, invisible and present, it is the one which gives to words the pomp and value of a beginning.

Roquentin, however, cannot suspend his knowledge that such "beginning" was not really there, because the future was not really there. There can be no shadings, no highlights, no "pomp and value" in the viscousness of a true present; only in the remembering, in the telling, can there be the beginning, middle, and end which mold our illusory orders. For Roquentin such recountings are merely the consolations of the unthinking, and have nothing to do with actual life. He retains the desire that life should unfold with the order of a memory: "I wanted the moments of my life to follow and order themselves like those of a life remembered," yet he knows the impossibility of this: "You might as well try and catch time by the tail."

Whatever Roquentin's and Sartre's views on the situation, there is an important strain of twentieth-century writing that has pursued the consolations of a "life remembered." If modernity in literature is in some sense a forgetting, then myth is preoccupied with remembering: a mode of writing and a portrayal of consciousness in which originality displaces or compromises itself by a type of repetition.

In talking about myth I want to restrict myself to one particular manifestation of it in twentieth-century literature, and that is its appearance within a text as an explicit, superior structure either known to the characters who participate in it, as in Mann's *Joseph and His Brothers* or Faulkner's *A Fable,* or made overtly, if subtly, available to the reader, as in Joyce's *Ulysses.* Myth in these instances retains what we have come to regard as its usual qualities: (1) it fulfills the broad Aristotelian function of story or plot, providing a shape to the events of a work, and (2) it performs this act by incorporating into the work, to a greater or lesser extent, a story of the gods or larger-than-life-size heroes. But the modern use of myth has a third function as well, that of exploring the relationship between present and past, new and prior texts, the individual creating mind and a given order.

However veiled its reference to archetypal heroic quests, however closely tied it may be to specific character motive, myth in its Aristotelian sense as plot or mythos always claims an integrity of its own— some degree of independence of the voices or characters who participate in it. It is an action or system that seems to originate outside character, having the quality of preexistent pattern, like a prophecy that is finally fulfilled. Pattern and character, of course, are never wholly separate, since the former can be made visible only through the consciousness and deeds of the characters. Yet there remains the sense of external control in the pattern as well as the idea of service in the characters.

Such an external pressure, which is basic to all our literary forms, is precisely what much of modern literature begins by trying to reject. Whether in terms of the imposed static conceptions of intellect or the Socratic-Euripidean misplaced faith in the representational accuracy of forms, modernism has been severely critical of any pattern that pretends to anticipate existence. Yet the fact remains that we can find in modern literature, in such works as *Ulysses, Joseph, A Fable,* "The Bear," *Dr. Faustus,* and *Four Quartets,* the most obtrusive kinds of mythic structure, instances of myth operating not merely as narrative frame or conventional lyric pattern, but myth as the largely undis-

placed presence of a prior source: *The Odyssey,* a major portion
of Genesis, the story of Christ, the history of America and the South,
the Faust legend, and—less susceptible to paraphrase in Eliot since he
is not writing a narrative—an orthodox Christian belief in the idea of
Incarnation, the oneness of time and Time.

Mythos in these works exaggerates its traditional authority, making
obvious the distance between structure and character, past and present.
Most studies of myth in literature emphasize the unity of these elements
so that myth and present action are seen as reinforcements of each other.
In the works I have mentioned, however, the distance is crucial. As a
result, the relationship between consciousness and context becomes central, a part of the modernist concern with the tools of expression and
with the idea of originality.

In *Ulysses,* with the title as the initial clue, Joyce asks us to explore
the points of contact between the classic text and the new one, even as
we remain wholly aware of the differences. Our ability to establish these
contacts—Joyce has laid enough traces to last any reader's lifetime—is
an exercise in consciousness similar to Joseph's attempts, in the Mann
tetralogy, to see his life prefigured in an anterior Joseph. In the case
of *Ulysses,* it is tempting to share A. Walton Litz's impatience with
excessive critical concern with the Homeric parallels, and "to conclude
that the parallel with the *Odyssey* was more useful to Joyce during the
process of composition than it is to us while we read the book." And
yet Litz may be erring in a new direction when he says, "It would be
a grave mistake to found any interpretation of *Ulysses* on Joyce's *schema,*
rather than on the human actions of Stephen, .and Molly, and Mr.
Leopold Bloom."[17] The Homeric analogy is not the same as a scaffold-
ing which we can ignore, since it is not there, once the building is up;
and the human actions of the characters *are* set ingeniously within the
framework of a prior text. Our reading of *Ulysses,* like our reading of
Joseph, is an exploration of the territory between that text and these
actions, a region in which originating and remembering interact.

In *Joseph* we follow each character in his deliberate study of how
what he is, and has always been, bears on what he does; in *Ulysses* we
are ourselves participants, reading Leopold and Ulysses into whatever
identities we can imagine. The concern of each work is the passage from
the modern desire to invent new forms to the reconciliation with existing forms, while at the same time preserving both the fictiveness of *all*
forms and the power of the individual imagination. This is not so much
a rejection of modernity as the attempt to describe an original consciousness willing itself into the pattern of preexistent fable, and making that

pattern responsive. The shift from a more radical modernism is that the imagination no longer seeks to invent a wholly original pattern but to make space for itself within the given. There is a folding back into "literature" that we do not find in *Nostromo* or *The Castle, Esthetique du Mal* or *Absalom, Absalom!*, a willingness to borrow the shaping power of an older order. But the vitality of the hero as *conscious pretender* is still present: this Joseph who *knows* that he is "Joseph," this figure whose pride takes the form of a deliberate concession to the past, who dresses himself in quotation marks as if his initial appearance were an encore.

Whatever the differences between *Ulysses* and *Joseph,* both novels can be said to stress the arbitrary rather than the inevitable unity of consciousness and structure, the precariousness rather than the solidarity of fictions. In this respect the mythic method is consistent with the general thrust of modernism and its emphasis on the dubious reality of forms, with the important exception that the fictive orders of myth are not vulnerable to collapse. The external structure of a work like *Joseph* is invested with what Richard Chase, in a passage I quoted earlier, calls an "impersonal magic force or potency"; or what Philip Wheelwright, more grandly, refers to as "transcendental forces peering through the cracks of the visible universe."[18] Unlike the various orders of *Absalom, Absalom!*, for example, invented by imaginations within the novel, and having a frailty intimately related to their beauty and power, the hovering mythos of *Joseph* or *A Fable* or "The Bear" has a firm, unquestionable authority. And unlike recent examples of mythos, such as the plot of *Tom Jones,* this authority has a spiritual dimension as well. Its possible illusoriness only triggers the power of faith. The act of consciousness, modifying its originality and repeating what it knows to be nothing more than a prior text, becomes something like a religious act.

The invisible communal ethic of Frenchman's Bend in *The Hamlet,* the Christ story in *A Fable,* the journey of Ulysses, the story of Joseph, Eliot's "still point of the turning world"—all these survive as testaments, to be repeated and made "real" by minds haunted, like Roquentin, with disorder, but who choose to will their lives into lives "remembered." There is a leap from contingency to the past, to an idea of precedence in whose wake consciousness performs as if it were repetition. Invested with faith, structure assumes the position of a real yet strangely dependent god: like a pillar of fire or cloud that points out the proper route only to a clear and believing eye. The past has a reality and an effective power seldom demonstrated in modern literature, yet this power still resides partly in the ability of the conscious mind to *see,* if not to contrive. But seen or not, the order abides. The cloud points toward Canaan no matter where the Hebrews may turn; and it confers on their movement an idea of direction, toward or away from a promised land.

The intention of the modern mythic method may well be, as T. S. Eliot observed in his essay on *Ulysses,* to provide "a shape and a significance to the immense panorama of futility and anarchy which is contemporary history."[19] But Eliot's emphasis is too much on the need for tradition and too little on the individual talent; too little on the way in which a new text (especially in *Ulysses*) takes a prior structure on terms suitable to itself. Much of twentieth-century archetypal criticism makes, and compounds, a similar error in emphasis. Such criticism has often used the mythic elements in modern literature as a way of shoring up the ruins of its fragmentariness. Mythic analogues become a means of demonstrating that the disruption in twentieth-century writing is only superficial, that these texts in fact have conventional structures that it is the business of the myth critic to bring to light. In doing so, however, the critic frequently ignores the special status of the archetype in its new context, as well as the implications of what is taking place *between* present and past, the modern mind and its predecessor.

Throughout Faulkner's novels we find abundant mythic allusion, implicit and explicit references to gods or heroes from various traditions.[20] Yet I would argue that Faulkner does not write a "mythic" novel—that is to say, a novel in which a superior structure becomes an effective agent of order—until *The Hamlet* in 1940. Clearly there is a difference between mythic reference as a means of adding weight and texture to a novel, and myth as a means of organizing a novel. In pointing out mythic allusions, critics have often tried to collate them into an organizing pattern. This is a natural step in archetypal analysis since allusion to myth is always allusion to a narrative of some sort or other: "In literature," Northrup Frye writes, "whatever has a shape has a mythical shape, and leads us toward the center of the order of words."[21] By "backing up," in Frye's terms, from the aesthetic object, we can begin to see the larger patterns that organize it. Ideally, for the archetypal critic, there is *no* work of fiction that will not yield itself to a traditional shape if the critic will only retreat far enough away from it.

The problem with such a criticism is that it makes distinctions among texts difficult: distinctions between those texts, such as "The Bear" and *A Fable,* in which myth plays a vital, controlling role, and a text such as *The Sound and the Fury,* in which it has much less importance. In

The Sound and the Fury mythic allusion fails to pass over into a determining mythic structure. There are numerous mythic references: an Easter weekend, a castrated idiot who happens to be thirty-three, a good Christian woman who serves that idiot with love and respect. In terms of structure, however, what do we do with these references? Does *The Sound and the Fury* repeat in any significant way the life and meaning of Christ? Does that ancient pattern, or any other that the novel invokes, unify the work at all, so as to include most of what goes into the monologues of Benjy, Quentin and Jason? Dilsey, of course, understands perfectly the Christian ordering of the world and conducts her life in accordance with it. But what of the Compsons themselves, particularly the three sons whose respective consciousnesses consume so much of the novel? They are scarcely aware of the Christian myth: they do not adhere to it or rebel against it, nor can it be said that they serve it unknowingly. Moreover, the narrative implicit to that myth does not organize the novel at any level. The fragmentariness of the book does not heal itself convincingly through the myth, even as the four versions of the Compson experience yield no comprehensive view of its meaning. One can say this use of Christian myth is ironic, it does not operate in the Compson world, and "that is the point." But if Christian myth does not operate, it is not ironic—it is irrelevant; it has nothing to do with the novel, and *that,* I think, is the point.

R. P. Adams has pointed out in detail a number of myths alluded to in *The Sound and the Fury.* He believes that Faulkner "organized it by means of the mythical method, using patterns that appeal to civilized minds, in order to achieve his artistic aim of stopping motion so that it can be seen." Nevertheless he admits that these myths, "no matter how we try to put them together . . . do no fit. Therefore no one of them, or combination of them, can be made to serve as a simple key or explanation to account for what Faulkner is doing. They contribute structural patterns to Faulkner's work, but they do not govern in it."[22]

Now myth that contributes "structural patterns" yet does not "govern" is myth that has been emptied of its mythos power. And insofar as the work resists this power it becomes, despite its allusions, antimythic. Perhaps it is true that, as Adams has hypothesized, Faulkner read at least parts of *Ulysses* and Eliot's essay on mythical method in *The Dial* before writing *The Sound and the Fury,* and consciously employed them in working out the novel.[23] But Faulkner's Easter, though similarly concealed, works quite differently than does Homer's *Odyssey* for Joyce. *The Odyssey* does to some extent "govern": it brings Bloom home to Eccles Street, Ulysses to Penelope, *Ulysses* to its conclusion, with at least something of that inevitability that the use of myth creates. Faulkner's Easter does none of these. The book has the quality of ending because its author has stopped writing, because four "failures" is enough—although "none of them were right."

As I Lay Dying is closer to an ironic use of mythic form. It is for reasons of its irony that I would distinguish this novel from Faulkner's later mythic period. Unlike the Easter weekend of The Sound and the Fury, the journey in As I Lay Dying is hardly irrelevant; it controls the whole novel. The irony is that the Bundrens' assent to the mythos is so compromised by their self-interest. The power of the myth is deflated even as it serves as a pattern through which the Bundrens (excepting Darl) can express their grief. In Thomas Mann's terms, which I will elaborate on shortly, this journey myth is merely a "prescribed feast," present as a "jest," although it serves to bring the Bundrens to their various destinies in Jefferson, and Addie to the end of her long dying.

If one of the difficulties with myth criticism is its failure to distinguish between myth as effective structuring agent and myth as mere allusion, another is its failure to distinguish between sincere and ironic uses of myth: whether the presence of mythic order affirms or ridicules the pressure that the past brings to bear on the present. In his essay "Freud and the Future," Thomas Mann makes a distinction between ironic and sincere examples of myth that is helpful in defining the different ways in which modern writers have used myth. Mann describes two kinds of mythic literary situation. In one the character assumes that he is the sole creator of his life, failing to recognize that there is a structure that outlives him, and that his own life is to fulfill. In the other, the character puts on the writer's own knowledge; he is able to see, in the midst of action, the overriding pattern that provides action with meaning and purpose.

> [The first] character is a mythical role which the actor just emerged from the depths to the light plays in the illusion that it is his own and unique, that he, as it were, has invented it all himself. . . . Actually, if his existence consisted merely in the unique and the present, he would not know how to conduct himself at all; he would be confused, helpless, unstable in his own self-regard, would not know which foot to put foremost or what sort of face to put on. His dignity and security lie all unconsciously in the fact that with him something timeless has once more emerged into the light and become present; it is a mythical value added to the otherwise poor and valueless single

character; it is native worth, because its origin lies in the unconscious.

Such is the gaze which the mythically oriented artist bends upon the phenomena about him—an ironic and superior gaze, as you can see, for the mythical knowledge resides in the gazer and not in that at which he gazes. But let us suppose that the mythical point of view could become subjective; that it could pass over into the active ego and become conscious there, proudly and darkly yet joyously, of its recurrence and its typicality, could celebrate its role and realize its own value exclusively in the knowledge that it was a fresh incarnation of the traditional upon earth.[24]

It is this second instance, "life in the myth, life as a sacred repetition," in which myth becomes sincere: the character celebrates his knowledge of the prophecy his life fulfills. "[There is a] mythical slant upon life, which makes it look like a farce, like a theatrical performance of a prescribed feast, like a Punch and Judy epic, wherein mythical character puppets reel off a plot abiding from past time and now again present in a jest. . . . [There is also a mythic slant which may] pass over and become subjective in the performers themselves, become a festival and mythical consciousness of part and play."[25]

Mann's two "mythic slants" describe the two kinds of mythic novel Faulkner writes. The first—the mythic view that issues in farce because the feast is only prescribed, not consciously renewed—has obvious anti-mythic implications. This view suggests the essential quality of *As I Lay Dying*. The characters become the puppets of Addie's desire, practicing an ancient ritual of interment which embodies and assuages an appropriate grief, but which is also the Punch and Judy debacle of ritual not altogether understood or believed. The controlling pattern is stripped of much of its meaning and most of its dignity: it abides from the past as a jest. The Bundrens know the myth they follow, but in their hands it becomes the agent of new desires: an abortion, a toy train, a set of false teeth. The second form of myth is the mode of Faulkner's later novels, in which the actors knowingly confirm and revitalize the patterns that guide them.

In works like *The Hamlet*, much of *Go Down, Moses, A Fable, Intruder in the Dust,* and *Requiem for A Nun,* the external structures of community, Southern history, the Christ story, become the enduring patterns of individual lives, whose essential act is to take those patterns upon themselves. To the sometimes dazed yet finally rooted members of Frenchman's Bend, to Lucas Beauchamp, Ike McCaslin, and Molly Worsham, to the Corporal and the Old General, to Chick Mallison, to

Nancy Mannigoe, existence becomes, in the living of it, an "adventure": "a life remembered."

The extent to which Faulkner may have been influenced by Mann, Joyce, and Eliot in his use of the mythic mode has yet to be determined. His respect for at least two of them is well-documented: "The two great men in my time were Mann and Joyce. You should approach Joyce's *Ulysses* as the illiterate Baptist preacher approaches the Old Testament: with faith."[26] Once asked if he had read Mann's *Joseph and His Brothers,* however, Faulkner replied, "I never heard of him."[27] But given his occasional praise of Mann it seems likely that Faulkner had read some of the *Joseph* series (published in English in 1934, 1935, 1938, and 1944) by the time he wrote *Go Down, Moses.* In any event, the work of his last phase bears a similarity to *Joseph,* portraying life, even in the chaos of war, as what Mann calls "a kind of celebration": "it is a making present of the past, it becomes a religious act, the performance by a celebrant of a prescribed procedure; it becomes a feast. . . . The feast is the abrogation of time, an event, a solemn narrative being played out comfortably to an immemorial pattern; the events in it take place not for the first time, but ceremonially according to the prototype."[28]

Joseph and His Brothers is the supreme twentieth-century version of the mythological novel. It is controlled throughout by the foreknowledge of the major characters who participate in it. They all see who they are, the roles they have inherited. Whatever the event, whatever crime performed or suffered, whatever glory or embarrassment, there is the recognition of a pattern that inevitably is being fulfilled. Isaac knows the truth of his sons Jacob and Esau, knows, for all his claim to love the latter most, who is to be the bearer of his blessing, and *they* know also: "the clearer it became *who they both were,* in whose footsteps they walked, on whose story they were founded, the red man and the smooth man, the huntsman and the dweller in tents." Isaac goes blind, with strange deliberateness, "like the dying moon, and he lay in darkness that he might be betrayed, together with Esau, his eldest son." Once again the conflict of brothers has recurred. Jacob is the Abel, the Isaac, the *preferred,* to this Cain, this Ishmael, even as Joseph will be the Jacob to his jealous brothers.

But actually nobody was deceived, not even Esau. For if I am venturing here to write about people who did not always know precisely who they were . . . yet this occasional lack of clarity had to do only with the individual and the time-conditioned, and was precisely the consequence of the fact that everybody knew, perfectly well outside of time, and mythically and typically speaking, who the individual was, and so did Esau. . . . He wept and raved, of course, after the betrayal, and was more murderously minded against his favoured brother than Ishmael had been against his—indeed, it is true that he discussed with Ishmael an attack upon Isaac as well as upon Jacob. But he did all that because it was the role he had to play; he knew and accepted the fact that all events are a fulfillment, and that what had happened had happened because it must, according to archetype. That is to say, it was not the first time, it was ceremonially and in conformity to pattern, it had acquired presentness as in a recurrent feast and come round as feasts do. (Pp. 131–32)

Joseph is at the center of the novel because he, more than anyone else, lives openly and confidently in the knowledge of his destiny, even as he must struggle to work it out. His greatest skill is to think "mythically," to see and to declare the pattern of what he believes is his lofty end, whatever the risks from the envy of his brothers. He is aware of it always, even in the apparent contradictions of his humiliation and his suffering. He links the present to a pattern that alters the meaning of the present, rescues it from the limits of immediate anguish and transforms it into a necessary phase in a larger sequence.

He was a true son of Jacob, the man of thoughts and dreams and mystical lore, who always understood what happened to him, who in all earthly events looked up to the stars and always linked his life to God's. Granted that Joseph's way of dignifying his life by attaching it to the higher law and reality was not the same as Jacob's, less spiritual, more shrewdly calculating; yet he seriously held that a life and activity without the hall-mark of higher reality, which does not base upon the traditionally sacred and support itself thereupon, nor is able to mirror itself in anything heavenly and recognize itself therein, is no life or activity at all. He was convinced that nothing in the lower world would know how to happen or be thought of without its starry protoype and counterpart; and the great certainty guiding his life was belief in the unity of the dual, in the fact of the revolving sphere, the exchangeability of above and below, one turning into the other, and gods becoming men and men gods. (P. 389)

This mythic consciousness, it is well to point out again, is nothing like the primitive consciousness Ernst Cassirer describes in *The Philosophy of*

Symbolic Forms and elsewhere. Joseph's awareness is not that of a passive witness to the sudden incarnation of the god in an inanimate object, but an extremely sophisticated perspective that knowingly accepts a past formula as its own. His understanding of himself as the second or hundreth Joseph depends on a mature sense of how the mind confirms and celebrates itself as the reincarnation of a prior being.

This is a new version of the modernist quest for originality and autonomy. The creative mind adopts an inherited form yet asserts a familiar freedom by the very willfulness and arbitrariness of that adoption. From the ritual of duplication, from an idea of collective being, the mind carries away the consolations of self-knowledge.

As I have argued in the previous chapter, this is a mode of modern writing that Faulkner is only occasionally able to handle with the kind of aesthetic success he achieved earlier in his career. By and large, myth becomes in his hands a heavy and sterile form, a controlling authority of which he is not master but servant, making entries in ledgers ruled in stone. Faulkner comes to a mythic fiction still powerfully attracted to the dominant high modernist mode, a fiction that wants to forget more than it remembers. Unlike writers like Mann and Joyce, he is unable to combine those allegiances or to manage the difficult transition from one to the other. Behind him, not to be equalled by his later work, perhaps not to be surpassed by any modern writer, is the unique power of his major novels: where his words come magnificently alive because they labor in the world's confusion; where meaning is eternally and hopelessly human, and resides nowhere but in the perpetual creation of forms.

Notes

Preface

1. See, for example, the important book by Joseph Reed, Jr., *Faulkner's Narrative* (New Haven: Yale University Press, 1973), which contains a rigorous analysis of narrative technique.
2. Malcolm Cowley, Introduction to *The Portable Faulkner* (New York: Viking Press, 1946), p. 18. In an early review Dudley Fitts suggested that the Benjy section be read last: "Two Aspects of Telemachus," *Hound and Horn* (April-June 1930), 445–47, reprinted in *William Faulkner: The Critical Heritage,* ed. John Bassett (London: Routledge & Kegan Paul, 1975), p. 88.
3. George Marion O'Donnell, "Faulkner's Mythology," in *William Faulkner: Three Decades of Criticism,* ed. Frederick J. Hoffman and Olga W. Vickery (East Lansing: Michigan State University Press, 1960), pp. 82–93.
4. Frank Kermode, *Continuities* (London: Routledge & Kegan Paul, 1968), pp. 68–69.
5. Richard Poirier, *The Performing Self* (New York: Oxford University Press, 1971), p. 45.
6. Northrop Frye, *Fables of Identity* (New York: Harcourt, Brace & World, 1963), p. 131.
7. For a fuller discussion of the role of process in modern literature see my essay, "Process and Product: A Study of Modern Literary Form," in *Massachusetts Review* 12 (1971): 297–328, 789–816.
8. Paul de Man, *Blindness and Insight: Essays in the Rhetoric of Contemporary Criticism* (New York: Oxford University Press, 1971), pp. 20–35.
9. Ihab Hassan, "The Critic as Innovator: A Paracritical Strip in X Frames," *Chicago Review* 28 (Winter 1977): 19.

10. T. S. Eliot, "Ulysses, Order, and Myth," in *The Modern Tradition: Backgrounds of Modern Literature,* ed. Richard Ellmann and Charles Feidelson, Jr. (New York: Oxford University Press, 1965), p. 681.
11. Roland Barthes, "The Structuralist Activity," trans. Richard Howard, *Partisan Review* 34 (Winter 1967): 86–87.

The Sound and the Fury

1. Joseph Blotner, *Faulkner: A Biography,* 2 vols. (New York: Random House, 1974), 2: 1208. For an early interpretation see Carvel Collins, "The Pairing of *The Sound and the Fury* and *As I Lay Dying,*" *Princeton University Library Chronicle* 18 (Spring 1957): 114–23.
2. Frederick L. Gwynn and Joseph Blotner, eds., *Faulkner in the University, Class Conferences at the University of Virginia 1957–1958* (Charlottesville: University of Virginia Press, 1959), p. 207.
3. James B. Meriwether and Michael Millgate, eds., *Lion in the Garden, Interviews with William Faulkner 1926–1962* (New York: Random House, 1968), p. 147. Faulkner repeated this account on several occasions: in a 1955 interview with Cynthia Grenier; a 1956 interview with Jean Stein (both reprinted in *Lion in the Garden*); in *Faulkner in the University,* pp. 1, 31–32; in Joseph L. Fant and Robert Ashley, eds. *Faulkner at West Point* (New York: Random House, 1964), pp. 109–11; and in two recently printed drafts of an intended introduction to the novel, written in 1933: James B. Meriwether, ed. " An Introduction for *The Sound and the Fury,*" *Southern Review,* n.s. 8 (October 1972): 705–10, and James B. Meriwether, "An Introduction to *The Sound and the Fury,*" *Mississippi Quarterly* 26 (Summer 1973): 410–15.
4. Meriwether and Millgate, *Lion in the Garden,* p. 244. Blotner's accounts of the writing of both novels indicate that Faulkner, while exaggerating a bit the ease with which he wrote *As I Lay Dying,* was fairly accurate in his comments. See *Faulkner: A Biography* 1:566–79, 587–90, 633–42. The manuscript of *As I Lay Dying* seems to have been completed in forty-seven days, the typescript a month later. Faulkner's attitudes toward the relative merits of these novels were not always the same. In a 1932 interview with Henry Nash Smith he thought *As I Lay Dying* his best work (*Lion in the Garden,* p. 32); by the time of his 1955 interviews in Japan he thought it his worst, or the one he "like(d) the least" (*Lion in the Garden,* p. 180).
5. Ibid., pp. 226, 99.
6. Michael Millgate, *The Achievement of William Faulkner* (New York: Random House, 1966), p. 106. See also André Bleikasten, *The Most Splendid Failure: Faulkner's "The Sound and the Fury"* (Bloomington:

Indiana University Press, 1976), pp. 51–66. This is a major study of the novel, valuable not only for its interpretation but for its collation of the criticism.

7. Faulkner, "An Introduction for *The Sound and the Fury*," p. 710.

8. Frank Kermode, *The Sense of an Ending* (New York: Oxford University Press, 1967), p. 140.

9. Gwynn and Blotner, *Faulkner in the University*, p. 6.

10. Millgate, *The Achievement of William Faulkner*, p. 98.

11. My position here should not be confused with that of Walter Slatoff, "The Edge of Order: The Pattern of Faulkner's Rhetoric," in *William Faulkner: Three Decades of Criticism*, and *Quest for Failure: A Study of William Faulkner* (Ithaca: Cornell University Press, 1960), who has argued that Faulkner deliberately fails to resolve *any* of his novels, "that every one of Faulkner's experiments with form and style . . . is a movement away from order and coherence." The quest in Faulkner is not for failure but for form, to move *toward* coherence but only in ways acceptable to the modern writer. The attack on conceptual art, the need to create an illusion of process in fiction, to create persuasive yet not static forms—these are the motives of the great twentieth-century writers, who refuse only the kinds of resolution Slatoff is insisting on, not resolution itself.

12. William Faulkner, *The Sound and the Fury* (New York: Random House, Vintage Books, 1954), reproduced photographically from a copy of the first printing, 1929, pp. 1, 12, 53, 51. Subsequent page references within this chapter will be to this edition.

13. Meriwether and Millgate, *Lion in the Garden*, pp. 147–48.

14. Henri Bergson, *Creative Evolution*, trans. Arthur Mitchell (New York: Random House, Modern Library, 1944), p. 7. For a discussion of Bergson and a note on Faulkner's knowledge of his work, see Part Four.

15. Bleikasten, *The Most Splendid Failure*, p. 86.

16. John W. Hunt, *William Faulkner: Art in Theological Tension* (Syracuse: Syracuse University Press, 1965), p. 89.

17. See, for example, Olga Vickery, *The Novels of William Faulkner* (Baton Rouge: Louisiana State University Press, 1964): "that [Jason's] actions are the results of clear, orderly thinking in terms of cause and effect cannot be disputed" (p. 31); and Floyd Watkins, "The Word and the Deed in Faulkner's First Great Novels," in *William Faulkner: Four Decades of Criticism*, ed. Linda Welshimer Wagner (East Lansing: Michigan State University Press, 1973): "Jason, however, is too sane and rational ever to make associations which are illogical and poetic" (p. 228). For a contrasting view see Edmond Volpe, *A Reader's Guide to William Faulkner* (New York: Farrar, Straus and Giroux, The Noonday Press, 1964), pp. 119–24.

18. Henri Bergson, *A Study in Metaphysics: The Creative Mind*, trans.

Notes

Mabelle L. Andison (Totawa, New Jersey: Littlefield, Adams & Co., 1970), p. 127.

19. Some of Faulkner's most important critics have seen greater resolution in the fourth section than I think is actually there. Concentrating on Dilsey, Olga Vickery writes that "her very presence enables the reader to achieve a final perspective on the lives of the Compsons" (*The Novels of William Faulkner*, p. 47). Hyatt Waggoner notes: "[the fourth section's] implicit perspective is based on judgments which we ourselves have been brought to the point of making" (*William Faulkner: From Jefferson to the World* [Lexington: University of Kentucky Press, 1959], p. 58). And Peter Swiggart writes: "The language of Dilsey's section suggests the point of view of a reader who has struggled long and arduously with *The Sound and the Fury*, and who now recognizes beneath the 'cluttered obscurity' an extraordinary clarity of action and theme" (*The Art of Faulkner's Novels* [Austin: University of Texas Press, 1962], p. 107). Margaret Blanchard, in "The Rhetoric of Communion: Voice in *The Sound and the Fury*," *American Literature* 41 January 1970), argues that the final section of the novel "provides no summing-up, no final interpretation," (555), yet asserts that the reader, because of the altered narrative perspective, can now "adopt . . . the narrator's tone, no matter how demanding its implications" (563). My own view is that this tone and interpretation of events must remain unacceptable to the reader, precisely because he has read the first three sections. Closer to me in interpretation is Beverly Gross, "Form and Fulfillment in *The Sound and the Fury*," *Modern Language Quarterly* 29 (December 1968), who argues that the fragmentation of the novel insures against a traditional conclusion that "convert[s] order out of disorder, equilibrium out of tensions, meaning out of mystery." Rather, the book concludes with the abiding effect of Benjy's last howls, "the novel's most intense depiction of sound and fury" (444).

20. For an exception to this common view see John V. Hagopian, "Nihilism in Faulkner's *The Sound and the Fury*," *Modern Fiction Studies* 13 Spring 1967): 45–55, who argues that the novel's nihilistic close explicitly denies Dilsey's Christian perspective. See also his bibliographical note on previous interpretations of Dilsey.

21. See Bleikasten, *The Most Splendid Failure*, p. 184.

22. "Notes Toward a Supreme Fiction," in *The Collected Poems of Wallace Stevens* (New York: Alfred Knopf, 1954), pp. 403–4.

As I Lay Dying

1. See André Bleikasten, *Faulkner's "As I Lay Dying"* (Bloomington: Indiana University Press, 1973), p. 44.

2. Frye, *Fables of Identity,* p. 22.
3. R. S. Crane, "The Concept of Plot and the Plot of *Tom Jones,*" in *Critics and Criticism,* ed. R. S. Crane, abridged ed. (Chicago: University of Chicago Press, 1957), pp. 66, 91.
4. William Faulkner, *As I Lay Dying,* corrected and reset edition, under the direction of James B. Meriwether (New York: Random House, 1964) p. 165. Subsequent page references within this chapter will be to this edition.
5. Ernst Cassirer, *An Essay on Man* (New Haven: Yale University Press, 1944), pp. 81, 83. See also Walter Brylowski, *Faulkner's Olympian Laugh* (Detroit: Wayne State University Press, 1968), p. 91.
6. Vardaman's primitive religious awareness also becomes an appropriate comment on Cora's Christianity. Cora speaks of "Christian duty" even in her secret contempt for Addie, while Vardaman, boring holes in the coffin lid so Addie can breathe, actually lives a religious experience.
7. Vickery, *The Novels of William Faulkner,* p. 58.
8. Calvin Bedient, "Pride and Nakedness: *As I Lay Dying,*" *Modern Language Quarterly* 29 (March 1968): 71. Bedient's essay is one of the best written on *As I Lay Dying.*
9. Bleikasten, *Faulkner's "As I Lay Dying,"* p. 86.
10. Bedient, "Pride and Nakedness," p. 72.
11. Gwynn and Blotner, *Faulkner in the University,* p. 15.
12. Bleikasten, *Faulkner's "As I Lay Dying,"* p. 127.
13. Cash seems at times, in his stoicism and silent suffering, a version of a Hemingway hero; even the occasional exactness of his expression may remind us of characters who speak of the need for names and the avoidance of abstractions: " 'How far'd you fall, Cash?' " " 'Twenty-eight foot, four and a half inches about' " (pp. 84–85). Cash, enduring the pain of his rebroken leg on the road to Jefferson, and Frederick Henry, silently rowing from Italy to Switzerland, are not incomparable.

We know of Faulkner's reservations toward Hemingway the artist; he felt that Hemingway's excessive control resulted in an inadequate range of vision: "Hemingway had sense enough to find a method which he could control and didn't need or didn't have to, wasn't driven by his private demon to waste himself in trying to do more than that." His may have been "the most solid work," but not "the splendid magnificent bust" of a writer like Wolfe (Gwynn and Blotner, *Faulkner in the University,* pp. 143–44). Cash Bundren, as man and artist, may be in part a parody of Hemingway's heroes and his style of writing; Faulkner may intend a similar parody in *The Wild Palms.* See Thomas L. McHaney, *William Faulkner's "The Wild Palms": A Study* (Jackson: University Press of Mississippi, 1975), pp. 3–24.

We must keep in mind, however, the fact that Faulkner's deprecating comments on Hemingway were not made until 1947, in a classroom interview at the University of Mississippi, and repeated several times afterward (Meriwether and Millgate, *Lion in the Garden*, p. 58). In 1931, nearly two years after completing *As I Lay Dying,* he said of Hemingway, "I think he's the best we've got" (Ibid., p. 21).

Joseph W. Reed, Jr., in his examination of Faulkner's narrative methods, sees less irony in Cash's precise craftsmanship than I do: "as carpenter, Faulkner saw himself as he saw Cash Bundren: a careful craftsman, conscious of the need for calculation and design, resourceful in adapting available materials" (*Faulkner's Narrative,* p. 7).

14. Ernst Cassirer, *The Philosophy of Symbolic Forms,* vol. 2, *Mythical Thought* (New Haven: Yale University Press, 1955), 241, 240.
15. The source of Darl's vocabulary, including "conical facade," "cubistic bug," and "Greek frieze" remains a puzzlement. Darl's last monologue refers to "a little spy-glass he got in France at the war" (p. 244). Is this true? And is that where he picked up his aesthetic language?
16. Bedient, "Pride and Nakedness," p. 61.

Light in August

1. Alfred Kazin, "The Stillness of *Light in August,*" in *William Faulkner: Three Decades of Criticism,* p. 251.
2. William Faulkner, *Light in August,* photographed copy of the first printing, 1932 (New York: Random House, Modern Library, n.d.), pp. 107–8. Subsequent page references within this chapter will be to this edition.
3. In *Faulkner's "Light in August": A Description and Interpretation of the Revisions* (Charlottesville: University Press of Virginia, 1975), Regina K. Fadiman demonstrates that in an earlier draft of the novel Faulkner made Christmas's black blood a matter of fact rather than conjecture. She also shows that chapters 6 through 12, containing the long flashback of Christmas's life leading up to the murder of Joanna Burden, were written only after most of the action in the narrative present was completed. Once simply a part (usually off-stage) of the Lena-Byron-Hightower story, Christmas "ultimately came to dominate the novel," as Faulkner "became more interested in the inner workings of Joe Christmas's mind" (pp. 64–66).
4. F. R. Leavis, *The Great Tradition* (New York: New York University Press, 1950), p. 180.
5. Vickery, *The Novels of William Faulkner,* p. 69.
6. Friedrich Nietzsche, *The Birth of Tragedy and The Genealogy of Morals,* trans. Francis Golffing (New York: Doubleday, 1956), p. 66. For a discussion of Nietzsche and modernism see Part Four.
7. The inconsistency in the novel as to whether Christmas was captured on a Friday or Saturday (on p. 322 it's a Friday; on pp. 331 and 343 it's

Saturday) is owing, like other inconsistencies in the novel, to the revisions Faulkner made, chiefly his raising the story of Christmas to central importance. See Fadiman, Faulkner's "Light in August," p. 51.

8. Biblical quotations are all from Matthew: Revised Standard Version.
9. Thomas Mann, *Essays*, trans. H. T. Lowe-Porter (New York: Alfred Knopf, 1957), p. 320.
10. Kazin, "The Stillness of *Light in August*," p. 264.
11. Volpe, *A Reader's Guide to William Faulkner*, p. 156.
12. The story of the death of Hightower's grandfather is inconsistently told: at one point in the novel he is shot from a galloping horse, at another he is killed in a henhouse. See pp. 57, 452, 458–59.
13. See, for example, Dorothy Tuck, "The Inwardness of the Understanding," *Approaches to the Twentieth Century Novel*, ed. John Unterecker (New York: Thomas Y. Crowell, 1965), pp. 97–98. Tuck's whole discussion of the novel is excellent.
14. Volpe, *Reader's Guide*, p. 162.
15. See Faulkner's own comment in Gwynn and Blotner, *Faulkner in the University*, p. 199: "there's a lambence, a luminous quality to the light, as though it came not from just today but back in the old classic times." The question of the origins of the title gains a new dimension in Blotner's biography. Sitting on their porch at Rowenoak one late August afternoon in 1931, Estelle Faulkner remarked:

> "Bill . . . does it ever seem to you that the light in August is different from any other time of the year?"

> He rose from his chair ."That's it," he said, and walked into the house. He returned and sat down again without explanation.

(Blotner, *Faulkner: A Biography*, 1:702.)
16. Irving Howe, *William Faulkner: A Critical Study*, 2d. ed. (New York: Random House, Vintage, 1962), p. 201.
17. Cleanth Brooks, Introduction to *Light in August*, p. xvii. See also the chapter on *Light in August* in Brooks's *William Faulkner: The Yoknapatawpha Country* (New Haven: Yale University Press, 1963).
18. Millgate, *The Achievement of William Faulkner*, pp. 133–34. For a more detailed discussion of these echoes, see Frank Baldanza, "The Structure of *Light in August*," *Modern Fiction Studies* 13 (Spring 1967): 67–78, and Francois Pitavy, *Faulkner's "Light in August"* (Bloomington: Indiana University Press, 1973), pp. 38–45.
19. For an interpretation of these patterns as "comic devices," resulting in the sense of "a puppet being moved through a pantomime on a highly artificial stage," see Richard Pearce's persuasive and imaginative essay, "Faulkner's One Ring Circus," *Wisconsin Studies in Contemporary Literature* 7 (Autumn 1966): 270–83. This is reprinted in his *Stages of the Clown* (Carbondale: Southern Illinois University Press, 1970).

20. Murray Krieger, *A Window to Criticism* (Princeton: Princeton University Press, 1964), p. 30.
21. "Chocorua to Its Neighbor," *The Collected Poems of Wallace Stevens*, p. 299.

Absalom, Absalom!

1. According to Blotner's account of the writing of *Absalom, Absalom!*, it is clear that from its origins as a short story called "Evangeline," begun in 1926, through his resumption of the tale in January 1934 as *A Dark House* (also, for a time, the working title of *Light in August*), to the novel's final form, Faulkner was concerned with the problem of telling. First "I" and "Don," then "Chisholm" and "Burke," finally Quentin and Shreve take the roles of two men trying to understand the past: "[Faulkner] was continuing to work at the problem that had perplexed him from the start: not the events in the lives of Sutpen and his children, but how to relate and interpret them," *Faulkner: A Biography*, 1:890.
   Between January 1934 and January 1936, when he completed the manuscript, Faulkner was besieged by his usual financial problems. He had to put the novel aside to write most of the stories of *The Unvanquished*, which he called "a pulp series," and *Pylon*, written largely in the last three months of 1934; he also worked on movie scripts for Howard Hawks. Yet, when the manuscript was done, Faulkner said to a Hollywood associate, " 'I think it's the best novel yet written by an American' " (2:927).
2. Nietzsche, *The Birth of Tragedy*, p. 131.
3. William Faulkner, *Absalom, Absalom!* (New York: Random House, Modern Library, 1951), p. 172. Subsequent page references within this chapter will be to this edition.
4. Kenneth Burke, *The Philosophy of Literary Form*, rev. ed., abridged by the author (New York: Alfred Knopf, Vintage Books, 1957), pp. 54, 18.
5. I am indebted to Hyatt Waggoner's essay on *Absalom, Absalom!* in *William Faulkner: From Jefferson to the World*, pp. 148–69, one of the first to explore the novel in terms of the creation of history. Another study, by James Guetti in *The Limits of Metaphor* (Ithaca: Cornell University Press, 1967), suggests that the novel is a failure because its subject, the failure of the imagination, is beyond literary art. I do not agree with Guetti's conclusions, but his account of the novel and the rigor of his argument make it one of the major essays on the subject.
6. Lyn Levins, in "The Four Narrative Perspectives in *Absalom, Absalom!*,"

PMLA 85 (January 1970): 35–47, sees each of the four major versions of the Sutpen history as corresponding to a distinct literary genre: Gothic fiction, Greek tragedy, chivalric romance, and the tall tale.

7. Vickery, *The Novels of William Faulkner*, p. 89.
8. Ernst Cassirer, *Language and Myth* (New York: Dover Publications, 1953), trans. Susanne K. Langer, p. 57.
9. Cassirer, *Essay on Man*, pp. 82–83.
10. Cassirer, *Language and Myth*, p. 58.
11. Vickery, *The Novels of William Faulkner*, p. 95.
12. Cassirer, *Language and Myth*, p. 98.
13. I disagree with Joseph Reed's contention that Quentin and Shreve's metaphors, unlike Miss Rosa's and Mr. Compson's, "are open-handed, with nothing self-indulgent or self-serving about them" (*Faulkner's Narrative*, p. 165). For much of their story the two boys, like the earlier narrators, are telling the tale most comforting to them.
14. Quentin and Shreve's interest in the possible incest between Bon and Judith often reminds readers of Quentin's preoccupation with incest in *The Sound and the Fury*, as if the two novels were parts of a single whole. The link between the two novels is a basic assumption of John T. Irwin's *Doubling and Incest/ Repetition and Revenge: A Speculative Reading of Faulkner* (Baltimore: The Johns Hopkins University Press, 1975). Although Irwin's book is one of the most provocative studies of Faulkner in existence, a penetrating discussion of Faulkner's work as a whole and of the idea of repetition in narration and life, I believe his close linking of the two Quentins forces him into some essential misreadings of *Absalom, Absalom!* The most crucial of these is his placing of Quentin at the center of the novel and the subsequent minimization of the importance or drama of the act of narration by Miss Rosa, Mr. Compson, and Shreve: "the other three only function as narrators in relation to Quentin" (p. 26). The brunt of my own discussion is that all three are involved in acts of narration that take their form from personal needs, that there are four acts of narrative repetition in this novel, not one. Irwin ignores the fact that Henry's incestuous desires for Judith are emphasized more by Mr. Compson than by Quentin (see pp. 79, 91–92, 96–97, and 99); and his suggestion that Bon is motivated more by a desire to gain recognition from Sutpen than by his love for Judith is contradicted by Shreve, the whole point of whose narration is to exonerate Bon from just such a charge. Irwin also assumes that there is a "true reason" (p. 119) for the murder of Bon, which Quentin knows and Compson does not, thus drastically reducing the importance of the novel as being about the imaginative act and its ability to invent (or repeat) the truth of the past. There is also the fact that the characterization of Charles Bon and his dual pursuit of recognition from Sutpen and the love of Judith is, to a large extent, dependent on

Shreve. Is he also repeating the events of *The Sound and the Fury?* Most important of all is the great difference in character between the two Quentins, one of whom is trapped in the fable of incest he has created as a substitute for his impotence, while the other completes, with Shreve, an imaginative breakthrough into the past which neither Mr. Compson nor Miss Rosa has been able to make. The two novels are different, with completely different conceptions of the powers of imagination, and this is a difference that Irwin neglects. In *Absalom, Absalom!,* of course, Quentin never mentions Caddy.

Faulkner had reasons for using his character again. In a letter to Hal Smith he wrote, "I use him because it is just before he is to commit suicide because of his sister, and I use his bitterness which he has projected on the South in the form of hatred of it and its people to get more out of the story itself than a historical novel would be. To keep the hoop skirts and plug hats out, you might say" (Joseph Blotner, ed. *Selected Letters of William Faulkner* [New York: Random House, 1977], p. 79.) What is important to Faulkner here is that the novel should be told from a critical although not unsympathetic point of view, so as to avoid the frequent sentimentality of historical fiction. Perhaps the soundest strategy on this point comes from Jean-Jacques Mayoux in "The Creation of the Real in William Faulkner," in *William Faulkner: Three Decades of Criticism:* "One needs, it seems to me, to forget the other Quentin while searching for the meaning of *Absalom, Absalom!"* (p. 167).

15. Brooks, *William Faulkner: The Yoknapatawpha Country,* pp. 436–38. See also Millgate, *The Achievement of William Faulkner,* pp. 323–24. In his examination of the manuscript of *Absalom, Absalom!,* Gerald Langford has discovered that Faulkner originally did not intend to withhold the knowledge of Bon's origins until the end of the novel. That he finally chose to do so is not an argument for or against the "truth" of Quentin and Shreve's interpretation, but it does emphasize the importance of that interpretation, making it the climax of the book (*Faulkner's Revisions of "Absalom, Absalom!"* [Austin: University of Texas Press, 1971]).

The Hamlet

1. Reed, *Faulkner's Narrative,* p. 225.
2. Howe, *William Faulkner,* p. 245.
3. William Faulkner, *The Hamlet* (New York: Random House, Vintage ed., n.d.). The subtitle, *A Novel of the Snopes Family,* was not in the 1940 edition. Subsequent page references within this chapter will be to this edition.

4. "Spotted Horses" appeared in *Scribners*, June 1931; "The Hound" in *Harper's*, August 1931; "Lizards in Jamshyd's Courtyard" in *Saturday Evening Post*, February 27, 1932; "Fool About a Horse" in *Scribner's*, August 1936; and "Barn Burning" in *Harper's*, June 1939. These publication dates do not necessarily reflect the order in which the stories were written. For a discussion of the writing of *The Hamlet* see Millgate, *The Achievement of William Faulkner*, pp. 180–85.

5. Crane, *Critics and Criticism*, p. 82.

6. Richard Chase, "Notes on the Study of Myth," *Partisan Review* 13 (Summer 1946): 342. For a fuller discussion of Faulkner's use of myth see Part Four.

7. Faulkner had conceived of a Snopes novel as far back as 1926, when he began writing *Father Abraham*, and had been continually encouraged by his friend and occasional mentor Phil Stone to work along these lines. He wrote Snopes stories periodically through the 1930s (see above, note 4); by December 1938 he was at work on *The Hamlet* and, as a letter to Robert Haas makes clear, had already conceived of a Snopes trilogy, to be called *The Peasants, Rus in Urbe*, and *Ilium Falling* (Blotner, *Selected Letters*, pp. 107–9). One of the reasons Faulkner bothered to project the largely unwritten saga so far ahead was that he was trying to borrow money from Random House and was using the Snopes novels as a guarantee of future productivity. By December 1939 he had finished the typescript of *The Hamlet* and knew the titles of the remaining volumes, *The Town* and *The Mansion* (Blotner, *Faulkner: A Biography*, 2: 1033). By and large, however, Faulkner seemed to be thinking primarily of a Snopes saga, not a Yoknapatawpha one. In other words, the sense was not yet strong in him of all his work being a single, unified history of a county in Mississippi; nor did he yet see that history as a formal structure for his fiction.

8. Melvin Backman, *Faulkner: The Major Years* (Bloomington: Indiana University Press, 1966), p. 142.

9. Viola Hopkins, "William Faulkner's *The Hamlet*: A Study in Meaning and Form," *Accent* 15 (Spring 1955): 127.

10. T. Y. Greet, "The Theme and Structure of Faulkner's *The Hamlet*," in *William Faulkner: Three Decades of Criticism*, pp. 332, 344.

11. Florence Leaver, "The Structure of *The Hamlet*," *Twentieth Century Literature*, 1 (July 1955): 78.

12. Gwynn and Blotner, *Faulkner in the University*, p. 66.

13. For information about Faulkner's use of southwestern humor in *The Hamlet* and elsewhere, I am indebted to T. W. Cooley Jr., "Faulkner Draws the Long Bow," *Twentieth Century Literature* 16 (October 1970): 268–77; J. T. Flanagan, "Folklore in Faulkner's Fiction," *Papers on Language and Literature* 5 (Supplement, Summer 1969): 119–44; R. K. Cross, "The Humor of *The Hamlet*," *Twentieth Century Litera-*

ture 12 (January 1967): 203–15; O. B. Wheeler, "Some Uses of Folk Humor by Faulkner," *Mississippi Quarterly* 17 (Spring 1964): 107–22; J. Arthos, "Ritual and Humor in Faulkner," *Accent* 9 (Autumn 1948): 17–30. For general commentary on southwestern humor, I am indebted to Walter Blair, *Native American Humor, 1800–1900* (New York: American Book Co., 1937).

14. Millgate, *The Achievement of William Faulkner*, p. 198.
15. Brooks, *William Faulkner: The Yoknapatawpha Country*, p. 182.
16. Backman, *Faulkner: The Major Years*, p. 147.
17. Hopkins, "William Faulkner's *The Hamlet:* A Study in Meaning and Form," pp. 132–33.
18. Howe, *William Faulkner*, pp. 247–48.
19. I am indebted in the following pages to Northrop Frye, *The Anatomy of Criticism* (Princeton: Princeton University Press, 1957) for his discussions of comedy, romance, and tragedy.
20. Backman, *Faulkner: The Major Years*, p. 154.
21. Meriwether and Millgate, *Lion in the Garden*, p. 244.
22. R. P. Adams confirms the significance of the nature imagery, by noting that Faulkner added it when he revised the story "Spotted Horses" for inclusion in *The Hamlet*. See *Faulkner: Myth and Motion* (Princeton University Press, 1968), p. 123.

The Last Novels

1. Mann, *Essays*, p. 318.
2. William Faulkner, *Go Down, Moses and Other Stories* (New York: Random House, 1942), p. 309.
3. Eric Jensen, "The Play Element in Faulkner's 'The Bear,'" *Texas Studies in Language and Literature* 6 (Summer 1964): 186.
4. In Part 4 of "The Bear," as throughout *A Fable* and *Intruder in the Dust*, Faulkner departs from the usual procedure in his use of quotation marks. The dialogue is in single quotes rather than double quotes. The effect is that of a dialogue within an encompassing dialogue, as if this piece of fiction were itself part of a larger story.
5. Although, as Marvin Klotz has demonstrated in his "Procrustean Revision in Faulkner's *Go Down Moses*," *American Literature* 37 (March 1965): 1–16, Faulkner took considerable pains to unify the several stories of *Go Down Moses* when he collected them (rarely to their advantage as stories), I find it difficult to accept the book as a novel as some have argued. Thematic relations or character repetition do not make a genuine fictional unity in themselves. Unlike *The Sound and the Fury*, which is also a series of separate narratives, the individual

stories can be read independently without significant sacrifice in literary value or understanding.

6. The mythic quality of the scenes in the woods is well captured by R. W. B. Lewis in "The Hero in the New World: William Faulkner's 'The Bear,'" *Kenyon Review* 13 (Autumn 1951): 641–60.

7. Klotz, "Procrustean Revision," p. 7.

8. William Faulkner, *A Fable* (New York: Random House, 1954), p. 17.

9. See note 4 above. The only exception to the practice of using single quotes occurs when the Old General observes Pierre Bouc, the "Peter" of the Corporal's band, trying to rejoin the others after his denial of them. The Old General now quotes from the New Testament (with a change in pronouns): '"Forgive me, I didn't know what I was doing"' (p. 336). This time there is a double quote within the single quote.

10. Adams, *Myth and Motion*, p. 163.

11. William Faulkner, *Intruder in the Dust* (New York: Random House, 1948), pp. 209–10.

12. V. S. Pritchett, "Time Frozen: *A Fable*," reprinted in *Faulkner: A Collection of Critical Essays,* ed. Robert Penn Warren (Englewood Cliffs: Prentice Hall, 1966), p. 241.

13. Andrew Lytle, *The Hero with the Private Parts* (Baton Rouge: Louisiana State University Press, 1966), p. 117.

14. This passage is quoted in Joseph Gold, *William Faulkner: A Study in Humanism from Metaphor to Discourse* (Norman: University of Oklahoma Press, 1966), pp. 431–44. Gold comments, "Faulkner's own description often reaches a symbolic minuteness that is extremely irritating." Irving Howe describes the prose style of the later novels in general: "In all these works there is a reliance upon a high-powered rhetoric which bears many of the outer marks of the earlier Faulkner styles, but is really a kind of self-imitation, a whipped-up fury pouring out in wanton excess. The very abandon with which Faulkner now uses language seems itself calculated and predictable, a device in the repertoire of a writer who senses the dangers of relaxation even as he approaches the dangers of exhaustion" (*William Faulkner,* p. 283).

15. William Faulkner, *Requiem for a Nun* (New York: Random House, 1951), p. 51.

16. Part of the reason for Faulkner's turn to myth during this period may well lie in his personal situation. In Blotner's biography we read the painful history of the later 1930s and early 1940s: of a financial situation constantly verging on disaster, of growing financial obligations with little prospect for increased earnings from his fiction; of constant rejections of short stories by the high-paying commercial magazines; of the need to leave Oxford and put aside the writing of fiction in order to earn money as a script-writer in Hollywood. In January 1946, shortly

before the publication of *The Portable Faulkner,* he could say: "In France, I am the father of a literary movement. In Europe I am considered the best modern American and among the first of all writers. In America, I eke out a hack's motion picture wages by winning second prize in a manufactured mystery story contest" (Blotner, *Selected Letters,* pp. 217–18). He also seems to have been deeply disturbed by the coming of World War II. In 1940 he wrote, "what will be left after this one will certainly not be worth living for" (p. 125).
Perhaps even more disturbing than these matters, however, was his own first awareness that his writing talent might have begun to fade. Referring to a letter Faulkner wrote in June 1940, Blotner observes, "He mentioned a complaint that was unusual for him, but one he would hereafter voice at intervals for the rest of his career: he had been unable to write" (*Faulkner: A Biography,* 2: 1046). That Faulkner should turn, in response to any or all of these conditions, to a mythos form for his fiction is not surprising.

17. Mann, *Essays,* p. 312.
18. Thomas Mann, *Joseph and His Brothers* (New York: Alfred Knopf, 1948), p. 389.
19. Vickery, *The Novels of William Faulkner,* p. 209.
20. Adams, *Myth and Motion,* p. 130.
21. Swiggart, *The Art of Faulkner's Novels,* p. 183.
22. For some of the terminology and the general approach here I am indebted to Krieger, *A Window to Criticism,* pp. 67–70.
23. Gwynn and Blotner, *Faulkner in the University,* p. 144.

Faulkner and Modernism

1. J. Hillis Miller, "Beginning with a Text," *diacritics* 6 (Fall 1976): 2.
2. De Man, *Blindness and Insight,* p. 148.
3. Ibid., p. 162.
4. Ibid., pp. 151–52.
5. Meriwether and Millgate, *Lion in the Garden,* p. 72.
6. Blotner, *Faulkner: A Biography,* 2: 1302.
7. For a discussion of Faulkner and Bergson as well as Faulkner's reading in general, see R. P. Adams, "The Apprenticeship of William Faulkner," reprinted in *William Faulkner: Four Decades of Criticism,* pp. 7–44. Of the nature of Bergson's influence on modern writers, Shiv Kumar's comment is instructive: "It should, therefore, be more appropriate to say that in his philosophy one finds a most effective articulation of that intuitive sense of fluid reality of which sensitive minds were becoming aware in the early years of this century" (*Bergson and the Stream of Consciousness Novel* [London: Blackie & Son, 1962], p. 13). A recent

book which deals at length with the moral implications, largely isolated from the formal, of Bergsonism in Faulkner is Panthea Reid Broughton, *William Faulkner: The Abstract and the Actual* (Baton Rouge: Louisiana State University Press, 1974).

8. Henri Bergson, *An Introduction to Metaphysics,* trans. T. E. Hulme (New York: The Liberal Arts Press, 1955), p. 48. Other works of Bergson cited in this discussion are *Creative Evolution,* trans. Arthur Mitchell (New York: Random House, Modern Library, 1944), and *A Study in Metaphysics: The Creative Mind,* trans. Mabelle L. Andison (Totawa, New Jersey: Littlefield, Adams & Co., 1970). Quotations from these works will be cited in the text with abbreviations IM, CE, and CM respectively. *Creative Evolution* and *An Introduction to Metaphysics* were first translated into English in 1911 and 1912.

9. Broughton, *William Faulkner: The Abstract and the Actual,* p. 131.

10. Friedrich Nietzsche, *The Birth of Tragedy and The Genealogy of Morals,* pp. 101, 133. Subsequent references to this book are to this edition and will be noted in the text as BT. For discussions of Nietzsche and modern English and American literature see Monroe Spears, *Dionysus and the City: Modernism in Twentieth-Century Poetry* (New York: Oxford University Press, 1970) and Patrick Bridgewater, *Nietzsche in Anglosaxony* (Leicester: Leicester University Press, 1972).

11. Edward Said, *Beginnings, Intention and Method* (New York: Basic Books, 1975), p. 203.

12. Thomas Hanna, *The Lyrical Existentialists* (New York: Atheneum, 1962), p. 117.

13. Franz Kafka, *The Diaries of Franz Kafka, 1914–1923,* ed. Max Brod, trans. Martin Greenberg with the cooperation of Hannah Arendt (New York: Schocken Books, 1965), p. 201.

14. Sigurd Burkhardt, *Shakespearean Meanings* (Princeton: Princeton University Press, 1968), pp. 24, 41.

15. Jean-Paul Sartre, *Nausea,* trans. Lloyd Alexander (New York: New Directions, 1964). This and the following quotations are taken from pp. 57, 171–72, 57–58.

16. Kermode, *The Sense of an Ending,* p. 133.

17. A. Walton Litz, *The Art of James Joyce* (New York: Oxford University Press, 1964), p. 40.

18. Philip Wheelwright, "Poetry, Myth and Reality," in *The Language of Poetry,* ed. Allen Tate (New York: Russell & Russell, 1960), p. 10.

19. Eliot, "Ulysses, Order, and Myth," p. 681.

20. Two books which explore myth in Faulkner in considerable detail are R. P. Adams, *Faulkner: Myth and Motion* and Walter Brylowski, *Faulkner's Olympian Laugh.* Two early, influential essays are Carvel Collins, "The Interior Monologues of *The Sound and the Fury,*" *English Institute Essays* 1952 (New York: Columbia University Press, 1954):

29–55, and "The Pairing of *The Sound and the Fury* and *As I Lay Dying.*"

21. Frye, *Fables of Identity*, p. 38.
22. Adams, *Faulkner: Myth and Motion*, pp. 247, 237.
23. In his biography Blotner more or less confirms the first point. Sherwood Anderson had read the novel by the time Faulkner knew him in New Orleans (p. 417) and doubtlessly recommended it to Faulkner. Mrs. Faulkner, in a 1931 interview, said that Faulkner gave her *Ulysses* to read on their honeymoon (*Lion in the Garden*, p. 26). Blotner makes no mention, however, of Faulkner's ever having read Eliot's essay on *Ulysses*.
24. Mann, *Essays*, pp. 317–18.
25. Ibid., p. 321.
26. Meriwether and Millgate, *Lion in the Garden*, p. 250.
27. Blotner, *Faulkner: A Biography*, 2: 1012.
28. Mann, *Essays*, pp. 320–21.

Index

203